Jock Mahoney

Jock Mahoney

The Life and Films of a Hollywood Stuntman

GENE FREESE

McFarland & Company, Inc., Publishers
Jefferson, North Carolina, and London

LIBRARY OF CONGRESS CATALOGUING-IN-PUBLICATION DATA

Freese, Gene Scott, 1969–
Jock Mahoney : the life and films
of a Hollywood stuntman / Gene Freese.
p.   cm.
Includes bibliographical references and index.

ISBN 978-0-7864-7689-3
softcover : acid free paper ∞

1. Mahoney, Jock, 1919–1989.   2. Actors—United States—Biography.
3. Stunt performers—United States—Biography.   I. Title.
PN2287.M242F84 2014   791.4302'8092092—dc23   [B]   2013039058

BRITISH LIBRARY CATALOGUING DATA ARE AVAILABLE

Front cover image: Jocko jumps off a rooftop onto
stuntman Al Wyatt on *The Range Rider*, early 1950s

Manufactured in the United States of America

*McFarland & Company, Inc., Publishers
Box 611, Jefferson, North Carolina 28640
www.mcfarlandpub.com*

Acknowledgments

The author had correspondence or conversations in regard to Jocko with his family, friends, acquaintances, and co-workers Ray Barrow, Grady Bishop, Stephen Burnette, Don Burt, John "Bud" Cardos, Camille "Caz" Cazedessus, Mike Chapman, Greydon Clark, Roydon Clark, Bobby Copeland, Patrick Culliton, Robert Dix, James Drury, Eric Dyck, Donald Carl Eugster, Al Fleming, Peter Ford, Robert Fuller, Tom Goldrup, John Hagner, Lois Laurel Hawes, Will Hutchins, Loren Janes, Russell Johnson, Dick Jones, Gene LeBell, Ruta Lee, Clarke Lindsley, Esther Luttrell, Jim Martin, Denny Miller, Diane Miller, Ron Nix, Jim O'Mahoney, D. Peter Ogden, Judy Pastorius, Gordie Peer, Phil Petras, Robert Potter, Marty Rendleman, Burt Reynolds, Don Kay Reynolds, David Rothel, Gene Ryals, Bill Sasser, William Smith, Steve Stevens, Kalai Strode, Neil Summers, Gregory Walcott, Tom Warner, Rodd Wolff, Don Young, Jack Young, and Jim Zabel.

Special thanks to Doug Smith of Davenport, Iowa, for his invaluable research and recollection of conversations with Vic Siegel and George "Sonny" Franck. Many thanks also go out to Bob Callaghan and his Jock Mahoney Tribute Site for putting me in touch with both Tom Warner and Gene Ryals, who answered many questions. Judy Pastorius and Esther Luttrell were quite generous in sharing information. Phil Petras answered many Tarzan questions and Mike Chapman was a huge help. Thanks to Peter Ford for his memories and providing documentation of Jocko at his birthday party, as well as Greg Ray for digging up the Jocko article in the Australian *Man* magazine. Another big thank you to George T. McWhorter of the Burroughs Bibliophiles for tracking down a difficult-to-find *Burroughs Bulletin* and being kind enough to share information on Jocko.

James Drury put me in touch with Robert Fuller who helped contact Dick Jones. Will Hutchins wrote a great letter. William Smith shared a workout at World Gym. All these TV cowboy stars were quite accommodating and helpful. A special nod goes to Denny Miller for his correspondence and providing a photo of the Tarzans together. Neil Summers was extremely giving and cordial at the Wild Western Festival in Glendale, Arizona. Grady Bishop shared his heartfelt memories and helped contact Ray Barrow. Gary Kent was instrumental in contacting John "Bud" Cardos. Old Tucson Studios guide Marty Freese found Robert Potter. Bill Sasser was a tremendous help in providing recordings of several film festival panels. Thanks also to Boyd Magers of *Western Clippings* and Chuck Anderson of *The Old Corral* for sharing information.

Further thanks to Kristine Krueger and Janet Lorenz of the Motion Picture Academy Library for their reference assistance, Joshua Crawford of the National Archives, and Gail

Heninger and her Davenport High students Austin Overman, Zach Hendershott, Sara Schwind, Luke Seyfert, Mandy Taylor, and Scott McKillip for finding Jocko in their old school annuals. The photos are courtesy of the respective studios and intended for publicity purposes. Larry Edmunds Bookshop was a great source for these. Finally, a very special thanks to Rodd Wolff for his personal memories and help in identifying some of Jocko's stunt work.

Table of Contents

Preface

My subject is television and film actor Jock Mahoney. He is considered one of Hollywood's greatest all-around stuntmen and one of the only members of that profession to become a successful leading man and character actor. Mahoney starred in the popular TV westerns *Range Rider* and *Yancy Derringer* prior to becoming the big screen's thirteenth Tarzan. Mahoney's portrayal was the closest to writer Edgar Rice Burroughs' original creation of an educated and articulate man who chooses to live in the jungle.

I became interested in Mahoney through watching his Tarzan films and was particularly intrigued by the physical hardships he faced filming in real jungles around the world. I wanted to learn more about his athletic accomplishments, military background, and the often anonymous work he performed as a stunt double for actors Errol Flynn, John Wayne, Randolph Scott, Gregory Peck and others. I cover Mahoney's entire life from his Iowa upbringing to the stroke and motor vehicle accident that claimed his life in 1989 at the age of 70. His professional career as a stuntman and actor is described in full detail. Less interest is paid to private aspects of his personal life, although these are discussed where pertinent or noteworthy.

In researching Mahoney's life I viewed hundreds of individual film and television projects and collected background information on these titles from the Academy of Motion Picture Arts and Sciences library. I utilized all previously published Mahoney articles and interviews available in books, newspapers, periodicals, and the Internet. An Iowa historian was consulted for background on his childhood, and I received his military record from the National Archives. I had personal correspondence with more than 50 friends, family, and co-workers who knew or worked with him. This is the first scholarly book on the life of Jock Mahoney.

Introduction

I was born in 1969. By this time Jock Mahoney's star in Hollywood was quickly descending into the "whatever became of?" status. In fact, the great stuntman had taken a sabbatical from acting during this period. It was an odd time for a man who once proudly rode the back lot range as a 1950s cowboy star and swung through real jungles as the most athletic screen Tarzan. A 1973 stroke hindered his attempts at a screen comeback. Like so many things in his life, the stroke was something "Jocko" overcame through tremendous will and determination. He was able to regain his health and mobility. However, he never regained star status in the motion picture industry.

I became aware of him in the afternoon Tarzan movies of my youth. Like any athletic kid, I was fascinated by the Edgar Rice Burroughs character, and Jock Mahoney was a ubiquitous presence throughout the modern Tarzan films. He played the villain in Gordon Scott's final adventure in 1960, starred as the jungle lord in two films, and went back to playing the bad guy multiple times opposite Ron Ely in the *Tarzan* TV series of the late 1960s. All these received heavy airplay in the following decade, no doubt because they were in color. I don't recall seeing any of Johnny Weissmuller's black and white Tarzan films. I do remember the first book I ever bought. It was called *Tarzan of the Movies* and contained a memorable chapter on Jock Mahoney and the physical toll the film *Tarzan's Three Challenges* had on him. It nearly killed him. He fought through adversity and extreme physical illness to complete the picture. It was an inspirational story and one I always remembered as I battled fatigue on the athletic fields. I was competing in college in 1989 when Jock Mahoney passed away from another stroke. At the time, his death did not make much of an impact on me. As it turns out, his life would.

I never forgot Jock Mahoney. Through the years I came into contact with people in the film industry who had known Jocko and spoke highly of him. I filed the information away. I always thought his life would make an interesting biography and hoped that one day someone would write a proper historical account. As time went by, that book never materialized. Through the years, many of Jocko's films and TV shows became available on DVD, and I found myself enjoying the stunts and the old westerns. The Internet also made it possible to track down history in the form of newspaper articles, magazine features and photos, and to make contact with a number of interesting people who had known Jocko. I began to realize that I had the resources available to write that book.

I'm probably one of the younger fans of Jock Mahoney. However, now that so much is available for viewing, perhaps others of my generation or the next will rediscover his fantastic athleticism. That is my hope. I found watching all the old westerns, Tarzan features, and Three Stooges shorts highly entertaining. At times my nine-year-old daughter sat down and watched these black and white oldies with me. "I don't know why," she said, "but I'm kind of into these *Range Rider* things, Dad." I think I know why. His name is Jock Mahoney.

1

The Athlete

Jacques Joseph O'Mahoney was born in Chicago, Illinois, on February 7, 1919, barely nine months beyond the day his working class parents were married in Kansas City, Missouri. The future athletic actor's lineage consisted of Irish, French, German, and a dash of Cherokee Indian blood in his veins. Jacques was the son of 25-year-old laborer Charles James Mahoney and his attractive 19-year-old bride Ruth Eugenia Miller. The Nebraska-born Charles hailed from Irish and German roots, the only surviving son of John J. Mahoney and Berthe Thoeming after four siblings were lost to tuberculosis. The Kansas-born Ruth comprised the French background and presumably the one-eighth Cherokee that Jacques claimed influenced at least some of his athleticism and proclivity for outdoor skills.

The Mahoney family went by the shorter and easier to pronounce version of their last name, although Jacques was proud of his County Cork ancestry and began to go by O'Mahoney as he reached manhood. In Hollywood in the 1940s, following World War II, he was less inclined to publicly mention the German stock in his family.

Jacques was born into a frigid world pounded by the cold winds of Lake Michigan, but things would heat up by the summer of 1919. Chicago was deeply affected by a steel-worker strike, race riots, and a World Series baseball scandal involving the hometown White Sox. Gangster Al Capone arrived within the year, ushering in a deadly era of violence to the city streets. It wasn't the best environment to raise a youngster. As the legendary stuntman, cowboy star, and oldest screen Tarzan later told *The Waterloo Daily Courier*, he stayed in Chicago "only long enough for three diaper changes."

When Jacques was one year old, the family moved west and settled in his father's hometown of Davenport, Iowa. The family's address was 2204 Rockingham Road, a stone's throw from the area where the infamous Highway 61 would one day snake along the Mississippi River. This property contained a row of small homes owned by Jacques' grandmother's family, a line of butchers who ran Thoeming & Eckhardt's Meat Market in downtown Davenport. Jacques' parents moved often between established relatives in Illinois, Iowa, and Missouri, but Davenport was where his father was raised and where the family formed their deepest roots.

His dad worked as a switchman for the Milwaukee Railroad and dabbled as a salesman for an oil company, jobs that oftentimes put him out on the road to places as far away as Texas. Charles Mahoney eventually took a government job as the head of shipping and receiving at the Rock Island Arsenal. This early exposure to change no doubt influenced the boy's adaptability. He would forever be a man on the move in his adult years and even somewhat of a vagabond.

Davenport, known as "The City Beautiful," is located on the banks of the Mississippi River in Scott County along the Iowa border directly across from Rock Island, Illinois. The communities of Bettendorf, Iowa and Moline, Illinois, complete the area which came to be known as the Quad Cities. Davenport, the gateway to the early west, has the distinction of being the only city situated on an east-to-west section of the giant river known as the Big Muddy. The remainder of the city in the 1920s was surrounded by farmland and a steep hill to the north that young Jacques traversed countless times. The population at the time approached 60,000 people. Much of the city's commerce relied on the river, with the Rock Island Railroad a major employer in the area. A bridge over the water connected the train tracks between Davenport and Rock Island.

Growing up, the adventurous Mahoney tyke spent ample time exploring the banks of the Mississippi and the Rock Island Rapids in the great tradition of Mark Twain's fictional characters Tom Sawyer and Huckleberry Finn. Watching the riverboats float by was an activity that piqued his imagination. Always by his side was his loyal dog Shadow. Clad in his favored moccasins, he no doubt uncovered many an Indian arrowhead from the Sauk and Fox tribes that once inhabited the area. This experience created a lifelong interest in Native American culture and tradition in him. The long cold winter months in Davenport were spent skating, sledding, and shoveling snow.

The French name Jacques seemed a bit dandified among midwestern folk, so the young-ster generally went by the Americanized Jack Mahoney or Jack O'Mahoney at Monroe Elementary School and beyond. Over the years he would acquire the nickname Jocko, a combination of his first name and the first letter of his real last name. The moniker fit, especially seeing as how he went on to become a noted athlete and sports jock. Even his good-humored disposition could be described as jocular by nature. Jocko quickly became the name he preferred and responded to amongst friends and colleagues.

Like many boys his age, Jocko was fascinated by cowboys and Indians and enjoyed the Saturday matinee westerns starring straight-shooters Tom Mix, Buck Jones, William S. Hart, and Hoot Gibson. Jocko was also enamored with Edgar Rice Burroughs' Tarzan character and the swashbuckling style of Douglas Fairbanks in *The Mark of Zorro* (1920), a film Jocko watched repeatedly. His childhood play was spent emulating the action of these celluloid heroes.

When Jocko was nine years old, Tom Mix and the circus came to Davenport. Jocko and a group of children spent the day helping the circus workers raise the tent. In the afternoon he came face to face with Mix himself, and the movie cowboy said hello to the boy and showed him his horse Tony. The meeting with his cowboy hero made quite an impression on the young Jocko. Little did he know as he rode horses, practiced a quick draw, or shot a bow and arrow made from green willow wands that he would one day be employing those skills on the big screen himself. Another fantasy Jocko held from a young age was to build a boat and sail around the world; so obviously the boy had dreams of lofty adventure not confined to the city limits of Davenport.

His dad had been an athlete in high school and promoted exercise. Jocko heeded his father's advice and set out to be as active as possible in order to maintain his health. From an early age he began a calisthenics and deep breathing routine employing free-hand exercise to keep fit. Every day after school, young Jocko visited the YMCA to play basketball and swim. There were plenty of other athletic endeavors for the youngster to partake in, such

Tarzan Goes to India (1962).

as little league baseball, tennis, and horseback riding. Gymnastics and acrobatics afforded him great control over his body and taught him how to fall and tumble with the least amount of damage. For several years he trained with German Turnvereine and Turngemeinde gymnastic clubs where he mastered the balance beam, the vaulting horse, the horizontal bar, the parallel bars, and the Roman rings.

Jocko's mother had influence over him as well. When he was five she enrolled him in tap dance classes and ballet at the Georgia Brown School in Kansas City, Missouri, where the family had relatives and Jocko spent a good portion of his youth. Jocko actually made his performance debut as a toe dancer in a school play. The experience was not enlightening in the least, as the youthful Jocko never entertained the idea that the stage was his calling. Although this dance background might be surprising considering the macho nature of Jocko's screen image, these classes helped give Jocko's legs the great spring and power he would display throughout the years in his films and TV shows. His mother also had him learn how to play the piano; Jocko often surprised people with how well he could finger the ebony and ivory keys.

Despite his dabbling in the fine arts, Jocko's natural inclination was toward manly pursuits in the area of health and fitness. In 1934 Jocko wrote a letter to physical culturist Charles Atlas and began to adhere to the instructor's Dynamic Tension workout routines, essentially pushing and pulling against his own body in a variety of positions for extended periods of time. The twice-daily isometrics were supplemented with hundreds of sit-ups, deep knee bends, and push-ups between chairs. His muscles responded accordingly with added strength and endurance. The Atlas courses became a lifelong devotion for Jocko, who preferred the free-hand exercise over weightlifting. He didn't want bulky muscles that would interfere with his participation in sports. As an athlete, Jocko began to stand out from the other kids in junior high track; he went on to set several school records in the broad jump. He kept up his devotion to gymnastics and trampoline work on the side, becoming quite adept at adjusting his long body in mid-air.

The Mahoney family travels during the Great Depression took them all the way to Texas, where young Jocko earned a dollar a day chopping cotton and improved his horse-riding abilities. In 1934 he returned to Davenport from Kansas City and enrolled in the ninth grade at West Intermediate School on the corner of Fifth and Cedar Street. During this period he became best friends with fellow athlete Kenny Dohse. Pickup basketball games were a common occurrence during the summer months, as was swimming at the huge outdoor Natatorium pool where Jocko worked as a lifeguard. The teenaged Jocko earned extra cash working at the Gordon-VanTine Company's lumber mill, a manufacturer of mail-order kit-homes. In addition to athletics, Jocko excelled in his scholastic studies. The school newspaper *The Sunset* stated he had a future as an algebra teacher based on his mastery of the subject. The paper featured Jocko in its "Perfect-Boy Column" due to his winning smile and fine teeth.

After the death of his grandmother Berthe, Jocko's family moved away from the Rockingham homes and settled in the heart of downtown Davenport at 436 West Eighth Street. This home was situated on a hill overlooking Davenport High some three blocks away. A steep set of stairs gave access to the house from the street below. Going up and down this staircase every day helped build Jocko's leg muscles and cardiovascular system, aiding him immeasurably in his sports activities. His continued horseback riding further built and conditioned accessory limb and core muscles that were hardly used in any other way. Strength in these supporting areas enhanced Jocko's immense natural ability to run, jump, and swim.

By the time he attended Davenport High, Jocko had become regarded as an all-around outstanding athlete; a tall and handsome brown-haired, blue-eyed Jack Armstrong type who excelled at everything he tried. At 6' 4" and nearly 200 pounds, Jocko was exceptionally large for that athletic era and attracted much local attention. He played all the major sports for the school's Blue Devils during his junior varsity years, including football, basketball, and track. He was the biggest player on the sophomore football team, leading the squad to a 5–2 record. They even beat the DeWitt varsity squad, the first time that feat had ever been accomplished by a Davenport sophomore team.

Jocko had such raw natural talent that he didn't have to work especially hard at any of the sports he tried. Happy-go-lucky Jocko preferred having fun over studying the playbook, listening to a coach's instruction, or practicing endlessly to perfect his skills. Nevertheless, he became a force to be reckoned with in the Mississippi Athletic Conference and especially distinguished himself as a swimmer and three-meter diving champion, winning a number of titles and trophies in those sports in YMCA and American Athletic Union meets. He was the captain of the Davenport Swim Team, and in diving he was crowned Iowa state champion. Davenport High was so successful in sports during this period that they soon ran out of room to display all their trophies.

Jocko was a varsity letterman in both football and basketball his junior and senior years. The 1936 football season was a rebound year for the school as legendary coach Jesse Day lost the previous year's entire starting line and two backs to graduation. The inexperienced Blue Devils still managed to post four wins against four losses with one tie, taking second place in the Quad City race. The highlight was a shutout victory of a tough Maplewood, Missouri, team. Jocko wore number 39 and played end on both sides of the ball, taking the place of the future University of Minnesota All-American and New York Giant pro George "Sonny" Franck. These were big shoes to fill, but Jocko was up to the task. He even set his eyes on romancing Davenport student Norma Hill, whom Franck had been sweet on.

Jocko was the tallest man on the basketball squad and served as both center and backup guard for coach Paul Moon. The team posted an impressive record of 15–6 and reached the state tournament after picking up momentum as the season went on. While Jocko had become known as a football hero in his hometown, he wasn't far behind as a basketball player. His height and agility served him well in the sport. A personal highlight for Jocko during his junior season was a game-winning basket in overtime versus Iowa City. In the state finals, Davenport lost 33 to 30 in overtime to Newton. The loss was tough, with Jocko losing a pivotal jump ball to Newton's exceptional center Bill Green. Although Jocko was taller than the 6'1", 185-pound Green, he found himself bested several times in the jump by Newton's combination track and football star. It was a big stage on which to be humbled, and the experience taught Jocko the importance of technique and focus in addition to raw ability.

Jocko's athletic failures during this period were few, and his senior year at Davenport brought more accolades. The 1937 football season saw the team cruise to a record of 7–3 under the new Municipal Stadium lights, outscoring their opponents 164 to 43. The Blue Devils won the city crown over St. Ambrose Academy and finished second in the Mississippi Valley Conference. Co-captain Jocko, wearing number 68, earned honors as a selection on the All-State team, despite suffering a knee injury during the season. No doubt Jocko's big body and long arms made an attractive passing target on offense and a threat to any opponent trying to run around end on defense. Jocko's senior yearbook termed him a "football hero."

The basketball team was even more outstanding in Jocko's senior frame, posting a 20–2 record and outscoring their opponents by more than 300 points. The Blue and Red quintet was so wildly popular in the community that extra bleachers were brought into the George Edward Marshall gym to accommodate the record crowds. A New Year's Eve game against Moline drew more than 3000 enthusiastic fans. The Blue Devils won the Mississippi Valley crown, the city crown, and the Class-A sectional title. They tied with Moline for the Quad City title. Jocko was one of the team's scoring leaders alongside teammates Kenny Dohse and Vic Siegel, a future All-American at the University of Iowa. In the second game of the season, a win over Dubuque, Jocko scored 11 of his team's 24 total points during the defense-oriented era. Unfortunately Jocko was only able to play half of his team's games due to early mid-year graduation. The Blue Devils were undefeated with Jocko on the court, and he led the team in scoring in his final game. Without Jocko, Davenport faltered in their quest for a state title, falling to Dubuque 29–26 in the District Championship. They had easily beat Dubuque earlier in the season when Jocko was at the helm.

Jim Zabel was a year behind Jocko at Davenport High and captained the track team. He knew Jocko well through their mutual involvement in athletics and Jocko's ability to stand out from the crowd. After attending the University of Iowa, Zabel went on to a long and distinguished career as a sportscaster for the Iowa Hawkeyes on WHO-AM Radio in Des Moines. Zabel remembered Jocko as "a big, good-looking guy" who was "a good athlete and a colorful character."[1] He told Mike Chapman of the *Iowa History Journal*, "Even way back then, if you asked me who I thought from our school would be a movie star, I would have said Jock Mahoney."

In addition to his involvement in Davenport High and YMCA sports, Jocko was a member of the Boys Glee Club and the A Cappella Chorus at his mother's urging. He sang first tenor under the direction of Kent Gannett and Clara Thomas. The January 1936 school musical *Hi-De-Hi* featured Jocko as a cowboy in the act titled "Dude Ranch." He sang lead tenors in the school's Gilbert and Sullivan operettas, most notably the May 1936 production *The Gondoliers* where he was cast as the Venetian gondolier Antonio and the 1937 production *Pinafore* in which he played the able-bodied sailor Ralph Rackstraw opposite leading lady Evelyn Van Walterop. Vic Siegel recalled Jocko occasionally breaking into a slightly ribald song on the team's basketball bus to the delight of the other players. While still in his teens, Jocko put together a professional adagio hand-balancing act with himself performing as the strongman.

At Davenport High, Jocko served on the student council, the class committee and the senior prom committee, and was the stage manager for the senior class play. Socially he and his fraternity friends squired their dates to tux and tail dances at venues such as the Black-hawk Hotel or the Coliseum Ballroom where the big bands played, lending Jocko an early sense of maturity and sophistication. One of Jocko's girlfriends during this period, Lucille Hobart, had dated Vic Siegel. There were also minor league baseball games to be enjoyed at Municipal Stadium in the form of the pennant-winning Davenport Blue Sox of the Mississippi Valley League, allowing Jocko the opportunity to see firsthand the way crowds became attached to their athletic heroes.

Upon high school graduation in January of 1938, Jocko's swimming, diving, and gymnastic prowess earned him an athletic scholarship to the University of Iowa in nearby Iowa City. He took pre-med science and minored in physical education while swimming lap after lap in what was then the world's largest competition pool. As a collegiate swimmer Jocko was known for his speed as a sprint man. He established a national record in the 40-yard free style at a YMCA meet with a time of 18 seconds, shaving four-tenths of a second off the top mark and besting the Iowa state record by a full second. In the spring of 1939 he won a 50-yard event at a meet in Minnesota for coach David Armbruster and helped Iowa to an impressive showing in the Big Ten Conference. He was also involved in a record setting 50-yard splash and dash at a spring 1938 meet; he was added at the last minute after being excused from football drill. He barely lost this race, placing third and pushing the winner to a record time. Jocko managed to beat both Michigan's star Bill Holmes and Northwestern's top man in the hotly contested event. With proper preparation and seasoning, it was obvious that Jocko could be an exceptional water man for the school.

Jocko's strength as a swimmer was not limited to speed sprints. Nor were his exploits in the water confined to organized meets. On a return visit to Kansas City to see relatives, Jocko became enamored with the horseshoe-shaped lagoon at Swope Park's Lake of the Woods, one of the country's largest urban parks. Canoes could be rented to paddle around the nearly one-mile perimeter of the island within the lagoon. Jocko had no need for a canoe. He promptly dove in and swam the entire length of the lagoon simply to prove he could do it.[2] Onlookers no doubt thought he was slightly crazed, a label Jocko carried throughout his life thanks to his often off-the-wall antics.

Jocko didn't limit himself to one sport at Iowa, which may have hurt him in the long run. In addition to gymnastics, diving, and being a rising star on the swim team, Jocko played offensive and defensive end in football and center on coach Rollie Williams' basketball squad. There are a few brief mentions in Iowa City's *Daily Iowan* regarding his early college athletics. For the basketball team he competed with and pushed older students Ken Bastian and Charles Plett for playing time. Regional newspaper reports predicted he might soon be the starting center for the varsity squad. The Hawkeye five posted a winning record of 11–9 in 1938, followed by a losing 8–11 season in 1939, when Jocko was joined by his old Davenport teammate Vic Siegel at forward.

The college was in the midst of a terrible sports decade in football, continuously trounced in the Big Ten Conference by Michigan, Minnesota, and Notre Dame. The 1937 season under coach Irl Tubbs saw them struggle mightily and fall to a record of 1–7. The 1938 season saw scant improvement as they posted a record of 1–6, and a tie, with Jocko playing little more than in practice as a freshman backup to ends Erwin Prasse and Dick Evans. An outstanding player, Prasse also excelled on the basketball court and earned nine varsity letters. He would achieve All-American status in football and later be selected as Iowa's Best All-Around Athlete in school history. He was drafted by the Detroit Lions football team in 1940 and played both basketball and baseball professionally. The miserable team performance was in large part attributed to star player Nile Kinnick playing the entire season with an ankle injury, but in reality even a healthy Kinnick wouldn't have made a tremendous difference in the 1938 record. The 1939 football season would be something else entirely.

Coach Tubbs was fired in November of 1938 and Dr. Eddie Anderson was hired to coach the struggling Black and Gold football squad. Anderson had played alongside George Gipp under legendary coach Knute Rockne at Notre Dame and played professionally for the Chicago Cardinals. He brought along with him another Notre Dame veteran, former

All-American quarterback Frank Carideo. Anderson immediately went about toughening up the players with stringent conditioning that opened a number of eyes for its volume and intensity. The 1939 spring practice had more than 80 candidates show up for the squad, but only 35 made it to the fall season. Anderson's style of coaching and conditioning built a legendary squad of highly focused two-way "Ironmen" that was capable of playing the entirety of 60-minute games. The 1939 Iowa Hawkeyes were the surprise of the Big Ten Conference and reversed their previous season's record to finish with six wins, one loss, and one tie, including a monumental win over Notre Dame. Left halfback Nile Kinnick, all 5'9" and 175 pounds of him, made All-American and won the Heisman Trophy.

Due to his multi-sport commitments and periodic academic ineligibility, Jocko did not play a large or memorable role on this legendary team although later Hollywood publicity touted him as a college football star. There was little chance for underclassman Jocko to experience much in the way of individual glory. In fact he was one of the spring casualties, unable to devote the time or energy to football demanded by Coach Anderson. The surviving Ironmen became instant celebrities in their home state. Parades were held in their honor, and the 1939 squad was often labeled the greatest in the Hawkeyes' history. Jocko was no doubt disappointed not to share in the glory or experience. However, the hard-nosed philosophy of Dr. Eddie Anderson and his Knute Rockne influence undoubtedly rubbed off on Jocko's state of mind and his long-term outlook on life. He would have Anderson's stoic tough guy mentality throughout the remainder of his career.

While Jocko was eclipsed on the football field by the nationally recognized exploits of Nile Kinnick and Erwin Prasse, he did not go unnoticed at the college. Overall, the charismatic Jocko was quite the man about campus his first two years, noted for walking on his hands and daring leaps over the length of couches in the Student Union. These feats seldom failed to impress the girls. Jocko and a gymnast friend named Bob Vin set up a trapeze outfit *sans* net over the school's swimming pool and practiced an act, culminating with high dives into the pool. Delta Upsilon fraternity pledge Jocko even went one step further and ventured up to the second story of the Field House, opening a trap door in the wrestling room floor through which he dove into the pool below.

Jocko learned how to walk a tightrope on a high wire and dabbled in boxing and fencing for good measure. He was proficient enough in the latter skill to work as an instructor in the epee on campus. On occasion Jocko and other athletes mixed it up at the tough road-house Ken and Fern's, sometimes landing in mild trouble that merely added to their notoriety. At one point he jumped off the Burlington Street Bridge and did a cannonball into the Iowa River for kicks.

To earn extra money, Jocko cleaned the Field House after practices and worked in the University hospital's cafeteria with pal Gus Schrader for three free meals a day. He was supposed to be cleaning dishes for three hours a shift to earn his keep, but through charming the pretty dietician Miss Zimmerman, Jocko seldom spent more than an hour a day scrubbing. The majority of his time in the kitchen was spent doing special favors for Miss Zimmerman. His most frequent occupation became scooping ice cream into dessert dishes for the nurses. Needless to say, the giggling nurses were going back for seconds. Gus Schrader later became a newspaper columnist and described Jocko in the *Cedar Rapids Gazette* as "a light-hearted, likable kid," even if he did cut a swath among the nurses that made all the other boys envious.

Fun-loving 20-year-old Jocko enjoyed a good time and the simple joys that attention and athletic exhilaration could bring to an individual. He didn't mind making a fool of himself if his actions garnered a laugh or a smile. All he needed was a challenge to send him into motion. At times his youthful folly bordered on impulsive craziness, but he was already gaining a strong feel for what his body could and could not do on a physical level. There was also the thrill of competition and doing something that no one else could achieve or dare to attempt, traits that carried over into his career as a professional stuntman. Jocko always attributed his extreme athleticism to a God-given gift, although he was also quick to credit his regular gymnastic workouts for keeping him in top condition. There was seemingly nothing that Jocko's body couldn't do and few physical challenges that he would back away from.

Jocko was in such demand in sports at the school that his grades ultimately began to suffer. The busy Jocko rarely had time to attend classes, much less devote the required period of study to master the challenging pre-med subjects. His noble intention to become a doctor was quickly becoming less of a reality. He later described himself to writer Mike Chapman as an "athletic bum" who spent most of his time at the University packing and unpacking to travel from one meet or game to the next. Each sport he was involved in had practices to attend. By his sophomore year he had varsity letters in swimming and basketball but was a long way from challenging Erwin Prasse. When a professor told him that he couldn't possibly pass Jocko since he hadn't attended enough classes; the young man reached a crossroads. "I was spending all my time jock-strapping and not getting an education," Jocko told the magazine *Guns of the Old West.*

Outside of school and during the summer break, Jocko found the energy to work part-time as a gym teacher, fencing instructor, delivery man, busboy, filling station attendant, and as a troubleshooting lineman for the local gas power company. During the summer of 1939 he was back in Davenport working as a menial machine operator for the Hansaloy Manufacturing Company, creating bread slicing blades. He didn't want to continue in any of these jobs for the rest of his life, especially in Iowa with its cold Midwest winters. He was tired of digging stalled motorists out of snow banks. On the personal front, his parents had gone through a divorce in the fall of 1938, adding a further distraction to his mental plate. He knew it was time for a life-changing decision that would have serious repercussions on his future.

Jocko was an outstanding all-around athlete with a chance to emerge as a major talent in his junior and senior years if he could keep his grades up, but in 1940 professional athletes in football and basketball were paid a minuscule fraction of the hefty contracts they would one day command. Jocko could make more money climbing poles full-time for the power company. Even Heisman winner Nile Kinnick turned down professional football offers to enter the University's law school for the hope of a more solid future. Olympic athletes could certainly reach stardom, but Jocko would have to give up football or basketball and concentrate all of his energies on swimming or diving if he wanted to stand out. It would take a lot of hard work, and the United States and its allies was in the midst of skipping the 1940 Olympic Games altogether to protest Germany's power moves in Europe. There was no guarantee the U.S. would even participate in 1944, and all Jocko's training could go for naught. With Hitler's 1939 invasion of Poland, there were also serious rumblings that the nation would be drawn into war before then. Jocko no doubt would be called into service of his country.

Jocko's Irish restlessness began to draw his mind to the state of California. His hometown of Davenport had been hit hard by the Great Depression, with many families losing their farms. Jocko saw hungry local citizens forced to stand in long bread lines or receive meager coal rations to heat their homes. Jocko wanted no part of that cold, bleak future. He was far too cognizant of the lure of a better life among the enticing citrus groves, the moderate temperatures, and the crash of waves on a sunny beach. He had bold dreams of dating a different Hollywood starlet every day of the week.

Jocko decided to drop out of the University of Iowa during his sophomore year and check out the situation in California before he was called off to war. His original intention was to eventually transfer his credits to Stanford University and resume his studies at some point. Although the decision no doubt disappointed his parents and puzzled his community, it would prove to be the best decision of his life. It's only unfortunate he never tapped his full athletic potential on the collegiate, Olympic, or professional level. He certainly had the size, speed, and agility to play football or basketball professionally, and he was already being recognized nationally in the water. Jocko arrived in Los Angeles in early 1940 with only $5 in his pocket, but he was full of hope and dreams, athletic self-assurance, and a unique skill set that would immediately set him apart from others even in the land of Hollywood movie stars.

2

The U.S. Marine

Jocko quickly found work as a lifeguard and swimming instructor at the trendy Los Angeles Athletic Club. Located downtown at the corner of Seventh and Olive, it was a premier fitness center for the city's elite. The club had the finest gymnasium, boxing ring, wrestling mats, indoor track, and spa in all of Southern California and often sponsored athletes for Olympic training. It was noted for being the first building to have an Olympic swimming pool on the upper floor. There were also shooting galleries and saloons on the premises. One of its long-time members had been no less than Jocko's boyhood hero Douglas Fairbanks, who died of a heart attack mere weeks before Jocko arrived in California. Fairbanks was 56 years old.

Having gained access to one of the best sponsorships in the nation for an amateur athlete, Jocko set about training in earnest for the 1944 Olympic Games as a swimmer and diver. He eventually transferred to the castle-like Pacific Coast Club in Long Beach, which was equally magnificent and next to the ocean. In addition to lifeguarding, Jocko offered tennis and swim instruction and drew upon his dancing background to teach both a rumba class for children and ballroom dancing. He also supervised a horseback riding class for problem children. Jocko enjoyed all the activities immensely and earned roughly $50 a week for his good times.

In anticipation of the looming war, Jocko joined the U.S. Army Reserve Officers Training Corps program in 1940. He went through basic training and continued to serve part-time on weekends over the course of the following year. He advanced to the rank of sergeant within the program. Jocko had the germ of beginning an acting career in the back of his mind upon arriving in California, but he was having so much fun on the beach that he seemed to forget any notion of pursuing acting for the time being. He did, however, pick up some work at Paramount Studios as a stand-in for cowboy actor Russell Hayden, who was busy at the time on Hopalong Cassidy features.

A stand-in takes the place of a star for camera and lighting set-ups. They are generally the same height and coloring as the star. When the cameras are rolling, the stand-in is out of the picture and watching on the sideline. Jocko was intrigued when he saw the rough-and-ready stunt doubles step in for action scenes. He learned that a stunt double sometimes makes more money than the star himself, and Jocko filed this information away. He watched what these macho men were called upon to do. Given his athletic background, Jocko knew he had what it took to be a stunt double. He still longed to be an actor, but the notion of speaking on camera left him shaking his head.

15

He didn't have any problems with self-confidence when he was in a pair of swim trunks. The dashing young athlete struck quite a figure at the beach with his lean, hard physique and attracted the attention of many a girl as he swam, surfed, and paddled in the Pacific Ocean on his Tom Blake hollow board. Utilizing his status as a Red Cross instructor, Jocko picked up extra cash lifeguarding at Palos Verdes Peninsula, where he befriended a surfer named Gard Chapin. It wasn't easy to befriend the roughneck Chapin, often noted as the sport's first surf bully. Jocko's new friend would become the stepfather of a young boy named Miki Dora, who went on to be one of the legends of the surfing world after Chapin taught him to catch a wave.

It was at Long Beach that Jocko met pretty 18-year-old USC coed Lorraine Mae O'Donnell, daughter of Sequoia Field financiers Lloyd and Gladys O'Donnell. Lloyd O'Donnell was a prominent Long Beach oil man and aviator. Gladys O'Donnell was a distinguished aviatrix who had competed against Amelia Earhart in the Powder Puff Derby, finishing second in 1929 and winning the national cross-country Woman's Transcontinental Air Race the following year. Lorraine's parents no doubt felt their daughter rated more than a college dropout turned beach boy, even if he was training for the Olympics. Jocko set out to prove them wrong.

Mother Nature lent a hand in creating a major upheaval in Jocko's life. An earthquake did serious damage to the Pacific Coast Club, and Jocko temporarily lost the bulk of his sustenance as the club retrenched its foundation. As the country mobilized for the impending war, Jocko set aside his idyllic beach existence and planned for the future. Taking an interest in aeronautics, he found a job in August of 1941 as an aviation mechanic at Sequoia Field near Visalia, a private school for aviation cadets founded by the O'Donnells. Jocko also learned to handle heavy ground machinery and became skilled in driving light and heavy trucks, motorcycles, tractors, and Caterpillar bulldozers. It didn't take Jocko long to abandon being a grease monkey and begin training as a cadet to get his own flying license. He intended to be a commercial pilot and flight instructor.

At Sequoia Field, Jocko learned the airline business from the ground up and earned his keep working as a tower operator, flight dispatcher, and maintenance purchasing agent for a full year as he built up hours piloting aircraft in his free time. Jocko's take-home pay for these occupations amounted to roughly $150 a month. Jocko primarily learned how to fly a 65 horsepower Porterfield and a 450 horsepower Beechcraft at Sequoia Field, logging 100 hours of certified flying time. All but gone was his intent to swim and dive in the 1944 Olympic Games.

When the Japanese bombed Pearl Harbor on December 7, 1941, the nation entered World War II and there was a clamor for all able-bodied men to join the war effort. Jocko was as able-bodied as anyone but opted to complete his flight training, then volunteer his services as a civilian flight instructor for the Army Air Corps. In the back of his mind was the idea of eventually becoming a fighter pilot. Jocko's newfound dedication to flying apparently quelled the objections of Lorraine's parents. The young couple was married in Las Vegas in March of 1942. A daughter named Kathleen Jacqueline O'Mahoney was born in March of 1943, and a son named James Dennis O'Mahoney was born in August of 1945.

Jocko continued working and flying at Sequoia Field until August of 1942. From September of that year to January of 1943 he attended ground school aviation courses as a Navy pre-flight cadet in Lone Pine, California. From September of 1942 to May of 1943 he was also busy flying out of Ross Field in Manzanar, California, logging over 230 hours in 65 horsepower and 220 horsepower Waco single engine land planes. In April 1943 he obtained his commercial pilot's license from the Harry Ross Accredited School of Aeronautics in Manzanar and began to pick up side jobs hauling air freight. He flew nearly 200 hours of unlogged time in 255 and 450 horsepower Beechcraft planes. Jocko was now bringing in roughly $200 a month as a pilot and civilian instructor.

The summer of 1943 saw Jocko stationed at Falcon Field in Mesa, Arizona, located a few miles east of Phoenix. It was there that Jocko took a refresher course as a certified instructor. In addition to American cadets, members of the British Royal Air Force were learning to fly Stearman PT-17 biplanes and North American Aviation AT-6 Harvard Monoplanes at Falcon Field. The British pilots were assigned their training exercises in the clear blue skies of Arizona because they were considerably safer than the foggy skies over war-torn England. Jocko was no doubt enticed by the picturesque mountains and miles of open desert surrounding the area. Despite the peaceful atmosphere, there were several casualties amongst the pilot trainees and even a few of the instructors.

In addition to a baby daughter, there were two other major events shaking up Jocko's home life. In July of 1943, Lorraine became ill and Jocko was forced to return to California until she was feeling better and able to care for baby Kathleen. The second major upheaval was that Jocko's mother arrived on his doorstep with a two-year-old half-brother in tow. Since divorcing Jocko's father, Jocko's mother had not only remarried but had a child at the age of 40. When her health suffered and she became too incapacitated to work, both she and the child were abandoned by her new husband. Ruth had a long history of living with relatives and now turned to her adult son for a helping hand. Jocko's mom and half-brother Lew Miller moved into Jocko and Lorraine's Chatsworth home. This no doubt interrupted Jocko's well laid-out plans and created a suddenly hectic homefront with two ill women and two small children under his roof.

Jocko remained determined to complete his flight training and receive his full instructor's rating. In August of 1943 he took another refresher course at the Army Primary School at Mira Loma Field in Oxnard, California, where he flew a 220 horsepower Stearman. Civilian flight instructor seemed a safe and smart occupation for a man with so many family obligations. However, that Irish restlessness was stirring once again. In September 1943, a gung ho and patriotic Jocko felt he wasn't making enough of a contribution and enlisted in the U.S. Marine Corps at the Reseda Recruiting Office, signing up for the duration of the national emergency. Jocko announced that his primary interest was in being a Marine Aviator fighter pilot with a secondary choice to be a Marine Raider with the Fleet Marine Force's naval division. Private First Class O'Mahoney was assigned serial number 875832.

The National Archives contain Jocko's military record. He achieved solid if unspectacular numbers for his Marine Corps entry aptitude tests. On the Army General Classification Test he scored a 112 and received a label of Grade II. On the MA3 he scored a 119, also a Grade II qualification. On the ROA-1 X1 he scored a 103. This was a Grade III classification. On a traditional letter grade score, these marks would categorize him as a B-student. He also scored a 40 on the Narith Test and a 57 on the Thuradio Test. His physical showed the 193-pound Jocko to be in excellent health with 20/20 vision.

Jocko was sent to the Marine barracks at San Diego's Camp Pendleton for seven weeks of recruit training, and no doubt the tough physical regimen came easily to the athletically gifted Jocko. Push-ups, chin-ups, sit-ups, runs, marches, and obstacle course navigation were a day at the beach for him. Singled out for his physical skill, he became an assistant drill instructor by November and led other leathernecks through the exercises. Jocko always regarded himself as a leader, not a follower. The Marine Corps would also be where Jocko learned many of the hand-to-hand combat techniques and basic judo moves that he later utilized for his movie fights. His military record notes he is a "qualified swimmer." On the rifle range he was introduced to the M-1 carbine and classified as a Marksman with a score of 268. Jocko's shot would improve considerably over the years as he became an avid hunter and sports rifleman.

In October 1943, Jocko's picture appeared in the *San Diego Union* newspaper as he accepted a receipt for $43.13, the "smoke money" his platoon collected in a cigarette fund for active duty Marines serving in the Pacific. In January 1944 he was assigned to Aviation Training Squadron 131 at the Marine Corps Air Depot in Miramar, California. Jocko soon applied for an Aviation Refresher Course and was accepted in February. First he was assigned to study AVN ordinance for 16 weeks at the NATTC AOM Ordinance School in Norman, Oklahoma, with Training Squad 27. Jocko studied all aspects of guns, cannons, bombs, fuses, ammunition, and installations. He graduated 84th out of a class of 163 with a score of 86.50 on a scale of 1 to 100.

By all accounts he was a model Marine. He consistently scored ratings of very good to excellent in his Professional Conduct Record, which graded military efficiency, neatness, military bearing, and intelligence. He maintained perfect scores in the areas of sobriety and obedience throughout his time as a Marine. His final average in this record was 4.7 out of a possible five. He earned his Aviation Sergeant stripes in June of 1944.

Many Marine units were seeing front-line combat in the Pacific, but the military had other ideas for Jocko and his interest in becoming a fighter pilot. He was initially assigned to take a refresher flight training course as a Student Naval Aviation Pilot at the Naval Air Training Center in Corpus Christi, Texas. This assignment was changed across the Gulf Coast to the Naval Air Training Center in Pensacola, Florida (the Annapolis of the Air) before Jocko ever set foot in the Lone Star state. While in Florida, Jocko drew upon his aquatic background and became a swimming teacher for downed fighter pilots, instructing them on how to survive at sea. He completed his flight training and received his Navy Wings at Pensacola in December 1944 with a promotion to Technical Aviation Sergeant.

As he neared completion of his training in November 1944, Jocko requested additional training in CV aircraft flying off of and landing on aircraft carriers. He continued to study in Pensacola through the early part of 1945, attending ground school in the subject before beginning to fly F-4U Corsairs off the aircraft carrier U.S.S. Guadalcanal. Throughout his training exercises in the spring of 1945, he searched for German submarines in the Atlantic Ocean. Later studio biographies often mentioned Jocko's fighter pilot background, but in reality Jocko never actually saw combat. Germany had all but surrendered by May of 1945, and Jocko was not officially certified as a Naval Aviation Pilot until May 6, 1945. That's not to say that his flying was without danger. Jocko's former University of Iowa teammate Nile Kinnick had followed a similar career path and joined the U.S. Navy as a pilot. Kinnick was killed in 1943 during a training exercise when his F4F Wildcat crashed off the coast of Venezuela.

During this period Jocko added his mother and half-brother as dependents he was supporting in accordance with the enlisted man's Class B Family Allowance Act. His pregnant wife Lorraine and daughter Kathleen were considered Class A dependents. The small bump to Jocko's monthly Marine paycheck of approximately $100 was divided accordingly between his wife and his mother. In May, Jocko received a temporary duty assignment to the Marine Fighter Operational Training Unit at the Naval Air Station in Jacksonville, Florida. The military granted him a 15-day furlough between assignments and allowed him to travel from Pensacola to Jacksonville in his civilian vehicle, a bright yellow 1942 Mercury Club Coupe convertible.

Jocko continued flying out of Jacksonville through July of 1945, awaiting orders to be assigned to San Diego and the Pacific Theater to fight the Japanese. He was also awaiting the birth of his son. A curious paperwork snafu occurred during this period as a number of events happened at once. At the beginning of August, Jocko's Pensacola commander issued an appointment request to Marine Headquarters in Washington for Jocko to be promoted to the rank of second lieutenant effective as of July 30, 1945. In accordance with such a promotion, the appointee needs to acknowledge and accept the new rank. The problem here is that Jocko was stationed in Jacksonville and headed to California on furlough for the birth of his son James. August also happened to be the month that the A-Bomb was dropped on the Japanese cities of Hiroshima and Nagasaki, effectively ending the war with that country's surrender. At the end of his furlough, new dad Jocko reported on September 1, 1945, to the Marine Barracks in San Diego and joined Squadron 46 at El Toro Marine Air Base in Santa Ana, California. In his mind he was still an enlisted man with a rank of sergeant. According to Washington, he was now an officer with the rank of second lieutenant.

By October, Jocko had filed the appropriate application to add his son James as a new dependent, listing his rank as Technical Sergeant on the app. At the same time, Jocko's wife and mother both mysteriously began to miss the Family Allowance paychecks they were reliant on. After the second consecutive check did not arrive, they wrote individual letters to the Paymaster in Washington D.C. Both received replies from Colonel E.E. Shaughnessey informing them that as of July 30, 1945, Jocko was no longer an enlisted man and in accordance with the provisions of the Serviceman's Dependents Allowance Act of 1942 they were no longer eligible for financial allotments from the government.

When Jocko learned of the mistake, he went to his immediate superior with his new unit. Jocko's commanding officer C.W. Nelson wrote headquarters on his behalf, explaining that Jocko was a Technical Sergeant with an enlisted man's status and that Nelson had never received any paperwork appointing Jocko to a commissioned rank. Nelson further verified that in Jocko's own words he had no knowledge of ever having an opportunity to accept such an appointment and was still being paid as an enlisted man. An official inquiry and investigation audit on the matter was launched in Washington and continued through January of 1946.

Jocko's financial shortages were eventually reconciled by the Paymaster, but the experience no doubt left a sour taste in his mouth. With the war finished and his obligation to the military over, Jocko opted to muster out of the Marine Corps as soon as possible. He filed the appropriate paperwork and set about exploring civilian possibilities. Many servicemen had no idea what to do with themselves outside of the military, but Jocko was literally bursting with ideas and couldn't wait to embark on his life's next adventure. Initially he thought he wanted to manage a South American airline but likely opted to stay in California for family reasons. Jocko was honorably discharged from the Marine Corps on February 15, 1946, and never looked back.

The combination of marriage, fatherhood, the Marine Corps, and the wartime atmosphere added a hard veneer to Jocko's youthful disposition. No longer was he a carefree beach boy. He was a man with adult responsibilities. Jocko set about buying, certifying, and selling surplus war planes. When that idea ran its course, he came up with the notion of breeding, raising, and training pure-blooded Arabian horses as jumpers in Chatsworth. He had been riding horses since his Iowa youth and especially enjoyed teaching children during his time at the Pacific Coast Club. His initial foray into the horse-breeding business met with struggle as he learned the ropes. One of his means of making money became supplying livestock to the motion picture business. He still harbored dreams of being an actor and began to take dramatic lessons at the Del Powers Theatrical School. He paid for these lessons by cleaning the theater after hours. Based on the release dates of motion picture credits, it is likely Jocko began to pick up some early stunt assignments riding for the pictures he was providing horses for.

In mid–1946 Jocko was at a social gathering and met a movie director by the name of Derwin Abrahams. It is likely Jocko knew him from his (Jocko's) time as Russell Hayden's stand-in, for Abrahams was then an assistant director on the Hopalong Cassidy films. As the two made idle chitchat, the director mentioned that he had an actor signed for a film who needed to learn how to ride a horse. Could Jocko teach the man in one week? Jocko agreed to the task and a week later had the saddle-sore actor looking confident astride a horse. Abrahams was pleased and rewarded Jocko with bit parts in two pictures he was making. They were a pair of Charles Starrett Durango Kid westerns entitled *The Fighting Frontiersman* (1946) and *South of the Chisholm Trail* (1947).

In *The Fighting Frontiersman* Jocko was assigned to play a background henchman named Waco, a "dog-ass heavy" by his own admission. When the script called for him to fight or fall, Jocko did his own stunts. Jocko's physical dexterity and willingness to put his body at risk impressed the filmmakers. He first appears in a line-up of the heavies in a saloon. Jocko is in the forefront and in profile, coolly smoking a cigarette. His screen presence is obvious, and he seems far too handsome to be a heavy. Although he never utters a line, he is seen throughout the film and engages Charles Starrett in a short saloon brawl midway through. Jocko throws a couple of good punches and reacts well to Starrett's blows. He even throws in a couple of flips, making it hard for any viewer not to notice this movie newcomer.

He did less physically in *South of the Chisholm Trail*, playing a henchman named Thorpe, but did have some dialogue. Jocko recalled that he froze in front of the camera the first time he was called upon to speak. In a scene with Smiley Burnette, Jocko has his arms folded over a chair. In another scene he is seen smoking a cigarette or fiddling with a weed. The pros on the film obviously gave him some bits of business to keep his hands occupied when the cameras rolled. Jocko seemed much more at ease taking a gunshot to the belly and falling face first onto the western street.

The Fighting Frontiersman was released in December of 1946 and *South of the Chisholm Trail* a month later. The Internet Movie Database credits Jocko with stunt work on a handful of Durango Kid films released earlier in 1946. It is possible *Fighting Frontiersman* and

Chisholm Trail stand out in Jocko's mind because they are the first films where he actually had screen roles. Jocko also appeared in a small role in Abrahams' medieval serial *Son of the Guardsman* (1946), where he appears in a couple of chapters with a few brief lines and stands a head taller than anyone else in the cast. Veteran character actor Terry Frost recalled Jocko in *The Westerner*, saying, "He was the greatest athlete I've ever met. First time I saw him he was in chain mail for a serial. I thought, "There's a good-looking guy who'll go far."

Jocko went back to his horse-breeding business and didn't hear anything more about movies for several weeks. Then a phone call came from the Durango Kid production team asking if he'd be interested in becoming a full-time stuntman. He was quite interested indeed. He told interviewer David Rothel for the book *Opened Time Capsules*, "When you're not good enough to be an actor — which I found out I wasn't after two quick pictures for Starrett — then you stay in the business any way you can."

3

The Stuntman

The Durango Kid filmmakers were offering Jocko an enticing $250 a week to be the main double for Charles Starrett in the B-western film series. Jocko could make even more based on the difficulty of individual stunts. Columbia Pictures made eight Starrett films a year, often shooting each movie in two weeks. It would be a solid beginning for a fledgling stuntman, but there was one catch in Jocko's mind. A veteran stuntman named Ted Mapes was the usual double for Starrett, and Jocko didn't want to take his job away. The producers told Jocko that Mapes was tired of the low-budget films and wanted to work on bigger projects. Jocko elected to talk to Mapes himself before agreeing to the deal. When he got the okay from Mapes, Jocko signed on the dotted line and was ready to make movie history. Mapes went on to become the main double for A-list stars Gary Cooper and James Stewart.

Jocko worked on the Durango Kid films from 1946 to 1951, appearing in nearly 50 Starrett pictures in total. The Durango Kid character dressed in black and wore a bandana over half his face to hide his identity. That detail made it quite easy for Jocko to take over for the 6' 2", 190-pound Starrett and still have audiences believe the star was doing all the action. Quizzical viewers, however, began to wonder how Starrett was suddenly growing amazingly spry as the Durango Kid entered middle age.

Jocko's first Durango Kid stunt called for him to drive a buckboard with two horses up to a house to deliver a message. Jocko had never driven a buckboard before, and the filmmakers wanted him to bring the horses around a fencepost at a fast clip. Although he was a bit nervous, Jocko was determined to make a solid first impression and got as much speed out of the horses as he could. Starrett recalled this stunt in *Paragon*: "Boy! He just took that fencepost down! He went right up to that house and pulled them up beautifully! They slid right into place and he stepped down. It was beautiful."

Jocko did all kinds of action on the Durango films including lots of fighting, horseback riding, and falls. Where he began to stand out from the crowd was in his high work. Jocko could scale walls and jump from roofs with the best of them. He had incredible spring in his legs, with witnesses recalling how he could stand flat-footed and literally jump over the top of a 15-hand horse and land on the other side. He could easily put himself in the saddle without ever using his hands. Legend has it he was able to take a running leap from the ground and clear three horses standing side by side. If a fourth horse was there he would land in the saddle and take off. Some of the Durango Kid films have been out of circulation for years, but there is evidence of Jocko clearing two horses and landing in the saddle of the third in the film *Blazing Across the Pecos* (1949). Jocko no doubt left many a jaw dropped in disbelief.

Veteran stuntman Roydon Clark was raised as a working cowboy on the Hudkins Ranch across the street from Warner Bros. As a young man he worked as a cowboy extra and remembered the first time he ever saw Jocko on a Durango Kid set. The cowboys were told Starrett had a new double, and the cliquish group immediately sized the lanky swimmer up as someone without a lot of horse sense. When they were told that the new kid on the block was going to jump over three horses and land in the saddle of the fourth, they all gathered around to watch him fall on his face as he attempted what they considered an impossible feat. At the call of action, Jocko made his running leap, cleared all the horses, and rode off in a successful take. The cowboys were left dumbfounded. "What the hell was that?" Clark recalled them saying to one another. "It was mind-boggling."[1]

The next time Clark saw Jocko, it was at Iverson Ranch on another Durango Kid film, *Whirlwind Raiders* (1948). Jocko would be attempting a transfer from a horse to a four-up team leading a stagecoach. When Jocko jumped from his horse to the team, he missed his grip on the Hames collar. That should have been the end of the stunt, but Jocko somehow managed to run alongside the horses and execute a quick Pony Express mount to stop the entire team and save the shot. Again, Clark and the cowboys were left speechless.

"He had an incredible agility and athletic ability for a big man," Clark said. "He was

The Durango Kid in *Six Gun Law* (1948).

in good shape and did some remarkable things physically. He had a slick body and a set of legs like a goddamn chimpanzee. It was a pleasure to watch him. He was a fabulous guy and a great part of that era. He brought a lot of excitement to the industry."

Along with Ben Johnson, Jocko would become known as one of the best horsemen in the stunt profession, especially adept at hard galloping and doing horse and saddle falls. He even rode horses off cliffs into bodies of water, an especially difficult stunt to get a horse to do. Jocko liked to say over the years that he "fell off every horse in Hollywood." Actress Peggy Stewart recalled Jocko was such a good rider that he could balance a glass of water on his head and not spill a drop.

There's one humorous aside regarding Jocko's horseback stunts on the Durango series. Columbia studio chief Harry Cohn insisted that the Kid's horse Raider be the whitest horse in the business. As Raider became dirty and soiled during filming, the film crew often resorted to whitewashing the horse for the camera. As a result, Jocko needed several changes of Durango Kid costumes because he often emerged from action scenes with white paint on his black outfit.

In addition to Derwin Abrahams, director Ray Nazarro was a frequent contributor to the series. Nazarro always wanted Jocko to come up with more dangerous stunts for the camera. Jocko joked that Nazarro was trying to kill him, but liked and respected the director all the same. It was a mutually beneficial relationship as Jocko negotiated higher pay for the more dangerous gags. On one film Jocko dove through the window of a moving stagecoach, a nearly impossible stunt to time successfully. He also devised a daring feet-first jump to the ground off second story balconies or rock ledges. Jocko was careful to build up his landing area with plenty of soft sand so he would not break his ankles or snap his lower legs upon impact. Another trick was to conceal a piece of $\frac{5}{8}$" plywood atop a pair of 4 × 4s that would create a spring effect and absorb some of the shock to his legs.

As word spread of his bravery, Jocko began to devise his most death-defying Durango Kid stunt yet, a jump between two rooftops that he measured at more than 20 feet across and 20 feet to the ground. Including take-off and landing, the leap would put him in the neighborhood of the long-standing world record long jump of 26' 8" held by the great track star Jesse Owens since 1935. With a pair of ambulances standing by ready to whisk him to the hospital, Jocko completed the running leap without a problem. The jump has to be seen to be believed. Not only is the distance between the buildings considerable, but Jocko reaches a perfectly balanced position at the apex of his leap that makes it appear as if he's sitting in a chair. He's nearly 25 feet above the ground at that point and there is easily ten feet between him and either building. It's not a stunt that got a lot of press, but surely one that drew gasps from every viewer who has seen it. The jump is also seen in recycled footage in *The Kid from Broken Gun* (1952).

The Durango Kid's daring athleticism began to draw minor notice within the film industry and major notice at the Saturday matinees, where the series was a huge hit with children. Box office receipts began to reflect the audience's appreciation for the more exciting version of the Durango Kid. Don Kay Reynolds (aka Little Brown Jug), a child actor who worked on the series, saw first-hand Jocko's daring feats of athleticism. This led to an especially strong case of hero worship. Durango Kid Charles Starrett took it all in stride, delighted to have a stuntman who made him look good to those who didn't know better.

"Jock Mahoney was kind of my idol," Reynolds said. "I made three Durango Kid movies, and I hung out with him a lot on the set. He was one of the greatest athletes I've ever seen in my life. Some of the stunts that he did were pretty outrageous. Jock Mahoney was the only man I ever saw that could take one step and jump up and land astride of a horse without using his hands. Dean Smith is the only other man I've seen who could even come close. Jock was one of the greatest stuntmen there ever was. He was also a hell of a nice guy, and I enjoyed working with him tremendously. He was one of my heroes, and I loved him. Jock was just a jewel."[2]

Starrett recalled in Bobby Copeland's book *Trail Talk*, "When Jock Mahoney started working in my films, he was all over the place. He did a lot of my fight scenes, stunts, and most of my riding. I kiddingly told some people I was only around to do Jock's dialogue. He was a tremendous athlete." Starrett continued praising Jocko in *The Great Cowboy Stars of Movies and Television*: "I can't say enough good words to describe my feelings for Jock Mahoney. He was superb. Excellent. He was perfect, in all respects. He was a fine athlete, a fine stuntman, a perfect double for me. He turned into quite a star himself, and all deserving. I personally can't praise Jock enough."

Jocko and Starrett developed a solid friendship that would last decades beyond their work in the B-westerns. Jocko told *Favorite Westerns*, "Charlie Starrett put a lot of beans on my table. As a stuntman, I've doubled many stars, but Charles Starrett is primarily responsible for my career — that's where I learned my trade — not only as a stuntman, but as an actor." In the book *The Adventures of the Durango Kid*, Jocko revealed, "Charlie only blew up on me once in four years. And we did eight pictures a year. Charlie was a damn good man to work for and with. I did the stunts and he did the acting. I think we made a good working team."

Jocko's most famous Durango stunt is likely the balcony dive onto stuntman Al Wyatt seen in *Horsemen of the Sierras* (1949). Jocko detailed the stunt for the book *The Adventures of the Durango Kid*: "I was 12 feet above him and 15 to 18 feet away. We dug up the street a little bit to cushion the fall. When I hit Al I dropped one arm over his shoulder and then laid my body right up next to his back. I grabbed him around the back in a bear hug, taking a good stiff hold of him. Then I took him to the ground, controlling his fall. He fell on top of me; we rolled together and rolled right up onto our feet."

Six-foot-four, 200 pound Al Wyatt was born in Kentucky and entered stunt work after service in World War II. A horseback specialist and an extremely able fight man, he worked especially well with Jocko. (Wyatt doubled Starrett whenever Jocko was unable due to his acting parts.) When the studios began to insist that Jocko have a stuntman, it was Wyatt who got the nod. Durango Kid female lead Lois Hall remembered the athletic duo for *Feature Players*: "Jocko and Al Wyatt working together was just like poetry."

It takes a courageous individual with a fair amount of moxie to be a stunt performer. Jocko didn't lack for intestinal fortitude. He was fresh out of the Marine Corps where he routinely made pinpoint landings on the deck of an aircraft carrier. He was also accustomed to Olympic dives, standing on a high board with intense focus on the task at hand as judgmental eyes monitored his every move. Most movie stunts were a piece of cake in comparison. When the call for action came, Jocko could deliver. When his life was on the line, he reached back for that something extra that he seldom had to call upon during his athletic days at Davenport and the University of Iowa. What emerged was Jocko reaching his full athletic potential as he tapped into his mental resources to aid the physical. He was an ace stuntman.

The stunt work also appealed to his sense of adventure and his heroic nature. He told his actress friend Mary Stuart that he sometimes felt as if he was born in the wrong era. He belonged in a time when he could gallantly ride in on a white horse and rescue a damsel in distress. Being a stuntman allowed him to fulfill his sense of heroic destiny on a daily basis. Jocko had found his calling.

Jocko began to branch out from the Starrett films and work other stunts, primarily at Columbia Pictures as a double for Jon Hall, Sonny Tufts, William Bishop, Willard Parker, Ken Curtis, and Jerome Courtland. In addition to westerns, he excelled at costume dramas such as *Slave Girl* (1947), *The Swordsman* (1947), *The Gallant Blade* (1948), *Barbary Pirate* (1949), and *The Rogues of Sherwood Forest* (1950). Two films from this period are excellent showcases for Jocko's talents: the swashbucklers *Prince of Thieves* (1947) and *Black Arrow* (1948). In the former he doubled for star Jon Hall playing Robin Hood of Sherwood Forest. In the latter he doubled villain George Macready. In addition to a multitude of fencing and fighting in these films, Jocko hung from his neck and was dropped through a trap door, scaled a castle wall, fell 40 feet from that wall, and climbed hand over hand up a drawbridge chain. The climax of *Black Arrow* saw Jocko fighting a jousting duel on horseback and taking a saddle fall while wearing 50 pounds of armor.

Fellow stuntmen began to notice. Jocko was one of several crewmen working under Dave Sharpe at Columbia on the Dick Powell drug smuggling film *To the Ends of the Earth* (1948). Sharpe wasn't yet familiar with Jocko and used his favored stuntmen for the majority of the gags. After a day's location shooting they were returning to their cars, which were bordered by several fallen logs. Sharpe took off on a run, hit a log and vaulted over the hood of a car. In quick succession all his men followed his lead one after another. When it came Jocko's turn, he simply ran and jumped over the entire length of the car's body. The bold action gained immediate notice and approval from Sharpe, who used Jocko regularly from then on.

In late 1947 Jocko cemented his reputation in the stunt business when he doubled for Errol Flynn in *Adventures of Don Juan* (1948) and made a daring leap from a 12-step staircase onto another man. Jocko had only a one-foot ledge to push off from, and it was a stunt which he often acknowledged was his most difficult. Flynn's form-fitting tights left no chance for a stuntman to pad himself around the knees or hips, and the angle of the camera set-up meant there would be no mattress to land on. Neither of Flynn's regular doubles working on the film, Don Turner and Sol Gorss, would even attempt the leap, and both those men were highly regarded within the business. The stunt called for Flynn to make a significant leap down a large stairwell onto his foe Robert Douglas. Stuntman Charles Horvath and unit manager Frank Mattison were on the Warner Bros. set and both let it be known to stunt coordinator Allen Pomeroy that there was only one man who might be able to make the leap: Jocko Mahoney. Director Vincent Sherman told them to find this daring new stuntman.

Jocko was summoned by Pomeroy from Columbia Pictures where he was working on a barroom brawl for the Sonny Tufts film *The Untamed Breed* (1948). His hair had been bleached light blond for that doubling assignment. Pomeroy set the price for the challenging stunt at a princely sum of $1000, but Jocko said he'd do it for only $350 in hopes that it would open doors for him at Warners and with Flynn. The next problem outside of darkening his hair was finding a willing stuntman to double Robert Douglas. From that great distance, a large body hurtling through the air could severely injure the man on the receiving end. Legend has it that in the early days of motion pictures, a stuntman was killed attempting such a stunt — another reason why all those on the film were so hesitant. Stuntman Paul Baxley, himself a former U.S. Marine, finally stepped forward to be the man at the bottom of the stairs. Baxley actually demanded and got $500 for his portion of the stunt. Jocko had the floor waxed to make his landing smoother, using the theory of a ski landing. If a body were to stay in motion once it landed, there would be less risk of injury upon impact.

The cameras were ready to roll, and Jocko said the silent prayer that he always did before a big stunt. Clutching Flynn's scabbard, Jocko pushed off from a standing position with all the power in his muscular legs. He flew magnificently out and over the steps, creating great space between himself and the descending stairwell. At the completion of the fantastic 18-foot leap, Jocko hit Baxley and rolled with him in a perfect take. Only upon getting up did he accidentally knee Baxley in the groin and hear mutterings under his fellow stuntman's breath. Jocko later recalled in *Leatherneck* magazine, "If either my timing or that of the other stuntman had been even a fraction of a second off, I'd have buried my head up to the heels in the sound stage floor."

Baxley was quoted in *American Classic Screen*: "I'd watch these guys come in and try it and I'd wince. I wasn't going to let them dive on me. They could have killed me. It wasn't dangerous but it was really a very spectacular physical feat. Most guys would try to do a jump like that upright. Jock realized that he had to go headfirst, in a dive to keep his feet up. When he hit me I didn't even feel it. He was like a bird, he was that good."

The action looked so impressive that director Sherman suddenly regretted that he had not captured it in slow-motion to showcase it for the screen. It was a career-making stunt, and Jocko was highly congratulated by all those on the set. Flynn shook Jocko's hand and offered him the use of his dressing room whenever he needed. That was especially gratifying to Jocko, as Flynn's *The Adventures of Robin Hood* (1938) had been Jocko's favorite film when he was in college. The star and the stuntman became good friends from that point on. Douglas Fairbanks and Flynn were Jocko's biggest influences, and the friendship and working relationship proved quite significant for the up-and-coming stuntman. Jocko doubled Flynn again in *Silver River* (1948), *Montana* (1950), *Kim* (1950), and *Against All Flags* (1952). In *Montana* he rode headlong into a stampede of cattle. In *Against All Flags* he made another fantastic jump, this time between two ships. Jocko always welcomed the opportunity to work with Errol Flynn.

Word of mouth spread about the *Don Juan* stunt, and Jocko became a hot property in the stunt world. Unfortunately, Flynn was having a rough time with his growing problems with alcohol, and filming of *Don Juan* was done in fits and starts. The film was not released to viewing audiences until nearly a year after Jocko performed his leap. Jocko continued doubling Charles Starrett at Columbia and began to branch out to other studios as well. He landed a plum assignment as one of the doubles for Randolph Scott in a fight scene with Forrest Tucker in the western *Coroner Creek* (1948). That fight was noted for its viciousness as Scott's character fought much of the battle with a broken hand, hurling his body at his opponent and even resorting to butting heads to gain an advantage. It was a perfect showcase for Jocko, who also doubled Tucker and George Macready in the film. In the climax, Jocko took a great fall for Macready from a 20-foot tower when a ladder broke. Jocko landed flat on nothing more than a simple bed mattress (this was long before the days of air bags). This was another gag that Jocko included among his most difficult. In other films he did falls as high as 60 feet into cardboard boxes, a tremendous height for that era. "It isn't the fall that's dangerous," Jocko would say, "it's the sudden stop."

Jocko doubled Randolph Scott in a number of other films, including *Return of the Bad Men* (1948), *The Walking Hills* (1949), *Canadian Pacific* (1949), *The Doolins of Oklahoma* (1949), *The Cariboo Trail* (1950), *The Nevadan* (1950), and *Santa Fe* (1951). He was a good match for the reliable 6'3", 190-pound cowboy star who had been riding the trail since the early 1930s. Jocko also doubled Joel McCrea and Gary Cooper, most likely in *Colorado Territory* (1949) and *Dallas* (1950). However, it was an assignment doubling Gregory Peck in the William Wellman western *Yellow Sky* (1948) that cemented Jocko's reputation.

Among the legendarily craggy boulders of Lone Pine, California, Jocko doubled Peck throughout the picture and performed one more breathtaking stunt that had audiences and his fellow stunt personnel gasping in awe. Stuntwoman Martha Crawford Cantarini worked on the film and recalled in her memoir *Fall Girl* the stunt Jocko performed. She and others watched as he rode a horse full-tilt down a steep decline in a style that only he could pull off. To add even more speed to the stunt, Jocko had the crew grease the slide to make it

Performing a bulldog on stuntman Bob Woodward in the Durango Kid film *Phantom Valley* (1948) (11 × 14 lobby card).

extra slippery. Jocko might not yet have been the best horseman in Hollywood, but his athleticism created a knack for being able to stay in the saddle at times when speed and gravity should have seen him thrown. Crawford Cantarini called him "more cat than human being" and said that he was "considered by his peers to be one of the greatest stuntmen in the business."

Star Gregory Peck broke his ankle on the film so Jocko got to do much more than his thrilling horse stunts. That's Jocko who pounces on female lead Anne Baxter and rolls around in the hay with her. Peck only came in to perform the close-up dialogue. Former U.S. Marine John Russell has a prominent role and takes part in a fight scene with Peck. The 6'3", 190-pound Russell would became a lifelong friend of Jocko. As had happened when he worked with Errol Flynn and Randolph Scott, Jocko's abilities and professionalism greatly impressed Peck. The two became friends, and Jocko doubled Peck again in the western *Only the Valiant* (1951) and the seafaring action picture *The World in His Arms* (1952).

Jocko was unique for a stuntman in many ways. He had an extremely light touch when doing the traditional bulldog stunt where one man jumps on another and pulls him from a horse to the ground. Bulldogs could be a dangerous stunt if the two bodies became entwined on their way down, but the actors and stunt performers who worked with Jocko barely if ever felt themselves touch the ground. It seems Jocko had the ability to hit a man on the horse with little impact and absorb the ground himself while shielding his fellow stuntman. Jocko gained plenty of experience on the matter: He had performed no less than 75 bulldogs for the cameras within his first two years in the business.

Even horses reacted differently when Jocko jumped on them. It's a natural instinct for a horse to move when it senses an object descending upon it, and that's one reason many stuntmen prefer working with automobiles rather than animals. In Jocko's case, however, horses barely flinched when he was flying off balconies toward them. They learned not to fear his light touch, and he could land in the saddle without a reaction from a well-trained horse. Jocko would hit first with his knees and tense his legs on the sides of the horse to slow his descent and protect his own groin area, then gallop off impressively in one take. New horses sometimes wore blinders so they couldn't see Jocko flying down upon them.

Legend has it Jocko once had a skittish horse on a Durango Kid set but managed to outsmart the animal when he was supposed to make a jump from a saloon balcony into the saddle. Jocko realized that the horse was familiar with set protocol and tensed up when it heard the director call out "Camera" and "Action!" Jocko talked to the director and crew beforehand to work out the shot. When everything was in place, the director called out "Lunch!" The horse relaxed, and Jocko landed perfectly in the saddle for the running camera.

As word spread through the industry about Jocko, many of the producers and studios assumed he was working under the tutelage of Harvey Parry, a veteran ramrod who headed up the premier stuntmen working on the major films. Parry had been around since the silent days and doubled James Cagney for a number of years. He was known as "The Dean of Stuntmen" and had a spotless reputation with the studios. When Parry realized that studios thought Jocko was working under him, he pulled the independent stuntman aside and was amazed to learn Jocko had no formal training in the proper way to pull off stunts for the camera. Parry offered to train Jocko in the correct way to do movie stunts. Jocko set about training with Parry and learning from the master. Parry and his men were tough on Jocko, but the experience gave him the polish he needed for his already solid foundation.

Jocko also trained under veteran stuntman Allen Pomeroy during this period. Jocko spent a majority of his free time at the Riverside horse stables in Burbank, where he rode constantly to improve his horsemanship. He practiced archery, fencing, gunplay, twirling ropes, and cracking a bullwhip, and brushed up on his skill with automobiles and motorcycles should he be called upon to participate in chases and crashes. Boxing and judo were other endeavors he gained expertise in. Many years later Parry rated Jocko among the best stuntmen of all time. He told *The Book of Movie Lists*, "For a big guy, he was about as gifted as you can get. There was very little he couldn't do. What a jumper!"

Jocko was signed to double John Wayne on the seafaring adventure *Wake of the Red Witch* (1948). The studio wanted Jocko to jump from a dock to a ship for the star and roll through a fire during a fight scene. When Jocko arrived on the Republic Studios set and donned the Duke's outfit, the star began to have second thoughts. Wayne took a long look at Jocko's fantastically trim hips and waistline and decided audiences would never believe that build belonged to the beefy Duke. When Jocko was done setting up and rehearsing the stunt, Wayne announced that he wanted to do it himself. He had Jocko paid off and sent home. Jocko liked to joke to friends that Wayne sent him home because Jocko was too pretty.[3] *Wake of the Red Witch* is often included among Jocko's credits, as it should be, for his work as a behind-the-scenes stunt coordinator. Despite being denied the opportunity to work, Jocko and the Duke found they had a lot in common. "We were always good friends," Jocko told the *Dallas Morning News*.

A few months later, Jocko was close to getting a call to double for Wayne on *The Fighting Kentuckian* (1949). The script called for the Duke to vault flat-footed onto a horse, and none of the stuntmen working on the film that day were deemed athletically capable or suitably photogenic. The film's stunt coordinator Cliff Lyons was in a quandary and ready to send a summons for Jocko. One of the utility stuntmen, Chuck Roberson, stepped forward and claimed he could make the leap onto the horse. The 6'4" Roberson nailed the leap and went on to be Wayne's personal stunt double for the next 25 years. Ironically, that particular stunt as described is not in the finished film.

Some sources list *The Fighting Kentuckian* among Jocko's credits, and Wayne himself seems to remember Jocko working on the film. According to the Wayne biography *Shooting Star*, Wayne describes Jocko as "our chief stuntman." It's quite possible Jocko worked with Wayne at other points in the Republic film. Wayne seems to remember that nobody (including Jocko) could do the horse vault, but had Jocko been there it would have been a piece of cake for him unless he was nursing an injury. That flat-footed horse vault was something he did routinely on the Durango Kid films.

The Fighting Kentuckian is full of horse and saddle falls, hard riding, and fast mounts, so there would have been plenty of work for Jocko. One stunt that could be Jocko has Wayne jumping from a second story balcony onto his horse for a fast getaway, the type of Durango Kid stunt that Jocko specialized in. There's another brawl sequence in which stuntman Dave Sharpe runs up a short flight of stairs with a mob chasing him. At the top of the stairs a tall man goes over the top of Sharpe's back and straight up into the air and down the stairs. Luckily the approaching mob of bodies is now there to break his fall. It's another gag that has Jocko written all over it, and if Wayne was describing Jocko as the chief stuntman

Jocko practices his cowboy skills by throwing a lasso on set.

on the film, it probably is him. No other stuntmen have claimed credit for these two difficult stunts over the years. It might have been interesting for Jocko's career had Wayne used him more prominently here or on future films. As it was, Jocko was not hurting for work as his reputation continued to grow favorably.

Normally it's acknowledged that it takes at least five years for a stuntman to get a small foothold in the business. They often begin with extra work, graduate to minor stunts, and upon earning the trust of stunt coordinators begin to obtain regular work. In many cases they are only as good as their last stunt or as long as they remain injury-free. By the time they begin to work and earn any money at the craft, their athletic skills might be declining with age. Only a small percentage of stunt people actually work with any regularity and they have a monopoly and first crack at all the top jobs. Jocko had risen to the top of the industry in less than two years and was reportedly making close to $30,000 a year, a nearly unheard-of sum for a stuntman in that era. It's been claimed that from 1946 to 1950 he did stunt work on approximately 175 films and amassed more than 350 individual stunts without ever missing a day of work. It was not uncommon for a top stuntman to work on as many as two or three films a day if the work was at the studios.

Jocko was outwardly so calm, cool, and collected when it came to doing stunt work that legend has it that he was sometimes found napping on the set between takes. There was little of the anxiety or nervousness displayed that many of his brethren commonly endured before a big stunt. In reality, Jocko liked to meditate and was so focused mentally on the task at hand that others mistook this for a cavalier nonchalance. He called it "controlled relaxation." Due to his fearless reputation he was often approached by producers with the most dangerous gags. Jocko knew when to say no, and that was often the end of it for all concerned. When planning a stunt, Jocko would figure out not only how to do it, but how to react with countermeasures if anything were to go wrong. Fellow stuntmen felt that if Jocko walked away from a stunt, no one else should want a part of it. One director of the day noted confidently that Jocko would tackle any stunt suggested. He was soon being spoken of in the same breath as Dave Sharpe, "The Crown Prince of Stuntmen."

Sharpe was an all-around stuntman who literally could do it all. A former gymnast with national championships to his credit, he could ride, fight, fall, and leap with such panache and style that fans are still talking about the stunts he did in Republic Studio serials decades later. He was brought into the business by Douglas Fairbanks and regularly doubled Douglas Fairbanks, Jr., in swashbucklers. For years when the major studios had a big stunt to do, they went to Sharpe first. Jocko held Sharpe in high regard and claimed that he was the greatest stuntman ever. In fairness to Jocko though, Sharpe stood about 5'8" and weighed roughly 160 pounds. Jocko was unique in the sense that he was a big man who could fly through the air in a similar fashion to Sharpe, and that fact was not lost upon those who worked with Jocko. Some took to calling Jocko the "King of the Stuntmen." Sharpe himself opted to label Jocko as the best big man in the business. Actress Peggy Stewart told *Favorite Westerns*, "Jock Mahoney and Davey Sharpe were like two graceful cats whose feet never seemed to be touching the ground."

As quickly as Jocko made it to the top of the stunt profession, he saw a new challenge in the sense that he was not yet considered an actor. He'd play small parts in the Durango Kid films billed as Jacques O'Mahoney or Jack O'Mahoney, but that was often done for the filmmakers to save on budget. By casting a stuntman such as Jocko, they didn't have to hire an actor if the part called for a stunt. Still, it was giving Jocko experience speaking in front of the cameras. One of his favorite sayings was "In every stuntman there is an actor trying to get out." Jocko had small acting parts in the films *Over the Santa Fe Trail* (1947), *Swing the Western Way* (1947), and *Smoky Mountain Melody* (1948) in addition to performing stunts for those pictures. He even had a bit part in *Jolson Sings Again* (1949). Actor Burt Reynolds told *The Book of Movie Lists*, "Jocko was too big and too damn handsome not to get his kisser on the screen."

Branching out from the Durango Kid films, Jocko began to play parts in a number of short films at Columbia starring the Three Stooges. Among the titles were *Out West* (1947), *Fuelin' Around* (1949), *Squareheads of the Round Table* (1949), *Punchy Cowpunchers* (1950), *Knutzy Knights* (1954), and *Hot Stuff* (1956). *Knutzy Knights* utilized recycled footage from *Squareheads* while *Hot Stuff* borrowed from *Fuelin' Around*. These were classic examples of the physical comedy the Stooges excelled in. In most cases, Jocko had little to do but look handsome and act earnest. He was typically cast as the romantic interest of female lead Christine McIntyre, playing characters such as Cedric the Blacksmith in *Squareheads* with noted unease. In *Fuelin' Around* he's a jail guard who gets his head stuck between the bars after being sweet-talked by McIntyre.

He does get to shine in *Out West* and *Punchy Cowpunchers* as the Arizona Kid; his screen presence and camera awareness is markedly improved. Jocko even manages to elicit his own laughs as he takes a number of pratfalls and drawls lines like, "I fell off my horse," "I forgot my guitar," and "I forgot to load my guns." *Punchy Cowpunchers* concludes with a visually amazing Jocko stunt as he's prepared to walk off into the sunset alone. To keep him, McIntyre hurls a ceramic vase that crushes against Jocko's head. With perfect timing Jocko goes into a full front flip and lands on his back. This is all done with a guitar in his hands. Jocko's son Jim considers this to be one of the most impressive stunts Jocko ever performed.[4] Even many loyal Stooge fans agree that Jocko managed to steal these films away from the talented comedians.

His greatest challenge as an actor in the Stooge shorts was not to burst out laughing as Moe Howard, Larry Fine, and Shemp Howard carried on with their spirited shenanigans. Jocko remembered the Stooges as distinctly different men off-camera: They all enjoyed betting the horses and were often on the phone with their bookies or drumming up poker games. Jocko didn't like to gamble and opted not to lose his money to any of the Stooges. Moe was the most serious of the lot and could be quite introspective when the cameras weren't rolling. The Stooges did spend a lot of time rehearsing the physical comedy but were free to ad-lib and often threw other performers off, something they took delight in doing. Jocko told *Favorite Westerns*: "The hardest part about that was keeping a straight face. Because I have the wildest sense of humor of anybody God ever put on this green earth.... There I was just learning to act, trying to be so serious at what I was doing. All the while, those lovable idiots were having a ball."

In 1948 former Olympic swimming champion Johnny Weissmuller was coming to the end of the line in his Tarzan films and a casting call was put out looking for a replacement. Jocko was one of the 1000-plus hopeful actors and athletes who auditioned to be the new King of the Jungle. Jocko made an impressive showing and was reportedly one of the finalists. The part ultimately went to 6'4", 210-pound Lex Barker, a handsome former Princeton University athlete and World War II vet already under contract to RKO. Barker played the part until 1954, when Gordon Scott took over. Barker, who was briefly married to actress Lana Turner, later went to Europe to star in films throughout the 1960s and died of a heart attack in 1973 at the age of 54.

Around this time, Jocko came to the attention of noted producer Walter Wanger, who signed the stuntman to an acting contract. However, no immediate acting parts in Wanger

The Three Stooges (Larry, Moe, Shemp) and Jocko in the Columbia short *Punchy Cowpunchers* (1950).

films materialized although there was a major western and a seafaring story in development titled *Anne of the West Indies*. Susan Hayward was set to star with Jocko. Wanger reportedly wanted to make action pictures around the world starring Jocko, but was known for his lengthy time spent in pre-production dealing with large budgets. Legend has it the contract had a "no stunting" stipulation and was torn up when Jocko was caught continuing to perform stunt work on the side while waiting for his big break to materialize. *Anne of the West Indies* was eventually made in 1951 by director Jacques Tourneur with Jean Peters and Louis Jourdan.

On a personal front, Jocko and his wife Lorraine went through a divorce. No doubt the abrupt changes in Jocko's life were at play, and it's highly likely the young couple were already going separate ways due to the time Jocko had spent in the service. They married young and they divorced young. It should be noted that the marriage of Jocko's parents Charles and Ruth had not survived either. Ruth and her young son Lew still were living with Jocko, who had to keep a watchful eye on his mother after she became involved in promoting a card club that skirted legal boundaries as a pyramid scheme. Jocko took some of the money he was making from his movies and purchased a string of beauty salons to keep his hairstylist mother otherwise engaged.

Lorraine settled in the Long Beach area with their children Jim and Kathleen and dabbled as a fashion model. Lorraine eventually married Charles Doyle and opened the Lorraine Doyle School of Modeling and Self-Improvement in Long Beach. Jocko began dating Durango Kid leading lady Virginia Hunter, an actress under contract at Columbia. Jocko temporarily took up residence in the guest house of comedian Stan Laurel of Laurel and Hardy fame. Jocko's actor pal Rand Brooks lived in the main house with his wife Lois Laurel, the funny man's daughter. Lois Laurel Hawes recalled both she and her husband were fond of Jocko and were happy to help.[5]

Jocko was free to play the field, and his name briefly surfaced as one of the many boyfriends of rising actress Shelley Winters. He was also friendly with young Columbia starlet Marilyn Monroe, who was under a six-month option at the studio in 1948. Jocko became engaged to actress Yvonne De Carlo in 1949 after they made the film *The Gal Who Took the West* (1949). On that movie Jocko doubled in a huge two-man fight scene between Scott Brady and John Russell in the tradition of the oft-filmed *The Spoilers*. The rugged furniture-crashing battle was another feather in Jocko's cap. It's full of impressive leaps and flips.

In his other top fight scenes from this period, Jocko doubled Sonny Tufts in a humor-filled saloon brawl with William Bishop and pals in *The Untamed Breed* (1948), doubled Randolph Scott in a battle with Victor Jory in *Canadian Pacific* (1949), and doubled Rod Cameron in a slugfest with Jeff York in *Short Grass* (1950). The *Untamed Breed* brawl saw a defeated Jocko go smashing through a glass partition, sliding under the saloon bat doors, and flipping down an outside staircase. One of his toughest fight scenes was doubling Willard Parker for a scrap with Joan Fontaine in *You Gotta Stay Happy* (1948), where he had to be especially careful not to injure the female star: Fontaine was four months pregnant at the time.

Jocko deservedly earned a reputation as a great motion picture fight man. His fights were always energetic and exciting with expert timing. There were few stuntmen or actors better at "selling" an opponent's blows. Jocko's body could fly around a room in reaction to a punch as well as anyone. He was also great at delivering a screen punch, throwing his fists from a wide enough angle so that the camera could see them. Realistic short punches are not effective on film. A screen punch should be shot over the shoulder and pass a few inches in front of the face of the man taking the punch. The taker throws his head in time with the passing punch to give the appearance of a hit. This was the method that Yakima Canutt and John Wayne developed for the cameras in their early B-western days. It revolutionized the way fights were filmed and saved a lot of shoulder and arm bruises.

Jocko was blinding quick with these telegraphed punches, so much so that there was never a need to under-crank the film, a common practice during this period to speed up the action for the audience's eyes. Jocko also had great camera awareness and was always able to quickly reposition his body within a take so that the camera couldn't tell his punches were swings and misses rather than swings and hits. This ability to keep the camera running created a need for fewer edits in post-production and gave a nice sense of flow and continuity to Jocko's fights.

There was little doubt that Jocko's unique abilities made him stand out from any crowd. It was a case of love at first sight for Yvonne De Carlo when she saw him on the *Gal Who Took the West* set. She described her hormones as raging when she eyed this Adonis and his physique. The leading lady immediately sent her stand-in Marie Bodie to get all the information available on the stuntman, and then the star and stuntman began to date. In her autobiography, De Carlo described Jocko as "something of a romantic." After several dates, he kissed her for the first time after an outing to the Circle J Ranch. The romance progressed over the ensuing months and Jocko slipped a simple diamond ring on her finger while they were in a country bar high in the Sierra Nevada Mountains. By her own admission, engagements made her skittish, but for the time being she was smitten with her stunt hunk.

Yvonne De Carlo was born Margaret Yvonne Middleton in Vancouver, British Columbia, Canada, in 1922. The dark-haired beauty entered show business as a professional dancer and took her mother's maiden name as her professional surname. She became a star with the lead in Universal's *Salome, Where She Danced* (1945) and began to top-line that studio's films throughout the late 1940s. She starred in *Slave Girl* (1947), one of the many costume dramas in which Jocko worked as a stuntman. She also began to date and publicly flaunt a succession of prominent men, including actor Howard Duff and eccentric billionaire Howard Hughes. She initially had high hopes that Jocko was the man she had been waiting for, even if she knew that relationships among actors rarely worked out due to the business itself.

Despite the distance often created by film locations, De Carlo and Jocko remained a hot item for roughly a year. At one point they looked at ranch property together in San Luis Obispo. A getaway to the Palm Springs Racquet Club yielded some noted publicity photos of the two enjoying one another's company both on horseback and at the pool. The relationship was the first to put Jocko's name in the syndicated newspaper columns and fan magazines. De Carlo spoke glowingly of Jocko to columnist Harrison Carroll: "Some of the muscle boys are dumb. But Jacques is intelligent. He's accomplished, too. He's a champion swimmer. I'm sure he's going places on the screen. Somebody's going to pick him up and make an action star out of him."

The turning point in their relationship came when De Carlo became pregnant. In her autobiography, she writes that she and Jocko were both looking forward to having a child but that a large ovarian cyst was discovered during a medical check-up. In the process of having the tumor removed, she lost the child in her first trimester. "Things were never quite the same between Jocko and me from then on," De Carlo wrote. "I think our greatest problems had to do with career. He may have resented my success and his own lack of it and while he said he appreciated my help trying to get him jobs, he probably resented that as well. He was a big man with an ego to match."

Jocko didn't like that their relationship always seemed to be played out in the gossip columns and accused De Carlo of using his "fame" as a stuntman for her own gain. "What fame?" she bluntly countered in Harrison Carroll's column. His only fame thus far had come from "being seen" with her. In reality Jocko was at the top of his profession. The only problem was that it was an anonymous profession in the eyes of the public. It's true that Jocko sought fame as a cowboy star, but he didn't like De Carlo's habit of turning their personal lives into public lives. After splitting up, Jocko and De Carlo briefly reconciled in late 1950 but the relationship was not meant to last; there were too many arguments. As De Carlo wrote, "The good times didn't come frequently enough to offset the bad."

After the break-up, Jocko briefly squired around buxom blonde actress Irish McCalla, who would go on to star on TV as *Sheena, Queen of the Jungle.* A date with McCalla was chronicled for publicity purposes in the January 1951 issue of the magazine *Eve.* Jocko and

Publicity photograph in Palm Springs while Yvonne De Carlo looks on. (Bernard of Hollywood.)

the six-foot McCalla danced at the Mocambo, saw Frankie Laine sing at Ciro's, rode the merry-go-round at Ocean Park Pier, and dined at Charlie Fox's. McCalla later recalled a memorable Jocko moment for her on-line biography. She had a second story apartment in Santa Monica and Jocko walked her up the steps to her door. Upon giving her a good night kiss, he closed his eyes and fainted over the landing. A shocked McCalla looked over the edge only to see a smiling Jocko looking up at her from the backseat of his strategically parked convertible. This was one of the hazards of dating a fall guy. Jocko and McCalla remained good friends, and she sought out his business and stunt advice upon landing her *Sheena* TV show.

Jocko's acting career was indeed on the upswing with encouragement coming from Charles Starrett. On the Durango Kid films, Jocko was elevated to lead dress heavy for the film *The Blazing Trail* (1949). Billed as Jock O'Mahoney, he plays town boss gambler Full House Patterson. It's a capable performance and shows the beginning of Jocko becoming comfortable with dialogue. Despite his hectic stunt schedule he still found time to study acting on the side. The film itself is full of Jocko. He engages in a fight with Starrett that sees Jocko laid out on the ground. Jocko had perfected taking a punch and flinging his body several feet into the air until his back was parallel to the ground before plummeting to the earth. The fight begins with a bulldog from a horse that has the two sliding down an embankment before resorting to fisticuffs. Al Wyatt likely wore the Durango Kid outfit for that stunt. In addition to playing the main bad guy, Jocko doubled Starrett extensively throughout the rest of the film for some nifty action scenes.

Jocko followed this up with a good guy supporting part in the Durango Kid film *Bandits of El Dorado* (1949). Jocko plays Texas Ranger Tim Starling, who for much of the picture is in pursuit of Starrett. At one point Jocko gets to chase himself as the Durango Kid climbs atop the town's buildings to make an escape, culminating with a second floor balcony leap into his horse's saddle. There's plenty more action in the film with Jocko doing some superb stunt work, including a leap from a wagon and a vault onto his horse. All ends well with new pals Starrett and Jocko in smiles at the end of the picture. Jocko was action coordinator for the Durango films and the studio gave him carte blanche to devise whatever stunts he wanted on the western town street. With Jocko also acting in the films, the stunts would be saved until the final days of the production just in case Jocko injured or killed himself.

Jocko was again called on to double Randolph Scott in *The Doolins of Oklahoma* (1949), a film in which he had a pivotal supporting role as an outlaw character named Tulsa Jack Blake. He's a good bad guy in a story filled with anti-heroes. As a double, Jocko got to display his keen horsemanship during a standout night-time chase scene through a narrow mountain passage filmed in Lone Pine. This chase included a wild ride down a steep decline. The second unit action for the film was directed by legendary stuntman Yakima Canutt and contains what Jocko considered to be his scariest stunt up to that time.

The outlaw gang is boarding a train and Jocko is the first man to make the transfer from horse to moving locomotive before they reach an upcoming culvert. Such a stunt is best done at fast speed to make the transition from the horse the smoothest. On Jocko's first attempt, the horse shied away from the train. On the second go-through the horse came close enough for Jocko to make his jump to the train. However, the horse pulled away at the last second, and Jocko nearly missed the handrail he was leaping for. His grip was far lower on the rail than he intended and his legs were perilously close to the train's powerful wheels. Worse, the second stuntman was making his own jump over the top of the dangling Jocko, who was finally able to pull himself out of harm's way with a great effort. The rest of the stuntmen quickly followed suit before the horses reached the culvert. Jocko wrote of the experience in *Man*: saying, "I am not a religious man, but I have a speaking acquaintance with the Guy Upstairs who looks after everybody, and He has grabbed me by the seat of the pants more than once and lifted me through that last couple of feet of space I could not have made on my own."

There's a very well-done fight scene in *Doolins* between Randolph Scott and Frank Fenton, with Jocko doubling Scott. At one point Jocko has a bullwhip wrapped around him and is flung about the room's walls and tables before rallying to knock out his opponent and anyone else who gets in his way. There's an amusing close-up of Jocko's Tulsa Blake character watching the action during the fight, lest the audience wonder why Randolph Scott suddenly looks like another established character in the film. Tulsa meets his maker in a big shootout that sees him shot in the back as he tries to make it to safety. Jocko takes a blind back fall down a short set of stairs, a stunt that few others would even attempt for fear of injuring their head or neck. The show business bible *Variety* thought Jocko was "well cast."

In *The Nevadan* (1950) Jocko doubled Randolph Scott for another tense and memorable fight with Forrest Tucker (doubled by Bob Morgan) during a mine cave-in for the film's finale. While filming the fight scene, Jocko was hit by a falling beam and had a splinter of wood ram three inches into his shoulder. He had a notable supporting role as the villain's loyal strong-arm Sandy. Early in the film he beats up and knocks out star Scott, only to have the "favor" returned a few scenes later. He also has an exciting horse chase with female lead Dorothy Malone that sees a fast-riding Jocko take a jump over a fallen tree straight into the camera. He then is knocked off his horse by a low-hanging tree limb in mid-jump. It's another ingenious stunt that placed Jocko at the top of his field for planning and execution.

In *The Nevadan* he plays the kind of role that gave him a chance to make an impact, and he doesn't disappoint, showing great promise as a tough bad guy. At the same time some of his heroic quality manages to sneak through. One wonders if his loyalty to bad guy George Macready is due to an attraction to Macready's daughter Malone. It's a plot point that is never resolved but an interesting bit of subtext for Jocko's character. In real life Jocko dated Malone during this period. It had to be unique that so many leading ladies were ending up with stuntman Jocko behind the scenes rather than their leading men. The ruggedly beautiful Lone Pine location helps makes *The Nevadan* a near-classic; and *Variety* made mention of Jocko's "neat performance."

Jocko knocked off a horse in mid-jump in *The Nevadan* (1950) (11 × 14 lobby card).

Gene Autry (left) and Jocko in *Rim of the Canyon* (1949).

The quality acting parts in *Doolins* and *Nevadan* came courtesy of producer Harry Joe Brown and star Randolph Scott. Jocko thought quite highly of veteran leading man Scott, describing him as a gentleman with a lot of class. It's noteworthy that Scott, a savvy businessman who often had a hand in the production of his films, kept requesting and hiring Jocko to double him. It became a running gag on the Scott sets that while Jocko performed some bit of fantastic daring, Scott would be relaxing in his set-chair with his nose buried in *The Wall Street Journal*. When Jocko had completed the action, Scott would often look up with a smile and ask, "How did I look?"

Singing cowboy star Gene Autry had recently made his home at Columbia and took notice of Jocko. Autry tapped Jocko to play a nasty villain in his film *Rim of the Canyon* (1949). Jocko had doubled for Autry at Columbia, though in truth he was a lousy physical match for Autry, who stood about 5'9" and was thick around the belly. If John Wayne had qualms about Jocko being a convincing double, Autry must have been delirious to think that audiences would believe he was Jocko on screen. Nonetheless, Autry was a top cowboy star and starring opposite him as a bad guy was a major break for Jocko. Their fight scene in an abandoned saloon is one of the top highlights in any of Autry's films, with Jocko leaping off of staircases and tumbling over tables with great gusto. This is also the film where Jocko and two other stuntmen jump their horses off a ledge into a lake. In regard to acting with the much shorter Autry, Jocko told *Guns of the Old West,* "When we were doing a scene together, I had to bend at the knees a lot. No one was about to suggest Gene should stand on a box so we'd be the same height."

Gene Autry told *The Westerner,* "Jock Mahoney was one of the finest stuntmen and action men in movies." Autry called on Jocko to stunt double him in *Riders in the Sky* (1949) as Jocko leapt from a stagecoach onto a galloping Champion. Autry quickly brought Jocko back for another villainous role and another big fight in a horse pen and through a western set's streets in *Cow Town* (1950). Autry was doubled in this fight by Sandy Sanders. Bolstered by impressive Lone Pine location work and directed by John English, it's one of Autry's better mounted features. Jocko looks great as the black-hat villain Tod Jeffreys, although in reality he is a rather ineffective heavy plot-wise. He is bested throughout the film by Autry until his character steps aside for the film's finale. However, that involves Jocko as well as he doubles fellow bad guy Steve Darrell for another big fight scene with Autry-Sanders. Jocko had obviously made an impression on Autry, who in addition to being a cowboy star was an astute businessman. Autry promptly purchased Jocko's contract.

4

The Cowboy and Serial Star

Columbia Pictures saw the potential in their resident stuntman and were quick to cast him in an extension of his bumbling Arizona Kid character from the Three Stooges shorts. Ray Nazarro's *Hoedown* (1950) co-stars Jocko as Stoney Rhodes, a one-film cowboy star who is dropped by his studio while on a publicity tour due to his overall lack of talent. Stoney is such a "Golly" and "Aw, Shucks" simpleton that his publicity manager (Jeff Donnell) doesn't know where to begin. He can twirl his pistols but that's the extent of his talent. Singer Eddy Arnold as himself is the film's top-billed star, but it is Jocko's movie all the way. He winds up at a country music hoedown where a gang of bank robbers plan to rob the till. The gangsters take turns beating up the clumsy and idiotic Jocko, who faints at the sight of his own blood. When the bad guys aren't pummeling Jocko, Carolina Cotton's jealous boyfriend "Big Boy" Williams knocks him around. Despite his ineptitude, Cotton is enamored with the handsome cowboy. By the final reel her kiss turns him into an instant action hero as he miraculously rounds up the bad guys and has multiple studios bidding for his services.

Jocko does plenty of stunts in the film. He falls out of haylofts, engages in fistfights, and does a variety of pratfalls. The climax sees him chase down a speeding car on horseback and leap onto it. Director Nazarro apparently had no problem with star Jocko doing so many stunts, as they had worked together on several Durango Kid films. Jocko also gets to sing the song "Can't Shake the Sands of Texas from My Shoes" to his horse, though the voice is actually that of Gene Autry. The movie playfully pokes fun at this bit of business and acknowledges that it is indeed Autry's voice. Jocko even speaks directly to a poster of the Autry film *Strawberry Roan* (1948). When Jocko is implored to sing a song of his own by the dumbfounded gangsters, he unleashes a croaky version of "Froggy Goes a Courtin'" to great comic effect. It's a silly but entertaining film with Jocko front and center getting a chance to showcase his athletic and comedic skills.

In the film Jocko drove a Cadillac convertible with steer horns on the front grill and wore fancy cowboy shirts designed by Nudie's Rodeo Tailors. Actor Michael Pate, living in Australia at the time, saw a publicity picture of Jocko from the movie and for years thought that was the car Jocko actually drove. In reality, Jocko purchased a Lincoln Continental for his mode of transportation when not on a horse. Jocko was partial to the Nudie Cohn shirts in real life, as were many of the day's cowboys.

Female lead Carolina Cotton (real name: Helen Hagstrom) was a popular country singer noted for her ability to yodel. *Hoedown* was her favorite of her own films. Cotton

Singing cowboy Stoney Rhodes with Carolina Cotton in *Hoedown* (1950).

and Jocko make an appealing couple on screen, and they embarked on a number of personal appearances together to promote the film. At the 1995 Charlotte Western Film Fair, Cotton recalled Jocko: "He was one of the nicest guys in the world. He was also a good kisser. We practiced a lot on *Hoedown*. Jock was great, a terrific sense of humor."

Reviews for the movie were mixed. The influential film trade journal *Variety* noted, "O'Mahoney does as best he can with a ridiculous role." *Boxoffice* magazine added, "Jock O'Mahoney may seem overly dim-witted as a bashful cowboy star on the downgrade, but he gives an ingratiating performance nevertheless." *The Hollywood Reporter* was the most ebullient in its praise for Jocko, noting, "Jock O'Mahoney practically steals the show with his amusing portrayal of the handsome but dumb, movie cowboy star who never knows his own capacities until he is awakened by a girl's kiss."

In the summer of 1949 Jocko received a two-week visit from his Kansas City relatives the Warners. This included his eight-year-old first cousin once removed Tom Warner. The family stayed with Jocko's mom and his half-brother for the duration of the trip and met Jocko's girlfriend Yvonne De Carlo. Tom's mom Vera had taken dance classes with Jocko when they were small children so it was a nice chance for them to reminisce about their Kansas City youth. Her husband Robert accompanied Jocko to the set of *Hoedown* to see how a movie was made. When young Tom wondered what a stuntman did for a living, Jocko promised to jump off the roof of the house for him before the end of their vacation. That feat never occurred, but young Tom still came away with memories that lasted a life-time. He was impressed by Jocko's engaging personality and especially the cool way he walked and carried himself. Over 60 years later, Tom Warner likened Jocko's fluid move-ments to those of "a deer in the woods."[1]

Columbia quickly followed *Hoedown* by giving Jocko a leading role in the 15-part serial *Cody of the Pony Express* (1950) for veteran action director Spencer Gordon Bennet and notoriously penny-pinching producer Sam Katzman. The quickie action serials were shown in weekly segments at theaters before the main feature and were enduringly popular with audiences. They were also proven moneymakers. Each roughly 10-minute chapter always ended with the hero in perilous circumstances. These cliffhangers were a hit with kids and kept them coming back week after week to see how the hero escapes.

Jocko's western serial was shot at the frontier movie lot Pioneertown near Yucca Valley in the fall of 1949. He didn't play title character William Cody, but billed as Jock O'Mahoney, he still had top billing as undercover agent Jim Archer. Cody is a teenager in the storyline played by Dickie Moore, who was chosen over Dick Jones in the auditioning process. The serial afforded Jocko plenty of opportunity to display his prowess at jumping into the saddle, but curiously little else.

The studio assigned stuntman Al Wyatt to do anything deemed too dangerous for their new investment. Wyatt got an easy paycheck, as Jocko resolved to do all the action allowable. As a leading man Jocko always made sure his stuntmen rehearsed the stunts and were paid fully before he did the stunts for the camera himself. The problem with *Cody of the Pony Express* was that when the action started, Jocko usually stepped aside and watched Dickie Moore handle the bad guys. It's curious why they would cast a stuntman in a lead role and then have him do so little action. Perhaps Jocko was so insistent on doing his action for the cameras that the filmmakers opted to write out the majority of his character's risk-taking for safety's sake.

Despite Jocko's presence, *Cody* is disappointing in the action department and suffers from the continuity problems that plagued many serials of the day. The rocky desert boulders tend to make more of a lasting impression than the cast. There are few Jocko action highlights outside of some quick mounts and an abbreviated fight scene or two. When Jocko squares off with bad guy Rusty Wescoatt, a real-life professional wrestler, he puts the beefy villain down with a single punch. Certainly there was a missed opportunity there for a show-stop-ping brawl. Veteran bad guy Pierce Lyden is the main henchman and it seems as if the serial will lead to a showdown with Jocko, but after 15 chapters nothing much happens at all. Even a handful of routine Jocko stunts would have gone a long way to improving the dis-jointed feeling the serial leaves the viewer. Figuratively tying Jocko's hands and cutting him off at the knees in this role is the serial's greatest weakness.

Many still came away impressed with the new chapterplay presence. Serial authority William C. Cline wrote in his book *In the Nick of Time*, "Of the rugged, rough-and-tumble heroes, none was more so than Jock Mahoney. A big, handsome fellow and an accomplished stuntman — having taken the licks and spills for many leading stars — he was a natural for serial stardom as a hero."

At least the heroic part was more serious fare than his previous bumpkin characters for Columbia, proving he was more than a one-trick pony. A lanky Jocko dresses in a fringed buckskin shirt and sports a pencil-thin mustache. He's flatfooted in moccasins but still stands a head taller than most of the rest of the cast. The *Cody* storyline provides only a hint of romance at its conclusion, but Jocko managed to work that in off-screen. Pretty leading lady Peggy Stewart, a mainstay at Republic Studios, became Jocko's real-life girl-friend. The two dated for over a year, often enjoying lunch dates with Jocko's mother and weekend trips to Laguna to see Charles Starrett and his wife Mary.

Stewart hailed from West Palm Beach, Florida, and seemed right up Jocko's alley. She had been a swimming champion at age ten and a riding instructor at 14. Despite their common interests, Jocko and Stewart would drift apart. Stewart later guest-starred on Jocko's TV show *Yancy Derringer* and always spoke highly of her leading man, telling *The Los Angeles Daily News*: "He was like a cat, you know. He'd take off on a jump, and he'd look like he was on baling wire. For that big a man, he was so fast and so light."

In August of 1949 Jocko made one of his first publicity performances, serving as a guest with Stewart at a Texas-style picnic for a Long Beach function. Jocko judged the watermelon and corn-eating contests. In October he appeared at Desert Hot Spring's Forty-Niners Centennial Festival and a Fire Hall Benefit with Carolina Cotton. Jocko and Cotton were guests on the TV show *At Home with the Harmons* in November, and in mid–December the two appeared in the Coachella Valley Christmas Parade in Indio–Palm Desert. At the close of the year, Jocko returned to the Pacific Coast Club to serve as the master of ceremonies for the Golden Slipper Ball. Personal appearances became an integral part of Jocko's growing celebrity.

Jocko was quick to land another leading role. The *Kangaroo Kid* (1950) was filmed Down Under in Sofala, New South Wales, with a handful of American actors. In this interesting curio, Jocko starred as American cowboy detective Tex Kinnane, chasing a criminal responsible for a series of gold robberies while finding time to romance Veda Ann Borg (who replaced Jocko's real-life former girlfriend Dorothy Malone in the part). Jocko makes a handsome and charming hero, even if he's too often forced by the script to play the ingénue in this foreign land. There's a decent saloon brawl with Jocko taking on two men, and he gets to perform a leap from the saddle to a stagecoach in close-up at the conclusion. The film was directed by the veteran Lesley Selander, who knew how to effectively stage action scenes.

Although some of the production facilities were not top-of-the-line, Jocko and the American crew enjoyed the location and loved the local Aussie people. Publicity photos showed Jocko interacting with the film's mascot, a kangaroo known as Baby Kangaroo Joe. Gene Autry presented Jocko with a new saddle as a parting gift before he left the States. Jocko was actually a late replacement in the starring role for his friend Guy Madison, but the Tex Kinnane character fit Jocko much better than his previous leads. He's a true hero here, able-bodied and stalwart, as he takes on the bad guys single-handed. The Australian crew gave him a boomerang and a kangaroo rug as mementos of appreciation. There was talk in the trades of Jocko returning to Australia in the fall of 1950 to star in a pair of *Kangaroo Kid* sequels, but Jocko ultimately became involved with other projects and was unable to make the trip.

Jocko received some of his first press from the film with a self-penned article appearing in the September 1950 edition of the Australian magazine *Man*: In "Break Your Neck for a

Thrill," Jocko detailed some of his biggest stunts to date. Jocko also began to be featured in the state-bound magazines *Western Stars* and *Movie Thrills* as well as gracing the cover of the Standard Comic *Western Hearts*. *Kangaroo Kid* didn't receive much in the way of a critical reception, although *The Hollywood Reporter* did note that Jocko "is a handsome figure of a man, who acts convincingly, rides and shoots well, and can put on a rugged hand-to-hand fight with the best of our western stars."

Columbia Pictures felt that 46-year-old Charles Starrett was beginning to get a bit long in the tooth and that Jocko was a logical successor. Jocko was offered the Durango Kid starring role, but turned it down out of respect for Starrett. This bit of chivalry allowed Starrett to continue in his trademark role for another two years with Jocko remaining as his double. It was an easy choice for Jocko as he had other offers in the making. Gene Autry was in the process of developing a television series for his Flying-A Productions and wanted Jocko to play a wandering cowboy called the Range Rider. Singing cowboys Rex Allen and Russell Arms were also in early contention for the role, but Jocko prevailed thanks to his superior athletic abilities. Veteran stuntman Neil Summers wrote in *Blazing West*, "Any other choice to play the role would have been ludicrous as Mr. Mahoney is acknowledged by his peers to be one of the premier stuntmen ever to grace films."

Jocko did agree with Columbia to begin playing more substantial parts in the Starrett films and was elevated to co-star status for the rest of the Durango Kid pictures. Ironically, Columbia chose to have him play a recurring character known as Jack Mahoney in much the same manner as Gene Autry and Roy Rogers played themselves on screen. Jocko told *Television Western Players of the Fifties*: "I was young and good looking enough to kiss the girl. The hero, Charles Starrett, a great guy, was older and only got to kiss his horse. There was no special reason why I played myself. Nothing about those B-westerns had much reason to it, but they were great fun to do."

Jocko treated the Columbia lot a bit like a college campus and remained the popular rascal he had always been, despite many of the contracted performers around him living in fear of the iron fist rule of studio mogul Harry Cohn. Even established stars on the lot such as Glenn Ford, Broderick Crawford, and Rita Hayworth had to be careful of being put on unpaid suspension or, worse, forced to make inferior films that could hurt a career. At a studio Christmas party, Jocko walked right up to Cohn and told him he hoped to spend many more years working for him because he wanted to get deep into the man's pockets. Anything involving money tended to make Cohn glaze over, and he stared at the grinning Jocko in amazement. Jocko certainly liked to have fun with people, even someone as powerful and intimidating as Harry Cohn.

On another occasion, Jocko was having lunch in the studio commissary with Jack Lewis and was called over by Cohn's chief hatchet man Jack Fier. He read Jocko the riot act about some minor infraction while Jocko stood there smiling. The commissary had grown quiet as all watched Jocko and Fier. When Fier was done, Jocko promised, "I won't do it again, booby," then bent down and planted a big kiss on Fier's bald head. The commissary broke into laughter as Fier shrank in embarrassment. Jocko walked away still chuckling. The daring required to take on the big guns wasn't that far removed from the courage it took to perform a death-defying physical stunt.

Jocko's favorite target of mischief on the Columbia lot was Ray Nazarro, a demanding director who wasn't particularly well-liked by many performers. Actor Marshall Reed recalled an especially humorous occasion when Nazarro was trying to direct a scene on a saloon set. Jocko had climbed high into the sound stage's rafters with an Indian tom-tom drum and beat on it continuously. Nazarro had no idea where the noise was coming from as he tried to set up his shots for the camera. Every time the exasperated director was ready to call "Action," the drumbeat ceased. However, Nazarro had no idea if it would stop or not. When the scene was finished, the tom-tom beating resumed. Reed told *Serial World*, "Jock had Ray Nazarro going nuts because Jock did it all day long and Ray didn't know where the hell it was coming from."

During this period, Jocko appeared as part of a charity gymnastic show at the Long Beach Hospital and met Beverly Washburn, the six-year-old sister of one of the young acrobats appearing in the show. Jocko always had a soft spot in his heart for children and enjoyed speaking to Washburn and her mother. A few months later he encountered them in the offices of Columbia Pictures where young Beverly was auditioning for her first acting role. Jocko went behind the door to talk to the casting directors and the child actress suddenly had her first part in the film *The Killer That Stalked New York*. In the book *Eye on Science Fiction*, Washburn commented, "I really feel that I would not have gotten that part if it hadn't been for Jock Mahoney putting in a good word for me."

So as not to be typed in westerns exclusively, Jocko showed up in a variety of fare. These appearances often went without billing and involved a stunt, but they were giving him screen time and building some facial recognition within the industry. In the Cold War espionage tale *David Harding, Counterspy* (1950) Jocko plays a strong-arm man in a suit and tie. Star Willard Parker throws him through a door. It's later revealed Jocko is one of the good guys and part of the David Harding intelligence team. Jocko's mostly standing tall in the background of several subsequent scenes, although he does have a nice bit where he gets to flash an engaging smile and reveal a talent for lip-reading. *The Tougher They Come* (1950) was a logging adventure with lumberjacks Wayne Morris and Preston Foster pitted against one another. They ultimately join forces to take down bad guy William Bishop. Jocko played a secondary role in the Ray Nazarro film in addition to doubling in rough-and-tumble fight scenes. In the swashbuckling period piece *The Lady and the Bandit* (1951) Jocko doubles star Louis Hayward on horseback and appears in the part of a troublemaker who starts a fight in a tavern. The highlight of that scene sees Jocko jump atop a table that is immediately overturned and he falls back against a wall. Seconds later he is hit by a chair thrown across the room.

Despite branching out into other genres, Jocko remained best known as a cowboy and was still the top stuntman on the Columbia lot. The studio allowed him to ramrod the stunts on the films he worked on now, meaning he got to design and choreograph as well as perform. He was top dog, and all the other stuntmen on the film answered to Jocko. Although not official or credited on the screen, this ramrod position is what became known as stunt coordinator a few decades later. The western roles got bigger and Jocko's name began to consistently reach the opening credits. Based upon his impressive showing in *The Doolins of Oklahoma*, *Rim of the Canyon*, *The Nevadan*, and *Cow Town*, Jocko began to get some of his best parts yet, playing bad guys.

In the Randolph Scott western *Santa Fe* (1951) Jocko plays a henchman named Crake and sports a fancy mustache. When he shows up at the railroad site, Scott knocks him into a wheelbarrow and runs him off, literally dumping Jocko into a ditch. Jocko sticks around throughout the film as a menace and has a big climactic fight with Scott atop a moving train's flat car. Scott was doubled in the scene by Bob Morgan until it came time to fall off the speeding train. At that point Jocko doubled Scott while Morgan doubled Jocko. Jocko as Scott then managed to climb back onto the train and resume the battle. Jocko once again became Jocko and Morgan became Scott. "Actually, I ended up fighting myself," Jocko told *Guns of the Old West.*

The climax called for Crake to fall off the moving train and down a steep decline. Jocko did not require a stunt double: He checked the location carefully and cleared himself a long path free of rocks and boulders. However, even Jocko's meticulous preparation was reliant on the skill of others. "Something went wrong in the timing," Jocko told *Guns of the Old West.* "Right after the director yelled for me to take a dive, I found myself bouncing off the boulders I had moved earlier. I was 20 feet from the path I had cleared!" Luckily, Jocko managed to escape injury, and the fight with Scott is considered a classic. Jocko earned the princely sum of $1,500 to fall from the train.

Santa Fe is a fine example of Jocko not only at the peak of his stunt career but emerging as an acting presence to be reckoned with. *Variety* noted of his performance, "O'Mahoney delivers nicely." It's a solid Randolph Scott sagebrush saga although Scott's best films were still a few years away. For director Budd Boetticher he made a series of tough westerns that rounded out the decade and solidified his reputation as a cowboy legend. Jocko no doubt could have continued on as Scott's stunt double indefinitely, but his own acting career was gaining too much momentum to be ignored. Al Wyatt took over as Scott's main double for his remaining films.

Jocko played another second-tier bad guy in action director Phil Karlson's Columbia western *The Texas Rangers* (1951). The film is a solid programmer for star George Montgomery with a mustached Jocko playing one of a group of super-bad bad guys led by William Bishop. Jocko is largely strong and silent through much of the movie until springing into action during the well-filmed climax involving a shootout on a train. There's a nice one-shot of Jocko dismounting his horse, running over a small hill, and jumping onto the train. Jocko doesn't pick the easiest landing spot either. He lands on a car filled with uneven pieces of wood. Jocko never misses a step though and is firing both his pistols into the engineer within seconds.

Montgomery makes it onto the train via a nice Jocko-doubled leap to engage in the shootout. Jocko wounds Montgomery in the arm, and the star takes a nasty headfirst fall between two cars before catching himself. It's difficult to identify Montgomery's stunt double, but it's likely Jocko once again doing this dangerous stunt. Montgomery then shoots a surprised Jocko, freeing the stuntman of his acting duties so he can concentrate on orchestrating the many stunts in the film's exciting climax which involves a brutal fistfight between Montgomery and bad guy Douglas Kennedy. Jerome Courtland and John Dehner are also in the cast, making it a busy picture for Jocko when it came time for the stunt doubling.

Jerome Courtland told *Classic Images:* "Jock Mahoney did a lot of the stunt work as well. He was kind of like a big brother to me. He'd take me out to Ralph McCutcheon's ranch and teach me all sorts of trick mounts and things of that nature. And, as with so many of the really good stuntmen, Jocko had the ability to even walk like the actors [he was] supposed to be, so there was never a point in the scene when the moviegoer knew for sure where the actor stopped and his double began."

Still from *Roar of the Iron Horse* (1951).

Jocko squeezed out one more starring role in a 15-chapter Columbia serial, *Roar of the Iron Horse, Rail Blazer of the Apache Trail* (1951). Jocko plays undercover marshal Jim Grant, who wears flat moccasins rather than cowboy boots. The moccasins allowed Jocko safer footwear in doing the many stunts the script called for, as well as hopping on and off the title train multiple times. The rest of Jocko's outfit ensemble consisted of good-luck gifts given to him by no less than Gregory Peck, Errol Flynn, Gene Autry, and Charles Starrett. Unlike *Cody of the Pony Express*, this serial affords Jocko plenty of opportunity to ride and fight, with Jocko slugging it out against veteran heavies Mickey Simpson, Pierce Lyden, Rusty Wescoatt, and Charles Horvath, a former judo instructor in the U.S. Marines. Much of the action was done on location in Carson City, Nevada. At one point Jocko and Pierce Lyden unintentionally went off an embankment with their horses and ended up in a snow bank at the bottom of a steep canyon.

Acting-wise, Jocko is smooth and pleasantly confident in his delivery. In many of his acting scenes he appears relaxed with his arms comfortably crossed or his hands draped in his gun holster, solving the age-old problem for an actor of what to do with their hands. Most importantly, Jocko seems to be listening to the other actors then responding with realism. He makes a fine cowboy hero in this above-average serial. As far as action, *Iron Horse* is far and away Jocko's best serial.

Co-star Tommy Farrell was particularly impressed by Jocko's graceful horsemanship, telling Boyd Magers' *Western Clippings* that Jocko was, "the best horseman ever to ride in any western." Female lead Virginia Herrick also praised her leading man when interviewed for the book *Ladies of the Western*: "On the set they'd talk about Jocko's good sense of humor. He was also a heck of a stuntman and a heck of a rider. I've never seen anybody mount a horse like him. Gosh, I used to watch that. He was fascinating. In one chapter, I actually jumped in his arms. That was a great thrill."

An amusing incident occurred during the making of the serial. The stuntmen were having a difficult time building up enough speed for a wagon transfer in which Jocko would actually be doubled jumping from one wagon to the next. The studio was still handling their new serial star with kid gloves and didn't want him hurt. This seemed a silly notion to Jocko, who by this time was arguably the top stuntman in the business and could no doubt perform a wagon transfer upon rolling out of bed. Utilizing local horses, the driver of the wagon couldn't build up the required speed to get next to the other wagon for Jocko's stuntman to make the jump. They tried several times without success. After lunch the wagon driver still couldn't get enough out of his horses. Jocko suddenly jumped into the wagon and began firing blanks from his gun. The horses took off with great speed. As they approached the camera set-up, Jocko bailed off into a bunch of rocks so as not to be in the shot. With the film in the can, an incredulous Thomas Carr told Jocko the studio would kill the director if they knew he'd let Jocko do such a thing. Jocko simply smiled and said, "Oh, I wouldn't get hurt doing that." Carr told *Western Clippings*, "He was one of the greatest athletes I've ever met. He had the most tremendous power in his legs. The way he could jump! He moved like a cat."

Yvonne De Carlo briefly re-entered Jocko's life in late 1950 despite the bitterness associated with their public split the prior year. In December Jocko was doubling a villain in the Gene Autry film *Whirlwind* (1951), shooting at Pioneertown, and suffered two fractured ribs and a torn ligament. De Carlo dropped what she was doing and raced across the desert to the *Whirlwind* set to tend to his aches and pains. This action on her part received press in the gossip columns. Their reunion was short-lived. They broke up for good when De Carlo realized there were other women entering the picture. In early 1951 Jocko briefly dated Willard Parker's ex-wife, former actress Marion Pierce. Later that year, when De Carlo came to pick up a few of her items from Jocko's place, she was met at the door by a cute little girl named Sally, daughter of Jocko's newest lady friend Margaret Field.

Jocko ended up starring in three serials, but they're hardly what he is known for despite the affection with which that genre is looked upon by many movie fans from that generation. As was the case with most serials, Jocko's suffered from the quickness with which they were made and sloppiness in the editing process. Much of the action was routine, perhaps due in part to Columbia's unwillingness to let their star get hurt since he was so insistent on performing his own stunts. It's a shame there aren't any notable extended fight scenes in Jocko's serials. Republic Studios benefitted from the presence of fine stuntmen such as Tom Steele and Dale Van Sickel. This prolific pair could throw together a thrilling fight scene on a lunch break and make it work for the screen due to their familiarity with one another. Jocko worked well on fights with Al Wyatt, but somehow they were not allowed to block out an epic fistic battle for these chapterplays. The Columbia serials were noted for the frugalness with which producer Sam Katzman and studio head Harry Cohn made them. Had Columbia unleashed Jocko, his serials might be regarded as classics instead of run-of-the-mill.

Although he made a fine and stalwart cliffhanger hero, Jocko didn't linger in the land of serial stars. Many of these leading men were never able to establish themselves cinematically in any other manner. Jocko's champion swimming pal Buster Crabbe was the acknowledged "King of the Serials," but that designation ultimately kept him out of bigger-budgeted features and more important roles. At the same time Jocko did showcase himself well enough in the serials to earn the trust that Columbia and Gene Autry were placing in him. He was also learning a lot about staging action for the camera from old hands such as Spencer Gordon Bennet and Thomas Carr. What Jocko needed now was a strong character that could showcase his talents as a stuntman and emerging cowboy star. He found that role shortly.

5

The Range Rider

In late 1950, the Gene Autry *Range Rider* TV series went into production for CBS with Jocko billed as Jack Mahoney and starring as the title character, a fringe buckskin-wearing no-name hero who roamed the Old West, taking on all manners of villainy with fists and guns. He was given a young sidekick in the form of Dick West (played by Dick Jones), who was nearly the Range Rider's equal in terms of horsemanship and fisticuffs. Together the two made a dynamite pair. Jocko is smooth and natural in the part, showcasing humor when necessary and always bravery and wisdom in the face of danger. He's a perfect ruggedly masculine hero and a fine mentor to his saddle partner. Jones garners many laughs in his role as the fast-talking, impetuous teenage cowboy who too often is swayed by a pretty girl. He sometimes gets Range Rider into trouble but just as often rides to the rescue to fight by his side. The duo's amusing interplay is nearly as entertaining as their fantastic tandem stunt work.

The first episode of *The Range Rider* was filmed at the tail end of 1950 and its last original episode in the spring of 1953. They generally filmed 26 episodes over a 13-week period, aiming to complete two episodes a week. After avoiding the desert heat of the summer, they resumed the routine. That was the extent of the show's structure. Multiple episodes could be filmed at the same time to make optimum use of locations, sets, equipment, and guest stars. Often the guest actors had to be reminded which character they were playing at any given time. This created a whirlwind pace as everyone constantly changed in and out of costume. Some shows might suffer because of this demanding schedule, but *The Range Rider* was held together by the strong presence and natural levity of Jocko and Jones.

The *Range Rider* production totaled 78 fun-filled half-hour segments. It was syndicated slowly at first in select markets but picked up momentum as it debuted around the country. In March of 1951 Jocko made a series of personal appearances for the New York TV station WCBS to help promote the series. *Variety* noted the pilot was a "topflight sagebrush vidpic series" and that Jocko "cuts an attractive figure in his buckskin outfit and with slick horsemanship." *The Chicago Tribune* predicted great success, stating that Jocko has "got everything John Wayne, Gary Cooper, and Joel McCrea have, and he's roughly twenty years younger." Iowa's *Muscatine Journal* called him "the greatest action star since Tom Mix."

When filming the first episode, Jocko pulled Jones aside and suggested that they should both do all of their own stunts on the show. That way, when children asked if it was really them doing all the action on screen, they wouldn't have to lie. Jones, an athletic young man of 23 who could ride and fight, readily agreed. At the tender age of four he had been marketed as "The World's Youngest Trick Rider and Trick Roper." Cowboy star Hoot Gibson noticed him, and he got his start in pictures working as a child stunt performer. "Dickie" Jones acted in many youthful parts and was eager to show what he could do as an adult upon returning to the business from time spent in the U.S. Army. From that first day on, it was all Jocko and Jones, who tried his best to stay in Jocko's "hip pocket" for the camera. Jocko would tell the cameraman ahead of time where he would be at the end of a piece of action and it was up to Dick to hustle along or be left out of the camera frame. They performed almost every bit of their own action on the show and developed a close friendship that would last their lifetimes.

In 1990, Jones was quoted in *The Westerner* as saying, "There'll never be anybody else like him. He was one-of-a-kind in his field of endeavor and one of the nicest men I've ever known. Doing *Range Rider* was the most fun I've ever had. We had a closeness that I imagine very few people in the industry have. Our lives were on the line, we had to be close. He is the end of an era. To say I loved him would be an understatement."

Western Clippings quoted a 1974 Jocko interview where he said, "Dick was a fantastic partner. Whatever I did, he watched me like a hawk and he'd do it. He is a very handy guy. All the stunts were choreographed. It got to the point where we worked together so much that we thought alike. We made the shows in three days. Dickie and I were always trying to figure out new punches and mounts. We did personal appearances until they were coming out of our ears.... Every day was fun. You couldn't have asked for a better boss than Mr. Autry."

Jocko sat tall in the saddle and rode his dependable horse Rawhide all over diverse California locations, including Alabama Hills and Lone Pine in the High Sierras, Vasquez Rocks near Agua Dulce, Bronson Canyon in Griffith Park, and the forests surrounding Big Bear Lake in the San Bernardino Mountains. Filming of the series was also done at the western sets of Pioneertown in Yucca Valley, Corriganville in Simi Valley, Iverson Ranch in the Santa Susana Mountains, and Gene Autry's own Melody Ranch in Santa Clarita Valley.

Rawhide was in actuality a 15-hand buckskin gelding named Buck. Jocko's own personal horse at this time was Golden Nugget, which he kept at stuntman pal Bill Ward's stables. He acquired the 16-hand Sans Souci and the colt Knothead during the show's run. Cowhand Dick Smith helped Jocko care for the horses, who were rewarded regularly with sugar, carrots, and applause for jobs well done. Unlike some cowboy stars, Jocko had a great affinity for horses.

In addition to lots of thrilling hard-riding, Jocko did fantastic mounts and dismounts throughout the course of the show including cruppers, scissor vaults, and Pony Express mounts. A recurring gag amongst the crew was that no one ever knew how Jocko was going to get off his horse from one shot to the next. It was never recorded for an episode, but a still photo from the period shows Jocko doing an impressive back-flip off his horse. The many ways he got onto the horse were every bit as ingenious. TV's *Sugarfoot* star Will Hutchins wrote in *Western Clippings* that Jocko and Dick had the "best horsemanship I've ever witnessed in a TV western. Their synchronized mounts have to be seen to be believed, and I still don't believe 'em."

One interesting difference between the Range Rider and traditional cowboys was that Jocko wore moccasins rather than boots, a trait already exhibited by Jocko's serial heroes.

Leaping onto Dick Jones' horse for a fast getaway on *The Range Rider*.

This allowed him to pull off his stunts with less difficulty and also made it easier for the cameramen to frame both Jocko and the much shorter Jones in the same shot. It also brought Jocko's towering height down to the level of the villains he was taking on in fight scenes. Jocko didn't want children seeing the show to think he was a bully picking on little guys.

Physique-wise Jocko looks a bit more muscular in the Range Rider part. He had always strived to keep himself at a lean 200-pound body-weight during his stunt career. This no doubt was to make him a suitable double for all the long drinks of water he had to double, such as Gregory Peck and Randolph Scott. With no pressure to stay extra lean for doubling assignments, it is conceivable Jocko relaxed a bit during his Range Rider years and carried an extra five to ten pounds of muscle on his large frame. He would need it since wearing the buckskin outfit in the desert kept him drenched in perspiration. Jocko showed off his superbly conditioned body in a few episodes as the Range Rider dives into a lake and goes for a swim.

A photo taken at Corriganville shows Jocko could press and support Jones over his head while his partner performed a handstand on Jocko's palms. This is known in gymnastic circles as a high hand-to-hand. According to Jones, it was Jocko who would swing him into this position and hold him there, harkening back to his adagio act. The impromptu gymnastics kept their bodies limber for when the cameras were ready to roll. They were constantly coming up with new tricks for the camera. Some of their bits involved fluidly flipping and catching objects between one another. In one episode Jocko vaulted over a hedge, turned and caught Dick in his arms as the young man followed. It was moments like these that delighted audiences. "We spent many long hours into the night trying to conjure up stunts for the next day," Jones said.[1]

Both men took great pride in performing their own screen action. Many segments had them jumping from boulder to boulder like mountain goats as they positioned themselves to pounce down on the bad guys. The beginning of every episode saw Jocko leap onto his horse, spin it past the camera, and take off on a hard gallop to perform a stage transfer while Dick hung off the side of his horse and fired his gun. One of their most visually impressive feats was a double leap they took off a ledge outside of Pioneertown in the episode "Jimmy the Kid." They fell about 15 feet onto a decline and then both proceeded to tumble end over end for another 60 or so feet down a steep hill in a single camera take. Jones downplays the jump because they landed in deep sand. "That wasn't a stunt," he said. "It was just a way of Jocko and I getting real dirty."[2]

Jocko told *The Book of Movie Lists*, "Doing your own stunts adds to the realism and adds to the audience's enjoyment. For an actor, it adds a little spice to the performance. But most of all, it's a lot of fun." He added for *Favorite Westerns*, "*Range Rider* was more fun than the law should allow. It might have been a little weak on story, but great on action." He told *Saturday Morning TV,* "We always had men on the set who got paid for whatever Dick and I did, but we did the transfers from horses to stagecoaches and wagons and all the fights. Everything you saw on *Range Rider* was our work."

Since Jocko was doing all of his own stunts as a leading man, the actors playing heavies on the show felt compelled to prove their own mettle. They often did many of their own fights. The end result was that Jocko ended up taking even more punishment since he wasn't always working with trained stuntmen on the fights. He sometimes took miscalculated punches from the actors and had his nose broken four times on the show, most notably by Bob Wilke. Each time he quickly reset the break himself so as not to delay filming.

Time was money on the show, which budgeted slightly under $20,000 an episode. Jocko estimated he saved a half an hour every working day by eliminating the need for a Range Rider stuntman, though Al Wyatt was often on hand. In the long run this added up to thousands of dollars saved for the production company. Jocko suffered a bad gash on his forehead when working a fight with actors Jim Bannon and House Peters, Jr. He merely had it patched up and kept on fighting. A little blood in the eyes couldn't stop Jocko Mahoney. "I've always been able to control pain pretty good," Jocko told *Saturday Morning TV.*

Jocko worked fistfights on the show with notable heavies Lee Van Cleef, Alan Hale, Jr., Marshall Reed, Gregg Barton, Denver Pyle, John Doucette, Tom Munroe, Terry Frost, Pierce Lyden, Harry Lauter, Myron Healey, Dick Curtis, James Griffith, Sheb Wooley, and Mickey Simpson. Jocko did have a number of stuntmen who worked regularly on the show. These included Wyatt, Fred Krone, Bob Woodward, Sandy Sanders, and Boyd "Red" Morgan, all good fight men. Wyatt did double Jocko once on the show when Jocko's ribs were injured. It was for a minor long-distance riding shot. Jocko was quick to identify Wyatt's presence on screen by his flapping arms. As soon as he was able, Jocko was back in the saddle again.

Jumping off a rooftop onto stuntman Al Wyatt on *The Range Rider*.

For *Range Rider*, Jocko put on some of the greatest fights ever committed to film, often taking on multiple opponents at once in battles he choreographed himself. Many of the fights involved the anachronistic use of judo throws and holds, which made them unique in the annals of cowboy fights. The majority of the fight with Jim Bannon in "Outlaw Territory" consists of judo throws with Bannon's double Fred Krone. Jocko can also be seen performing kip-ups on the show, hurling his body from a supine position to a standing position without using his hands. Jocko gave the fight scenes his all, and no prop seemed safe. In addition to demolishing sets, his trademark became his mussed-up hair falling over his forehead. His longish mane seemed to take on a life of its own as his head rolled with the punches.

Jocko and Dick often relied on a shared count as a cue in their fight scenes. They were so in sync that they could begin counting, leave the building, walk around the block, and still be at the same point with one another when they got back. As a result of this impeccable timing, they worked blind falls into the show as they brawled with the bad guys. Dick would take a punch and launch himself backward, confident that Jocko would be there to catch him at precisely the right moment. Jocko would turn from whoever he was fighting, catch Dick, and throw him back into the fray.

One of Jocko's best fights of the entire series came against co-star Dick Jones when the latter played a lookalike villain in the episode "Jimmy the Kid." Jocko and Dick do the entire acrobatic minute-long fight in nearly one continuous take that sees them bounce each other around every corner of a room and over all the furniture. Every thrown punch looks like a hit. It's a testament to both men's exceptional skill and timing. Jocko and Dick fight one another again in the episode "Dim Trails," with Dick taking a comic beating as Jocko knocks him all over a saloon. Slapstick often worked its way into the stories, and Dick was surprised that he was so often allowed to upstage the star with his humorous antics.

The Range Rider was so inventive and thrilling when it came to fight work that it's hard to pinpoint which ones are the best. Virtually every episode has fights that would be the single most memorable fight on any other show. For example, in the episode "Indian War Party," Jocko has a fight scene with real-life Chickasaw Indian Rodd Redwing in picturesque Big Bear, California. The fight commences with both men leaping from their horses to meet face to face on a giant fallen redwood tree. Redwing brandishes a knife and goes for Jocko, who hip-tosses Redwing's stuntman atop the tree. Both men bounce to the ground and continue their acrobatic melee. Later in the fight, Jocko flips the stuntman over the top of a horse. The fight ends when Jocko executes a flying leg scissors that upends the Indian. Redwing was not comfortable with the complicated moves that Jocko devised for the scene, claiming the fight demanded a stuntman. Since they were on location, Dick Jones donned Redwing's Indian outfit and did the outstanding fight scene with Jocko. "That turned out to be pretty good," he said with modesty.[3]

Another big bare-knuckle battle came in the boxing ring against former professional heavyweight Mickey Simpson in the episode "Fight Town." The 6' 5", 240-pound Simpson appeared on *Range Rider* several times and also fought Jocko in *Roar of the Iron Horse* and *Yancy Derringer*. Simpson commented on Jocko for the book *Feature Players*: "I would call him the most flexible stuntman there ever was. He could stand two feet behind a horse and spring and leap right into the saddle without a trampoline." Character actor Harry Lauter remembered Jocko at the 1986 Knoxville Western Caravan, saying: "I worked with Jocko a good damn many pictures. He was very responsible for me being able to unfortunately do all my own stunts. He was my teacher. He was fantastic. He and Davey Sharpe were remarkable."

During the course of *Range Rider* Jocko trained stuntman Fred Krone, a rodeo photographer whom he met through Carolina Cotton. Krone worked on more than 60 *Range Rider* episodes and went on to be acclaimed as one of the industry's best fight men. He would take incredible bumps in his fight scenes with Jocko, earning him the nickname "Krunch" because of how hard he hit the ground. Jocko's *Range Rider* fights influenced many others. Stuntman Hal Needham kept his hair long so it would fly around during fights the way Jocko's did. Actor Robert Fuller idolized Jocko and modeled his *Laramie* and *Wagon Train* fight scenes after those he watched Jocko do on *Range Rider*. TV cowboys Clint Eastwood of *Rawhide* and James Drury and Doug McClure of *The Virginian* were all shown the proper way to throw a screen punch by Jocko. Popular 1980s screen martial artist Steve James called Jocko taking on multiple opponents as a major influence in how he performed fight scenes. These men became the best in the business, and they were all in one way or another descendents of Jocko.

Stuntman Neil Summers wrote in *Western Clippings*: "The pairing of Jock and Dick was a dream team. The two actors-stuntmen were a perfect combination of humor and action. Every episode is a delight. The action from these two men is as fluid and perfectly coordinated as any to be seen, then or now. The two reasons I wanted to enter the stunt business are Jock Mahoney and Dick Jones."

Range Rider aired primarily after school on weekdays and was a favorite with kids. In some markets it routinely aired five times a week. But 45 percent of the audience was adults, with 75 percent of those adults being women. Jocko and his saddle partner Jones no doubt had something to do with that number. At the height of its popularity, Jocko was receiving thousands of fan letters a week. There were *Range Rider* coloring books, trading cards, writing tablets, jigsaw puzzles, cap pistols, spinning tops, pins, bracelets, and a series of 24 Dell comic books that were produced through the late 1950s.

One child who idolized Jocko as the Range Rider was Peter Ford, son of actors Glenn Ford and Eleanor Powell. Glenn Ford was an excellent horseman and loved doing western roles. He hung out with stuntmen Dave Sharpe and Red Morgan and knew Jocko well. They were friends at Columbia and routinely lunched together in the commissary. In 1952 Ford requested Jocko make a special appearance at Peter's seventh birthday party, which the cowboy was glad to do. Jocko showed up in his Range Rider outfit to surprise Peter in the living room of the Fords' Beverly Hills home. The event was documented for publicity purposes by *Movie Stars Parade*. "I was mightily impressed," Peter recalled nearly 60 years later.[4]

Range Rider Jocko realized his standing as a role model for children and toed the line appropriately in both his public and private life. He later told *Saturday Morning TV*, "You couldn't be a successful cowboy star then and not live an exemplary life.... The minute we got out of line we were finished. The proof of the pudding was that those who were not hacking it on the outside were quickly shuffled off and lost in limbo."

Producer-director Andrew Marton wanted Jocko to star as a World War II pilot in the adventure *Storm Over Tibet* (1952), but Jocko's *Range Rider* commitments kept him from taking the role. Rex Reason was cast instead. Jocko was offered the part of the deputy in *High Noon* (1952) opposite Gary Cooper but turned it down after reading the script. He didn't like the fact that the deputy was cowardly and wouldn't back the hero in the fight with the villains. Lloyd Bridges ended up playing the part. Cooper won an Oscar for Best Actor for the role of Sheriff Will Kane, but Jocko never regretted turning the film classic down. The part didn't feel right to him, and he trusted that sixth sense throughout his life.

John Wayne publicly lambasted *High Noon* as un–American and leftist. Jocko never went that far, but he had his principles.

Some newspaper accounts mention that Jocko stunt doubled for Cooper in *High Noon* but this has never been confirmed. It's possible he did brief work on the film as it shot on Columbia's western street; it's difficult to identify him in the finished product due to the editing and distance from the camera. It's far more likely Jocko doubled Cooper in the earlier western *Dallas* (1950), which has some Jocko-style specialty stunts.

Jocko continued to perform stunts for other films and TV shows during this early *Range Rider* period due to the great demand for his talents and the simple fact that he loved the action so much. The paychecks also had to be enticing. He was making only $250 a week for starring and doing the stunts in *Range Rider*. He could easily double that in an afternoon doing some of the very stunts he was performing for himself on *Range Rider*.

At Columbia, Jocko filled in for pal Jerome Courtland during fight scenes with John Russell in the adventure comedy *The Barefoot Mailman* (1951). He did some stunt work for his friend Guy Madison in the early days of the TV series *Wild Bill Hickok* (1951–1958), although Madison was usually doubled by Dave Sharpe or Richard Farnsworth. Madison talked to *Saturday Morning TV* about Jocko, saying, "We called him an antelope. He'd jump 25 feet across buildings. He'd damn near break the Olympic record just doing that."

Star friends Gregory Peck and Errol Flynn were still requesting Jocko's services because they knew he would make them look good on screen. At Universal, Jocko, Al Wyatt, and Sol Gorss split the doubling duties for Peck in Raoul Walsh's superior 1850s sea adventure *The World in His Arms* (1952). Jocko can be seen doubling Peck during the fiery climactic fight scene and takes a dive off a ship prior to it exploding. Al Wyatt did the big jump through the plate glass window, but it's probably Jocko taking the feet first two-story jump immediately after that. He had performed that difficult stunt in the Durango Kid films.

Universal was also the location for another of Jocko's magnificent stunts. In the pirate adventure *Against All Flags* (1952), Jocko performed a tremendous jump from one ship to another for his friend Errol Flynn. The stunt received no publicity, but it's doubtful anyone other than Jocko could have made the leap for Flynn. Jocko did a second stunt in the film, swinging across the same chasm on a rope with a stuntwoman in his arms and later slid down the length of a sail with a knife, recreating a famous Douglas Fairbanks–Richard Talmadge stunt from *The Black Pirate* (1926). After *Against All Flags*, Flynn ventured to Europe to make films. Jocko was unable to accompany him due to his many stateside commitments.

Jocko's name has come up as a double for Stewart Granger on *The Prisoner of Zenda* (1952), although it is Sol Gorss who doubles the star for the climactic fencing scene with actor James Mason. Gorss was an expert fencer who had worked on *The Three Musketeers* (1948) and tutored Errol Flynn on nearly all of his swashbuckling films. It is likely Jocko doubling Granger earlier in the picture for some limber gymnastic work, going up a tree and over a wall. There is also a nifty leap from a rooftop to a tree that is the type of stunt Jocko specialized in.

At this point of his career, Jocko rarely talked about the actors he had doubled, adhering to the old stuntman philosophy that it was best not to reveal the secrets of the trade and to maintain the illusion for the public that it was the stars themselves handling all the action on screen. As Jocko's acting career blossomed, the press was always quick to ask who Jocko had done stunts for. Jocko needed the publicity, but he also didn't want to jeopardize future work by offending the stars he had worked with. Dick Jones said, "He was very close-mouthed and tight-lipped about things he had done, especially doubling jobs. I never pushed him to find out things."[5]

Columbia still wasn't sure what do to with Jocko. Initially TV was looked down upon by those making their living in film. Worse, he still insisted on working as a stuntman for other studios. Jocko did make a cameo appearance as himself in a nine-minute Columbia short entitled *Screen Snapshots: Meet Mr. Rhythm Frankie Laine* (1952), suggesting that Columbia believed he had achieved at least some level of celebrity. This was to promote singer Laine's newest film *Rainbow 'Round My Shoulder* (1952). Other stars under contract to Columbia such as John Derek, John Ireland, and Joanne Dru also appear as themselves, visiting Mr. and Mrs. Laine's Hollywood antique store. Handsome, athletic John Derek was one of Jocko's good friends on the Columbia lot. Jocko had first met Derek at a horse ranch in the early 1940s and became like a big brother to the young actor.

After the first season of *Range Rider*, the busy Jocko co-starred opposite Charles Starrett in the final series of Durango Kid films. Relying heavily on stock footage at this point, some of these movies were completed in only one week. Jocko customarily played the character of Jack Mahoney. The last name of Starrett's character changed from film to film, but his first name always remained Steve.

In *Pecos River* (1951), Jocko is an easterner named Jack Mahoney, who is taken for a bit of a dandy by the bad guys until he bests them in fisticuffs. Starrett teaches him how to handle a pistol like a cowboy, and by the end of the picture Jocko and Starrett are taking on the villains in tandem. *The Hawk of Wild River* (1952) saw Starrett helping frontier marshal Jocko take on dastardly Clayton Moore and his gang of crooks. In *Laramie Mountains* (1952), Jocko plays a half-breed Indian named Swift Eagle who joins forces with Starrett to fight off bad guys Bob Wilke and Boyd "Red" Morgan. A muscular Jocko is shirtless throughout the movie and gets to fire arrows and throw tomahawks in the film's conclusion. In *Smoky Canyon* (1952) he's a good bad guy on the lam, forced to fight Starrett as well as bad guy Chris Alcaide in a nice brawl that features a close-up bulldog into the camera. Jocko has the romantic lead in this and is cleared of any wrongdoing by Starrett in the end. It was the first film for tough guy Alcaide, who was tutored in screen fighting and horseback riding by Jocko. "Jock Mahoney was a great help," Alcaide told *White Hats and Silver Spurs*.

Jocko is given one of his best roles in the Durango series in *Rough Tough West* (1952) playing town boss Big Jack Mahoney. An old friend of Starrett's, Big Jack may or may not have turned into a greedy villain. Carolina Cotton is his girlfriend. In the film's climax, Jocko fights off the real villain Marshall Reed, is shot in the shoulder, and tries to rescue a child from a burning building. He succumbs to smoke inhalation before being rescued by Starrett. Jocko is able to lend some shading to this character role, foreshadowing the many villains he portrayed a decade later. He also doubles for Starrett in the film, doing a nice leap from a speeding wagon, then immediately scissor-vaulting onto Starrett's horse Raider to get out of town.

The Kid from Broken Gun (1952) concluded the Durango Kid series with Starrett stepping aside to allow Jocko center stage. Jocko has the romantic lead as a former prizefighter unjustly accused and standing trial for murder. He recounts his side of the story on the stand, and there's plenty of top-notch fighting with bad guys Chris Alcaide, Charles Horvath,

Jocko slides down the length of a sail for Errol Flynn in *Against All Flags* (1952).

Eddie Parker, and John Cason to keep audiences enthralled. There is also footage of one of the greatest stunts Jocko ever performed in his career, the 20-foot–plus jump between rooftops performed back in 1947 that approached Jesse Owens' Olympic record.

While making the Durango Kid films, Jocko became very good friends with Charles Starrett's on-screen sidekick Smiley Burnette. Smiley's young son Stephen often visited the set. Stephen recalled one morning at Iverson Ranch where the stuntmen were gathered around a campfire. Stephen was wearing a holster with his cap pistols, and Jocko offered to exchange his gun for the toy if Stephen could beat him to the draw. The boy beat Jocko and briefly got to exchange his cap gun for the real deal. The moment made quite an impression on the youngster, who went on to become a professional stuntman himself and worked over 30 years in the industry. "He was my hero," Stephen Burnette said of Jocko.[6]

On *Range Rider* Jocko was extremely popular with the female guest stars, who all spoke highly of their handsome leading man in later years. Among the actresses guest starring on the series were Lois Hall, Elaine Riley, Gloria Saunders, Gail Davis, Nan Leslie, and Donna Martell. Nan Leslie told *Western Clippings,* "Jock Mahoney was one Bootsie [Gail Davis] and I both agreed on — he was a pretty attractive fellow." Donna Martell told *Classic Images* that Jocko was "sweet" and "always a gentleman." In the morning she would find the phrase, "Good morning, Princess" written in lipstick on the mirror in her makeup room. She enjoyed the innocent flirtation, although she never dated Jocko. That wasn't the case with all of the female guests on *Range Rider*.

At the 1986 Knoxville Western Film Caravan, panel guest Harry Lauter gently teased Davis about her behind the scenes relationship with the *Range Rider* star. After a prolonged laugh of embarrassment, Davis finally summoned up enough air to say, "Jocko was absolutely terrific." Elaine Riley had dinner with Jocko on numerous occasions during filming. She commented on her leading man for the book *Ladies of the Western*: "I thought what a great guy Jocko is. He's tall and he was in shape. I think he had just come off being a stuntman type of thing. And oh, we laughed, between him and Dick Jones.... A sweetheart of a man." Lois Hall added to that assessment in the book *Westerns Women*: "Jocko and Dickie were as much fun off the set as they were on — it was a blast. They were fun and funny. Joking and playing tricks and hanging out with the wranglers, the crew and the cast. It was just a tight, fun family. I had a wonderful time doing those. Loved them."

Pretty 5'5" brunette actress Margaret Field made repeat appearances and attracted Jocko's attention as well. She had recently divorced Richard Field, and Jocko wasn't about to let someone else sweep this black-haired Irish girl off her feet before him. "Maggie" Field was born Margaret Morlan (McNamara) in Houston, Texas, in 1923 and was discovered by a Paramount talent scout while in the audience at the Pasadena Playhouse. She was signed to a late 1940s Paramount contract and appeared as a background-bit player in a number of Alan Ladd and Bing Crosby pictures while simultaneously attending Pasadena Junior College. The Edward G. Robinson film *The Night Has a Thousand Eyes* (1948) won her some notice, and she graduated to larger roles, most notably as the female lead in the science fiction film *The Man from Planet X* (1951).

Jocko married Maggie Field in Tijuana, Mexico, on January 21, 1952, and become stepfather to her two children Richard and Sally. The couple had a daughter of their own named Princess Melissa O'Mahoney, born in August of 1952. Jocko's huge Great Dane Du Barry and a Palomino Stallion named Prince completed the family. Jocko and Maggie were profiled in the April 1953 issue of *Movie* magazine, having a horseback picnic in Griffith Park. Their best friends were the married acting duo Barbara Hale and Bill Williams, the latter a former professional swimmer and veteran of the U.S. Army who was starring on the TV western *The Adventures of Kit Carson*. The couples dined together at popular upscale restaurants such as the Tail o' the Cock. They often got together in the

Jocko and wife Maggie in a publicity photograph.

evenings to go over scene work and rehearse with one another in hopes of improving their acting craft.

Maggie co-starred with Jocko in an episode of the long-running anthology western *Death Valley Days* in 1953. Jocko was the lead guest star in two episodes of the classic series, proving to producers that he was more than just the Range Rider. In his first episode

"Swamper Ike" he played a white man raised by Indians who tries to reintegrate into his original surroundings for the love of a woman. *Variety* reviewed the episode and noted, "Mahoney handles his role easily and seems perfectly at home in the setting." His second *Death Valley Days* was entitled "Husband Pro Tem" and saw Jocko cast as a young mining engineer attempting to broker a peace treaty with warring Indians. In the climax he's forced to fight the chief.

One benefit of doing *Range Rider* was that Jocko grew much more comfortable as an actor in front of the camera. Gone was the self-consciousness that plagued his earliest performances in the Three Stooges shorts. Jocko could now smoothly deliver the required dialogue, though in truth the part called for little exposition and Jocko attributed sheer exhaustion to his new relaxed attitude in front of the camera. One critic noted in the first season that Jocko's two favored expressions for the camera were "smile" and "don't smile," a review that amused Jocko; he was quick to quote over the years. He told *Saturday Morning TV*, "I was learning my trade at that point. TV was a marvelous school where I could try things and immediately see what the public reaction was."

Range Rider was nearly non-stop action, but Jocko paid attention during camera set-ups and had time to watch and learn from many veteran character actors such as Tom London and Lyle Talbot as well as series directors George Archainbaud, Thomas Carr, Don McDougall, John English, and Ray Nazarro. Jocko did get to stretch his talents in at least a couple of episodes. In "The Silver Blade" he masquerades as a dashing Spanish nobleman. In the amusing "Romeo Goes West" he pretends to be a Shakespearean actor staging *Romeo and Juliet* for a group of outlaws, with his partner Dick cast as a reluctant Juliet. Jocko does not embarrass himself in either assignment. At the 1990 Knoxville Film Festival, Lyle Talbot recalled Jocko, saying, "He was a hell of an actor. He was a great action hero and would do the most wonderful things."

Range Rider made Jocko a household name, even if it was Jack Mahoney. In the spring of 1952 he toured 20 cities to promote the show in different markets. He graced the cover of the August 1, 1952, issue of *TV Guide* and newspapers around the country regularly began running snippets and features on him. *TV Guide* ran additional articles on Jocko and *Range Rider* throughout the next three years. Jocko and Dick Jones made the cover of the March 22, 1953, *Parade* newspaper supplement performing a bulldog stunt. Jocko was considered an actor now and would never have to work as a stunt double again to earn his keep. Many over the years have said that making the transition from stuntman to actor in the industry is nearly impossible, but Jocko did it with seeming ease. The feat surprised few who knew Jocko and his strong will and determination.

Jocko was extremely popular with the public and toured extensively with Jones at rodeos and outdoor events until May of 1955, over two years after *Range Rider* ceased production. The two rode horses and performed 10-minute fight routines utilizing a truckload of real solid oak furniture for the appreciative audiences. At nearly every stop they tied in at least one trip to the local children's hospital, visiting the sick youngsters to lift their spirits. If a child was too tired to see them at the appointed time, Jocko and Dick were known to make repeat visits to ensure that no youth had been missed.

One of their first public appearances was at El Cajon's Western Days Celebration in September of 1951. Jocko served as grand marshal for the parade and Carolina Cotton appeared as the queen. Hundreds of children lined up to cheer the Range Rider and the

All-American Boy Dick West. The star trio repeated their El Cajon appearance the following year to a much larger turnout. The adoration had to remind Jocko of his own love for cowboys like Tom Mix while growing up in Iowa. Jocko was always happy to sign autographs and meet his young fans.

There was a *Range Rider* event in Salt Lake City in early 1952 and no one anticipated the huge turnout. Thousands crowded the auditorium, and the stars were forced to go outside to accommodate all the people. The police were called to do some crowd control. In March of 1952 they appeared at the Phoenix Rodeo in Arizona, taking time out to visit over a dozen local schools as well as the Phoenix Boys Club to sign autographs for all the kids. In June, Jocko was the grand marshal for the Days of the Verdugos Fiesta and rode with Dick in the Glendale, California, parade. On the Independence Day weekend they headlined the Coronado Carnival. Sensing they were onto something big, they began to explore the idea of putting on live shows throughout the markets in which *Range Rider* enjoyed healthy TV ratings.

In late July 1952 they did six shows for Tom Packs' Thrill Circus in Pittsburgh, entertaining over 90,000 fans. The capacity crowds spilled out into lawn seating at Forbes Field. While there, they surprised a group of underprivileged kids at nearby Camp O'Connell with an unscheduled visit. Jocko revealed to the local press that one of his dreams was to own a large ranch for underprivileged kids. Dick turned an ankle during the shows, and the smell of horse liniment was so strong that it nearly got them kicked off the flight back to Los Angeles.

In September of 1952 they appeared in support of singer Eddy Arnold at the Houston Fat Stock Show in Texas to great acclaim. That fall Jocko rode Rawhide through the streets of New York in the Macy's Thanksgiving Day Parade. Momentum was building for their appearances. Jocko and Dick's first starring engagement came in February 1953 at the Houston Fat Stock Show. They entered an agreement with promoter Jim Eskew, producer of the JE Ranch Championship Rodeos. As headliners they would perform 30 shows in Houston, making up to eight or nine engagements a week including matinees.

The highlight of the wildly successful Texas engagement was a Jocko injury. Jocko busted his shoulder falling from a horse that veered when it was supposed to go straight. Jocko promptly got to his feet and completed the fight routine without missing a beat. He received heat diathermy treatments at the Rice Institute and finished the rest of the scheduled performances with heavy taping and anesthetic injections. The shoulder didn't knit properly and bothered him for years, but at this point of his career it would take more than a few nicks and bruises to slow down Jocko.

In March of 1953 Jocko was invited back to Davenport, Iowa, to speak to the high school student body in the school gymnasium. He signed autographs at Parker's Department Store and nearly all of Davenport, Rock Island, and Moline showed up to see the homecoming hero. In July, he and Dick put on a live fight scene for 50,000 Boy Scouts at their National Jamboree in Newport Beach. *The Los Angeles Times* called their battle "a realistic looking motion picture fight that had the vast throng groaning in sympathy."

In the summer of 1953 Jocko and Dick toured the eastern cities of Providence, Philadelphia, Pittsburgh, and Cleveland, where Dick fractured his pelvis when his horse slipped in the Arena. They put on eight to ten shows at each venue and grossed a then unheard-of $273,000. The Providence Auditorium appearance in Rhode Island topped the previous record gates of Roy Rogers and Gene Autry at that venue by $20,000. Jocko and Dick had a percentage deal they split with the arenas and Eskew. Gene Autry's Mitchell J. Hamilburg Agency set the deal and took a cut as well. In September of 1953, Jocko made a solo appearance serving as the grand marshal for the San Gabriel Mission Parade while Dick continued to heal from his pelvic fracture. Two months after Dick's injury they were performing together at the Peninsula Celebration Rodeo in Redwood City, California.

Out west, Jocko and Dick headlined the World Championship Rodeo in Oakland, putting on five performances at the Oakland Ball Park to big crowds. In October of 1953 Jocko and Dick set the money record for the Boston Garden's Rodeo, nearly doubling what their boss Autry had done there the year before in a month-long engagement. In one appearance Jocko was kicked in the chest by his horse when he was doing a saddle fall. He announced to the crowd that he wasn't hurt and gamely climbed back on his steed. In fact, he had taken an incredible blow. It took six men to gingerly pry him off the horse, and he finally passed out after being taped up by a doctor. He was forced to emcee the next day's show from horseback while stuntman Dick Smith did the fight routines with Dick Jones. "When Jocko got hurt, it just about put us out of business," Jones said. "He was in real bad shape."[7]

Jocko was laid up in the Boston hotel suite with damaged ribs. The next day he took a hot bath and stretched out on the floor. He could barely move. This forced idleness bored Jocko to no end, and Dick decided to go to the lobby to get a magazine rather than listen to Jocko moan. Jocko jokingly told him to return with dancing girls. When Dick got on the elevator he encountered a gaggle of high school girls dressed to the nines for a social dance. The girls were ecstatic to meet Dick and were even more thrilled at the prospect of meeting Jocko. Dick invited them to meet the Range Rider, throwing open the door to their room to reveal Jocko stretched out on the middle of the floor wearing nothing more than a towel.

Jocko only missed the one show. The following day he was back to work doing his own stunts. His grit and determination were legendary, even in the face of better judgment. What was driving him outside of his own macho pride was that he had gambled on besting Autry's gate for the Boston shows in their percentage deal with the Garden. They literally had to put on the act to full or near-capacity houses for their paycheck. "The show's got to go on," he told Jones.[8] And it did.

In November of 1953 they appeared with the World Championship Rodeo at Madison Square Garden in New York. They stepped aside to allow Gene Autry to headline this show. Resuming the format of their Houston Fat Stock and Boston shows, Jocko and Dick entertained thousands of children at the Garden, always making sure to touch as many young hands as possible when they rode past. Outside of the arena, they staged a fight scene for patients at Bellevue Hospital and made a spate of TV and radio appearances in the Big Apple including the kid shows *Time for Adventure* and *Tootsie Roll Hippodrome*. Most notably they appeared on *The Ed Sullivan Show*. That appearance consisted of Jocko and Dick putting on one of their extended knock-down drag-out fight routines for the live audience and TV broadcast. As was his custom, Jocko inspected the saloon set prior to the show and told the prop men and the director what alterations needed to be made. Tables and the main bar both needed to be nailed to the floor as the men would be all over them. The director told Jocko that was impossible, as everything needed to be whisked away off the stage for the next live set-up. Jocko told them they had been warned.

The Sullivan set contained a spiral staircase and balcony that Jocko and Dick decided they would fight up and fall off of. However, when the show went live, the New York stuntmen portraying card-playing cowboys panicked when they realized Jocko and Dick would be coming down on their table. They let out a scream and ran away, upending the table in doing so. Jocko and Dick were suddenly looking down at dangerous table legs pointing in their direction as they fell. Jocko went to the left and Dick to the right, straight to the floor without anything breaking their fall. Justifiably upset at the New York stuntmen and the show's director, Jocko and Dick resumed the fight scene by smashing the table to pieces. Jocko pushed Dick into the main bar, which scooted nearly eight feet across the floor and took out the scenic backdrop behind it, ending up on the set for the next act. Jocko concluded the fight by throwing Dick into the bar and bringing everything smashing to the stage set in pieces. The Sullivan people were incensed. "We never heard the end of it," Jones said.[9]

During that fight, one of Jocko's punches caught Dick in the eye. When they later checked with Jocko's wife Maggie to see how it all looked on TV, she said it looked fine except for one punch that appeared to be an obvious miss. Both men knew exactly which punch Maggie was talking about. It was the one that actually connected and gave Dick a black eye. The mishap perfectly illustrated the powerful illusion of space created by the camera. Wide telegraphed punches that passed six inches in front of a face could look like solid punches with the right camera positioning. Given the length of their live battles, it is surprising Jocko and Dick didn't have more minor flubs, though on occasion Dick's shirt was unexpectedly ripped apart when Jocko would grab him for a flip or a toss.

The duo's enduring popularity led them to believe that *Range Rider* had ceased production too early and could have run successfully for at least another few years. In particular Jocko felt that a switch to color could have given the show new life. If that had happened, not only would the stars have been richer but the show might have had more staying power as well. As it was, the *Range Rider* episodes played in syndication around the world for years, expanding to over 150 markets. At the time, television was such a new entity that no one had an idea of its long-term impact. Gene Autry fulfilled his production contract for CBS and the sponsor Table Talk Pies and moved on. There was little thought given at the time to doing more than three seasons.

At one point in 1953 there was talk that Jocko and Jones would go to Italy for a series of films before meeting up with Autry for personal appearances that summer in England. It's not known what the subject matter of the Italian films would have been, as the spaghetti western genre didn't take off for another decade. Jocko and Dick ended up staying in the States due to the high demand for their public appearances and the prohibitive cost of going overseas. Autry was still considering starring Jocko in six cowboy films a year similar to the Durango Kid series, but as a savvy businessman he was realizing the power of television and the ultimate death of the theatrical B-western series. Autry's own cowboy film series ended in 1953. There was talk of another TV western starring a swimming cowboy but Jocko felt his future was in motion pictures as a leading man. Jocko decided to strike out on his own and exercised his right to walk away from both the Autry contract and the Mitchell J. Hamilburg Agency.

Jocko enjoyed working for Autry, considering him a boss who was good on his word. His checks never bounced. Autry had doubled Jocko's pay all the way up to $500 a week by the show's final season, a sum that was augmented considerably with personal appearances where he could stand to make as much as $1500 in one day. Still, it was but a modest wage for a TV cowboy star, and Jocko's free stunts inevitably saved Autry's Flying-A Productions thousands of dollars over the long run. But Jocko never complained about pay, merely grateful for the opportunity Autry gave him. He and Autry remained on friendly terms for the rest of their lives.

In addition to Autry, Scott, and Starrett, Jocko gained the respect of other cowboy stars of the era such as Lash LaRue, Jimmy Wakely, Monte Hale, and Rex Allen. He didn't get a chance to work with Roy Rogers during this period, but the two became good friends. Thirty years later they did work together on an episode of *The Fall Guy*. Another admirer was 1940s Republic Studios cowboy star Wild Bill Elliott. Jocko had been a fan of Elliott's westerns, and the two became good friends until Elliott's death in 1965 from lung cancer. Elliott gave Jocko a pair of his leather cowboy chaps, and Jocko cherished them as a sign of their close friendship.

At the height of their popularity Jocko and Dick spent nearly seven months out of the year making personal appearances. They became even closer out on the road interacting with the fans. For appearances on the West Coast they often drove with their horses Rawhide and Buster in a trailer behind them. The two married men shared a motel room to cut down on road expenses. Free time was usually spent rehearsing new fight moves and punches. Jocko sometimes killed time by the motel pool doing his endless pushups and chin-ups, but in reality the shows themselves usually involved enough action to keep the men in shape and tired all the time.

There was no temptation to seek out extracurricular mischief or get into trouble on the road. They were professionals and would not do anything that interfered with the precision needed for the next day's stage routines or stunts. The fans always came first. Jocko would later admit that he could put away beer in great quantities if inclined to do so, but there were many who knew him from this period who didn't think he ever touched a drop of alcohol. Normally his near-constant physical movement and exercise routine kept him too busy to waste the day away drinking.

Jocko kept his large circle of friends amused with his extraordinary feats. To know Jocko was to know a life filled with one crazy or humorous adventure after another. When they were in New York City, Jocko and Dick arranged for their wives Maggie and Betty to visit them. Jocko announced he was going to surprise Maggie when she arrived at the motel, answering the door in the buff with a rose in his teeth. Dick asked about the presence of the bellboy, and they decided Jocko should hide in the shower. When Maggie arrived, the bellboy did a quick check of the room, throwing open the shower curtain to reveal a buck naked Jocko with a rose in his teeth. "Oh," Jocko said to the surprised bellboy.[10]

Another humorous story involved a ride back from Iverson Ranch with Jones in Jocko's Lincoln Convertible. Jocko was behind the wheel with the top down. Deciding to show off to his pal, Jocko stood behind the wheel of the fast-moving car so that his head was above the windshield and the wind was hitting him in the face. Jocko threw a cigarette in front of him and caught it in his mouth as the wind blasted it back. An amazed Dick couldn't believe his eyes and went through a pack of cigarettes trying to replicate the stunt. Jocko claimed he had never practiced the trick and merely got lucky on the first try.[11]

For Christmas of 1953 Jocko and Dick rode in the Toyland Parade through San Diego's

North Park. In March of 1954 they made six days of appearances at the Junior Chamber of Commerce Rodeo in Phoenix, Arizona. The spring of 1954 saw Jocko and Dick put on eight performances at the Uline Arena in Washington D.C. and another six rodeo shows at the Arena in Philadelphia. The crowds remained enthusiastic, but the gates couldn't begin to compare to their record-setting run the previous year.

While touring rodeos with Dick, Jocko continued to wreck havoc on his body with his penchant for doing his own action. Even though he didn't have to do stunts for other actors any more, he was still determined to do all of his own. Jocko broke his left elbow in April 1954 doing a fight with Dick at the JE Ranch Rodeo in Providence, Rhode Island. Jocko reset the injury and blamed it on fatigue, having landed off-balance while taking a routine fall. All the aches and pains had him wishing he could come out to an audience and sing a song like Gene Autry or Roy Rogers, but that's not what the paying customers came to see. They wanted to see Jocko riding, fighting, and falling and that's what Jocko was determined to give them even if he was in pain while doing so.

Jocko had amassed a long list of mostly minor injuries from his years of stunt work and it was probably fortunate that he made it to leading man status when he did. At least he was putting his life on the line with less frequency in his new occupation. Other injuries from his years of stunts included the aforementioned broken noses, a crushed sternum after a horse ran him into a tree, fractured ribs, a sword poked in his eye, a sword impaled in his leg, bruised heels, broken fingers, and a split kneecap when he dove from a runaway buckboard and landed on a bottle in an area he thought had been cleared. Another time he took an arrow hit and fell into a net but was unable to clear the area before a second stuntman fell on top of him. On *Range Rider* he had a 25-pound fake boulder dropped on his head and was kicked in the stomach by a horse. He once made an easy dive from a ledge into a lake he was quite familiar with only to realize that recent rains had significantly built up silt on the bottom. Jocko nearly broke his neck and vowed to always recheck every stunt before undertaking it. Still, his body showed an uncanny ability to withstand all the punishment, as did his psyche. Jocko told *The Waterloo Daily Courier*, "I have 16 scars on my head and my right knee keeps floating around somewhere." In all he humorously estimated he'd only lost "a couple of quarts of blood and a couple of pounds of skin."

With production on the *Range Rider* show complete, Jocko remained open to accepting film offers in the summer of 1953. He was looking for an appropriate project that could propel him to greater stardom but decided to make another quick serial to give the kids he encountered new product. Clayton Moore of TV's *Lone Ranger* was the top-billed Jocko's co-star in the 15-chapter *Gunfighters of the Northwest* (originally *Northwest Mounted*) (1954), producer Sam Katzman and Columbia's last chance to squeeze more work out of their stunt ace and veteran director Spencer Gordon Bennet.

Jocko played Royal Canadian Mounted Policeman Sgt. Jim Ward, taking on outlaws and Indians on the warpath. Jocko looked good in his Mountie attire and worked well with Moore. The film was shot completely outdoors in the San Bernardino Mountains and Cedar Lake, further setting it apart from the usual serial. Jocko gets to hang from cliffs, fall from horses, paddle a canoe amidst a storm of arrows, romance Phyllis Coates, and fight heavies Marshall Reed, Gregg Barton, Pierce Lyden, and Rodd Redwing. Jocko's character is knocked unconscious at a fairly regular pace, but like any good Mountie he manages to get his man in the end.

Moore and Jocko first met when they did a fight scene together in a mine shaft in the Durango Kid film *South of Death Valley* (1949). Jocko, doubling for Starrett in the scene, delivered a punch that sent Moore flying into an ore car. It turns out they had a mutual friend in trapeze artist Bob Vin, whom Moore performed with in the 1930s. Jocko became social friends with Moore and his *Lone Ranger* co-star Jay Silverheels, a Mohawk Indian who played the part of Tonto. The trio spent a lot of time with one another in the early 1950s, and Moore even squeezed in guest appearances on *Range Rider*. Moore wrote in his book *I Was That Masked Man*, "I went on to work with Jock several times and always enjoyed it. He was always clowning — what a great sense of humor. He was a great athlete too, legs of rubber."

Leading lady Phyllis Coates told Bobby Copeland for *Western Clippings* that working with Jocko on the serial was a great experience: "Everyone knows Jock is a fun-loving guy. I enjoyed working with him. He was a great stuntman and horseman." Jocko had several other good friends in the cast of *Gunfighters*. Heavy Gregg Barton recalled Jocko for *The Westerner*: "He was an awfully nice guy, a prankster, fun-loving guy, but always did a competent job ... very diligent about his participation and helpful to other people." Veteran B-western bad guy Pierce Lyden wrote, "He was catlike, so quick in his movements. He was the perfect star for action films — a good athlete, excellent coordination, and the right build and height."

Lyden remembered one Jocko stunt in particular in this serial, though he mistakenly attributes it to *Cody of the Pony Express*. Lyden told *Serial Aces of the Silver Screen*: "He rode alongside, bulldogging me off my horse. Then he picked me up, knocked me out, and threw me over his shoulder, carrying me to a tree. On the other shoulder he carried a lariat which he tied around my feet, threw the rope over a tree limb, pulled me up and tied it off. Then, running to his horse, he did a crupper mount and rode away to get another baddie, and all this with the camera running — one shot, one take! It's hard to believe the great coordination of mind, strength, and time to complete a gig like this."

Actor-stuntman John Hart has a small role in the serial as he was visiting his then girl-friend Phyllis Coates. Ironically, Hart had just finished playing the *Lone Ranger* on TV when Clayton Moore left the role for a year over a contract squabble. The 6'4", 200-pound Hart, who had been a serial star himself in *Jack Armstrong* (1947), actually served as Jocko's double in the serial but had little to do. He wound up doubling Moore in some riding shots after Moore was thrown from a horse. Around the same time Jocko injured his foot doing a fight scene but was walking fine the next day and still doing all his own stunts. When Moore asked Jocko how his injuries healed so quickly, Jocko left him with a mystical one-word answer: "Metaphysics."

Jocko became pals with Hart and gave him a holster. Many years later, Hart auctioned off the rig and shared his memories of being Jocko's double when commenting on the origins of the rigging: "It was ludicrous doing stunts for one of the best stuntmen in town. Every time something came up Jocko would say, 'I'll do it.' And he usually did. I spent a good part of that job sitting under a tree watching him execute gags. Ones that I was supposed to be doing. Anyway, we became good friends, and I enjoyed the time we spent together and time shooting. We had great times shooting rocks, cans, targets, etc. We were both very good with an old Colt shooting iron."

Gunfighters of the Northwest came at the tail end of the popularity of serials. It benefits enormously from the location work and the presence of its leading men, but it's not quite up to the action standards of Jocko's *Roar of the Iron Horse*. Still, it's not bad as Columbia serials go. Children at the matinee were ecstatic for the chance to see both the Range Rider and the Lone Ranger on the same screen. It was a lot of fun for the principals to make. Unfortunately it was obvious that the entire serial format was running out of steam with the emergence of television.

Producer Sam Katzman had plans to star Jocko in another 15-chapter serial entitled *Riding with Buffalo Bill* (1954) because he could recycle action footage he owned from *The Valley of Missing Men* (1942) and *Deadwood Dick* (1940). Jocko had soured on Katzman's penny-pinching ways and realized putting out inferior product at this point could harm the momentum *Range Rider* was providing him for a film career. Short of flat-out refusing, Jocko reasoned with Katzman that at 6'4" he couldn't fit into 6'1" Bill Elliott's old wardrobe and the costumes would need to be altered. Having to dig into his pockets changed Katzman's mind, and he ended up casting Jocko's friend Marshall Reed in the title role.

Jocko found the time to make one other film after the end of his run as the Range Rider, but it never saw the light of day. Character actor Smiley Burnette, sidekick to Charles Starrett and Gene Autry, includes among his film credits an unreleased Columbia film entitled *Panhandle Territory* (1953). The star is Mahoney. This was apparently an old Durango Kid script by Barry Shipman that was revised as a vehicle for Jocko. Fred Sears directed with Colbert Clark producing. There is no other information on why the film was unreleased, but it may have been intended as a series pilot and was scrapped. There is speculation that Harry Cohn himself decided to shelve it after butting heads with Jocko.

The studio still thought of Jocko as little more than a stuntman turned TV actor. They took Rock Hudson on loan-out from Universal for their A-western *Gun Fury* (1953), placed Jocko's friend George Montgomery into several B-westerns, and pushed the stolid Phil Carey as their new cowboy star in a run of routine films that had Al Wyatt tackling virtually all of Carey's action. Jocko no doubt felt he could have handled any of these leads for the studio. It was time for Jocko and the studio to part ways. *Panhandle Territory* was the last project Jocko worked on at Columbia.

With *Range Rider* in the rear view mirror, Jocko set his sights on a film career as a leading man of action. During the *Range Rider* run, he'd had a meeting with Jack L. Warner to discuss starring in a feature film, but his hectic personal appearance schedule between TV seasons prevented any starring role for Warner Bros. at the time. He was also in serious discussions with 20th Century–Fox, although the studio was reportedly using him as a bargaining chip to get their current western film star Dale Robertson to back off his contract demands. Fox's tactics worked, and Jocko was not needed as star of *The Gambler from Natchez* (1954).

Exploring the current offers available, Jocko opted to sign a five-picture deal with producer Edward Small in August of 1953. Their first project was an action western entitled *Silver Dollar*, which became *Overland Pacific* prior to release. Unfortunately, it would be the only film of the five-picture deal that made it to production. It's not known why the association did not continue but might have involved Jocko's insistence on doing all of his own stunt work. Insurance premiums on such a film star could be cost-prohibitive. Another factor might have been that other producers were still vying for Jocko's services even after he signed with Small. The Italian company Thetsis Productions was courting him in the fall of 1953 for a starring role in a cloak-and-dagger action film to be titled *Shadow of the Borgias,* which might have influenced either Small or Jocko's mindset. Small went on to produce such western and action films as *Southwest Passage* (1954) with Rod Cameron, *Lone Gun* (1954) with George Montgomery, *Khyber Patrol* (1954) with Richard Egan, and *Top Gun* (1955) with Sterling Hayden. These may have been intended as projects for Jocko.

Overland Pacific starred Jocko as railroad agent Ross Granger. He's out to stop former friend turned bad guy William Bishop from orchestrating Indian attacks on the builders of the transcontinental railroad. Director Fred Sears, a former actor who befriended Jocko on the Durango Kid films, punctuated the above-average oater with some great action scenes, including an Indian raid that sees Jocko hurling sticks of dynamite to keep the attackers at bay. The standout is a one-minute slugfest with veteran stuntman Fred Graham, John Wayne's double throughout the 1940s. At one point Jocko's body flips over a hitching post, only to rebound like a spring and keep on fighting. Jocko's body takes plenty of abuse in the picture, and he's even shot in the shoulder by Chris Alcaide. Jocko still proceeds to wrestle Alcaide to the ground and club him with a rifle butt. Peggie Castle is the female lead who helps him tend his wounds.

The film was a step in the right direction from his association with television and serials, proving he could headline a Technicolor theatrical release and be accepted as a romantic lead. Jocko often joked that on *Range Rider* he was only allowed to kiss his horse since the show was aimed at children. *Overland Pacific* was fairly violent and bloody for the period and definitely aimed at a more adult audience. Publicity played up the fact that Jocko was the first movie stuntman to become a star. Reviews were generally kind and box office receipts satisfactory. *Variety* noted, "Mahoney has authority in his heroics and gives the picture an action-plus touch in settling the trouble and winning the love of Peggie Castle."

Jocko returned to his home state of Iowa for the premiere and was met by an enthusiastic crowd of children. He made appearances at the theater in Cedar Rapids and the local Ellis Park swimming pool. The Montrose Hotel honored him with a luncheon, and Jocko appeared on local TV and radio stations. Cedar Rapids couldn't get enough of the cowboy movie star. It was quite a welcome for the former Hawkeye. In September of 1954, Jocko also headlined with Dick Jones at the World Championship Rodeo in Fort Madison, Iowa, where they partook in a pancake breakfast, rode in a parade, and visited the children's hospital ward. The Iowa return had to be somewhat bittersweet, as Jocko's father had recently (1952) passed away at the age of 59. Jocko also made personal appearances for the film in Omaha, Nebraska.

Jocko and Dick's rodeo appearances became more sporadic through the latter half of 1954 following a less than substantial box-office in the spring when Jocko had injured his elbow. They appeared in Oregon for the July Fourth Molalla Buckaroo Rodeo, then followed with a one-day appearance at the Los Angeles Sheriff's Rodeo where they supported Gene Autry. The announcer at this show accidentally introduced them too early while the star Autry was still making his side-pass for the audience. Jocko and Dick had no choice but to ride out on cue. Autry understood. Jocko made a solo appearance at the Arkansas State Fair Rodeo in the fall, while Dick stayed home tending to the birth of twins. In October of 1954 they returned to the Boston Gardens and sang with guest Ray Whitley at the City Hospital. That fall Dick's hand became infected from a cut, and no appearances were scheduled for

The star of *Overland Pacific* (1954).

the next several months. In December, Maggie accompanied Jocko for the annual Toyland Parade through San Diego. The last of Jocko and Dick's *Range Rider* rodeo appearances came in May 1955 at the Lions Club Rodeo in Sacramento, California.

Aspiring musician Johnny Western accompanied Jocko and Dick for the 1955 appearance at the Sacramento Rodeo, working as a substitute wrangler for Richard Smith. The popular singer wrote about Jocko for *Western Horseman*: "During the time we were there,

I had a chance to talk with Jock. I remember even yet what he told me about show business and one's responsibilities to it. During this time, I learned just how popular Jock was with the public. They mobbed him at the rodeo, and at the hotel there was someone at the door for autographs all the time. He was gracious and understanding with his fans and they loved him. Dick Jones was a fine showman and a great part of the act. Although his personality is altogether different from Jock's, they worked well together. The public loved Dick's sparkle and bright dialogue, and Jock's easy-going manner was the perfect offset for the two of them."

Jones went on to headline his own Gene Autry–produced western series, *Buffalo Bill, Jr.* (1955–1956). Dick once again pleased audiences with his thrilling riding and fights. After 52 episodes he decided his banged-up body had seen enough stunts to last a lifetime. Dick opted to semi-retire and move into real estate. He stayed in touch with Jocko through the years and became a popular guest on the western film festival circuit. One of the subjects fans most often asked him about was Jocko. At the 1997 Knoxville Film Festival, Jones commented, "Jocko Mahoney was probably the greatest stuntman in the business. He was a great person, and a wonderful personality."

6

The Universal Star

Jocko told the AP newspaper wire services about his decision to move away from stunts to purely acting roles: "I decided to stop risking my neck because no stuntman ever walks off into the sunset with the leading lady." There were reports that Jocko would star in a series of swashbuckling films in 1954 or an action-packed seafaring TV series, but nothing came of this. Jocko was reluctant to take on another series because he'd have to give up making personal appearances as the Range Rider and would in effect be in competition with himself.

One role that was Jocko's for the taking was that of Tarzan. Lex Barker was leaving the part, ironically to try to establish himself in cowboy roles. However, Jocko and his agent felt that if Jocko were to play Tarzan now, he might never get out of the jungle. Jocko passed on the opportunity, and an unknown bodybuilder named Gordon Werschkul was rechristened Gordon Scott and cast as the Ape Man. In August of 1954 Jocko signed a seven-year contract with publicist Helen Ferguson. For the minimum of either $200 a month or five percent of his income, Ferguson would be expected to place Jocko's name and photo appropriately into a variety of media outlets to keep him constantly in the public eye.

Seeking to prove himself as an actor and romantic leading man, Jocko made no less than six appearances playing different characters on television's *The Loretta Young Show* in 1954 and 1955 for producer Tom Lewis. In one of the episodes he portrayed a Broadway director. Jocko was a hit with the female viewers, topping letters of fan mail to Miss Young's show for his guest appearances. *TV Guide* ran an article featuring Jocko entitled "Loretta Young and Her Men" in the January 1, 1955, edition. Jocko considered Young a good friend and one of his favorite leading ladies. He also guest starred opposite Ann Sothern on a 1955 episode of *Private Secretary*. The idea of branching out into different genres achieved the desired effect, and Jocko soon came under consideration for roles that didn't require him to mount a horse.

Jocko did a photo spread in the May 1955 issue of *Modern Screen* teaching Barbara Stanwyck how to do horse stunts for her film *Cattle Queen of Montana* (1954). He helped her become comfortable climbing into the saddle, then demonstrated a quick way to get off a horse. Jocko did his patented back-flip off the horse's hind quarters for the camera. He was friendly with Stanwyck and also stepped out onto the dance floor with her for another series of photos. Stanwyck told columnist Hedda Hopper that Jocko was "one of the finest dancers I've ever met."

Jocko landed a supporting part as a sailor in Joseph Pevney's well-made World War II

Still from *Away All Boats* (1956).

drama *Away All Boats* (1956), a Universal Studios all-star action affair that top-lined Jeff Chandler and featured other beefcake actors such as George Nader, Lex Barker, and Keith Andes. A young Clint Eastwood had a minor part as well. Jocko managed to get himself noticed with some sarcastic banter and stands out as the unit's top sharpshooter when he's called to detonate a mine with a crack rifle shot. This scene was done aboard the U.S.S.

Randall with Captain Robert Theobald providing one of the ship's own marksmen to fire at the target with live ammo while Jocko fired with blanks. The ship's marksman missed five takes in a row, at which point Jocko asked for permission to try with the live ammo. According to studio publicity, Jocko hit the target on the first take.

While on location in the Virgin Islands, Jocko became lifelong friends with co-star Richard Boone, a rugged World War II Navy veteran and amateur boxer. Boone later gave Jocko a Colt revolver and rig from his popular *Have Gun—Will Travel* series. Jocko passed it down to his son Jim. Jocko and Boone stood out from the rest of the cast in the Virgin Islands due to their TV backgrounds. Television had invaded the island paradise and while Boone's *Medic* was a hit with adults, Jocko's *Range Rider* could win any popularity contest. Jocko signed hundreds of autographs and spent a lot of time talking with the local children. He made special appearances at ball fields and the St. Thomas Carnival to meet the demand, but that didn't stop nearly 2000 kids from camping out in the lobby of the Virgin Isle Hotel to get a better look at their cowboy idol.

Away All Boats featured gravel-voiced character actor Charles McGraw, a drinker of note. Others in the cast such as Boone were known bottle-tippers. The film became noted for much of the cast needing to be dragged out of waterfront bars every morning before filming could commence. Outside of partaking in 20-foot dives from the hotel balcony into the swimming pool with fellow stuntmen Charles Horvath and Bobby Hoy, Jocko behaved admirably and made a good showing for himself. Universal took note.

His solid report card on *Away All Boats* and the mounting fan mail from *Loretta Young Show* appearances prompted Universal to sign Jocko to a seven-year leading man contract at 40 weeks a year. He'd top-line B+ westerns and other features similar to what Rory Calhoun and decorated war hero Audie Murphy were doing for the studio. The contract also stipulated that Jocko would be able to continue his own lucrative personal appearances although he would need to cease performing stunts during them. In October of 1955 Rock Hudson and much of the cast of *Away All Boats* appeared at the Cobweb Ball in the San Fernando Valley for Halloween festivities. In July of 1956 Jocko made an appearance for the Salt Lake City premiere of *Away All Boats*, decked out in his cowboy duds for the World War II film.

Universal was quick to drum up publicity for their new talent, who would now officially be known and billed as Jock Mahoney. In 1955 Jocko was defeated for the post of Honorary Fire Chief of Universal City by the starlet trio of Julie Adams, Leigh Snowden, and Dani Crayne, the future wife of studio contractee David Janssen. It was lighthearted fluff and typical studio publicity that put the names of the contract actors and actresses in the newspapers. Jocko also appeared in a shirtless beefcake spread for the January 1956 pages of the fan magazine *TV Star Parade* and swim trunk photos for the February 1957 issue of *TV Screen Life*. Yet again, the handsome Jocko proved a resounding hit with the ladies.

Jocko realized his physique was integral to his career and considered his body a temple. He stayed in shape not only with riding and stunt work but with a workout routine that saw him in his swimming pool every morning and his home gym or backyard workout area every evening. He rarely if ever stepped into a commercial gym or health club, though he did work out for a brief time under the watchful eye of noted bodybuilding trainer Vince Gironda. At Universal he would take an occasional boxing workout and spar a few rounds in the ring with the guidance of trainer Frankie Van. At home he was fond of wrestling with his 165-pound Great Dane Du Barry.

Jocko was especially conscious of his diet. Breakfast was typically eggs and grapefruit. Lunch might be a barbecue chicken and fresh vegetable salad concocted by Jocko himself. Dinner was often more barbecue grilled meat. Quarts of homogenized milk were consumed throughout the day. Snacks consisted of nuts and honey for needed energy that was not already fueled by a prodigious intake of cigarettes and coffee. As Jocko entered his mid-thirties, his waist measurement remained a mere 31 inches and his weight stayed steady at 200 pounds.

Jocko would often be mentioned positively by legendary columnist Hedda Hopper, who called him "good looking" and praised his "very charming manner." She even went so far as to champion him for various roles for which he was in contention such as the part of aviator Charles Lindbergh in *The Spirit of St. Louis* (1957). Some of these films never made it past the early stages of development, but they are interesting "what ifs." Among the never-made films was a Rouben Mamoulian western about Buffalo Bill Cody. Hopper's fellow columnist Jimmie Fidler was also singing Jocko's praises, writing in his column that he was "impressed with his friendliness, fine personality, and his physical size." Darryl F. Zanuck, head of 20th Century–Fox, included Jocko among those actors he felt were "destined to secure stardom."

At the tiller of his boat in a 1956 Universal Studios publicity pose.

Jocko continued to be readily accessible to the public. In January of 1955 he appeared at the Connecticut Sportsmen's Show with Bill Williams, taking a trip to the Colt Firearm Museum while there. In February of 1955 he was the grand marshal at the 15th Annual Palm Springs Rodeo. He repeated that post at the February 1956 Temple City Parade and the September 1956 Barstow Parade. In July of 1956 he made a personal appearance in Estes Park, Colorado, for the Big Windup. In September of that year he headed a special parade for 5000 children at the Napa District Fair in Northern California. In December he rode as a special guest with the Sheriff's Mounted Posse in Baton Rouge, Louisiana. The 1956 holidays saw him participate in the North Hollywood Christmas Parade and San Diego's Toyland Parade with Dick Jones. Jocko also sought to display his engaging personality across the airwaves, appearing on television game shows such as *Truth or Consequences* and *It Could Be You*. He even made some movies.

A Day of Fury (1956) from director Harmon Jones was a Universal western co-starring Jocko and Dale Robertson as protagonist and antagonist. Robertson has a meaty villain role as a gunfighter who saves marshal Mahoney's life, then moves in on both his woman (Mara Corday) and his town, turning the citizens against each other. There is a fair level of tension developed throughout the film before the conflict reaches its resolution in the form of a gunfight. It's a decently handled film, and Jocko manages his role as Marshal Burnett ably. However, the script doesn't call for a lot of action on Jocko's part. There are no fistfights or fantastic leaps; although Jocko does perform his own saddle fall early in the film. Rather than take a fall onto a nicely dug-up spot of softened earth, Jocko chose to dive straight over a rock. Outside of his dialogue, there simply weren't enough physical challenges in the film for Jocko to tackle.

This was one problem with Universal's handling of Jocko: They didn't utilize his action skills to their fullest. The viewer wants to see Jocko doing what he does best, which is leaping about and being front and center in knockdown drag-out brawls. Universal released a new version of *The Spoilers* the same year with Jeff Chandler and Rory Calhoun taking part in a fight to rival the 1942 John Wayne-Randolph Scott version. Chandler and Calhoun were doubled throughout by stuntmen Bob Morgan and Chuck Roberson. Casting Mahoney in one of these parts might have enhanced the overall effect and made the battle one for the ages. Instead, the studio chose to cast him in minor fare. Part of the problem was Jocko himself, who was so eager to work that he'd go into studio executive Ed Muhl's office and insist on being put into a picture. Jocko hated sitting around idle. *A Day of Fury* was fortunately a good film on which to build on and still holds up well as an adult psychological western. Universal publicity played up his *Range Rider* popularity in advertisements.

Dale Robertson told *Universal-International Westerns* that Jocko was "one of the most fluid actors in the whole business. He was really wonderful, he was athletic, had great moves." Co-star Jan Merlin added that Jocko was "a wonderful guy." Mara Corday told *Westerns Women* that she didn't care for the technique of director Jones and thought none of the performances played well as a result, labeling Jocko as coming off "like a big stick" and her own performance as "horribly rigid."

Most of the trade paper reviewers disagreed. Of his performance *Variety* remarked, "Mahoney competently essays part of the lawman who intends saving the town his way." *The Chicago Tribune* noted, "Jock Mahoney and Mara Corday are good looking newcomers," while the *Times-Picayune* called Jocko "the best actor in the lot." *The San Diego Union* chimed in with, "Jock Mahoney is excellent as the forceful, level-headed sheriff who tries to clean up the town."

I've Lived Before (1956) was the least typical of Jocko's starring roles. In it he plays a pilot, but that's as close as Jocko's background came to matching the character. The Richard Bartlett film has fantasy overtones and deals with the idea of reincarnation, a popular subject at the time given the case of Bridey Murphy. The opening scene has Jocko as John Bolan about to land a commercial aircraft when he suddenly feels as if he is a World War I pilot engaged in a dogfight. The feeling of *déjà vu* is so strong that Jocko begins to feel he is this dead flying ace caught in a different time and place. The rest of the film explores the psychological toll the experience has on Jocko and those around him, including female lead Leigh Snowden. *I've Lived Before* has the potential for some interesting material but is undermined by the fact it is a cheaply made black and white second feature.

Walking through the movie as if caught in a daydream, Jocko doesn't get to play to his strengths, and the majority of critics were not kind to the film or its star. Jocko should receive plaudits for trying something entirely different. He considered it a groundbreaking film on a personal level as he was able to wear a suit and tie, proof that he was more than simply a cowboy stuntman. As with his appearance on *The Loretta Young Show*, his intention likely was to distance himself as far from his western persona as possible. In that sense his work should be deemed a success. His acting wouldn't win any awards, but he didn't embarrass himself either. *Variety* noted, "Mahoney turns in a credible performance," while *The Hollywood Reporter* observed, "Miss Snowden and Mahoney are adequate but not interesting enough to carry such a picture." *The New York Times* reported, "A chap named Jock Mahoney, former Range Rider on television, plays the afflicted pilot in a blank and bewildered way." Then again, that was the character as written.

Jocko's acting at Universal was short on emoting and long on silent intensity, an effective combination for him at the time. There would be no crying or wailing to the heavens on Jocko's part. He wasn't part of the emerging Method school of acting being popularized by Marlon Brando and James Dean. He was much more the strong silent type. Jocko would hit his marks, say his lines, and look good doing so. He was a near-perfect western actor and stuck primarily to that genre with only a few diversions into military roles for which he was also well-suited. His natural easygoing charm and engaging smile made him an effective romantic lead within the comforts of these rugged surroundings. Realizing his limitations, he still held out hope that he would find a role that would push him to the top of the film world in much the same manner as Gary Cooper or John Wayne.

Jocko attended acting classes at Universal City and worked hard to become a better actor in front of the camera. Universal brass recognized Jocko's dedication and kept him slotted as one of their rising leading men. At the studio, Jocko began running a gym class for his fellow contract actors incorporating gymnastic exercises, weights, and calisthenics. Future film superstar Clint Eastwood and TV star Doug McClure were among the men Jocko gave fitness pointers and fight scene tips. When he wasn't in the gym he was riding horses around the western sets, often teaching his fellow actors how to ride on the back lot. Other Universal contract players at the time included John Agar, John Saxon, John Gavin, David Janssen, and George Nader. The top Universal stars were Rock Hudson, Tony Curtis, and Jeff Chandler.

Actor William Campbell had been hired by Universal to co-star opposite Kirk Douglas in the western *Man Without a Star* (1955). Unfortunately, Campbell had no idea how to ride a horse. He had the studio wranglers put him on a horse but was obviously struggling and frightened. It was at this point that Campbell looked up toward the sun and saw silhouetted against it atop a hill a lone figure on horseback. Campbell remembered for *Feature Players* that his immediate thought was, "There's the cowboy God." The striking figure rode down to Campbell and presented itself as Jock Mahoney. Jocko offered to meet Campbell every morning at the studio for the next two weeks to teach the actor how to get on and off the saddle and ride like the wind. Campbell felt forever indebted to Jocko as his newfound skill astride a horse opened up a whole new genre of work for him.

Jocko also became well-known and popular with aspiring stuntmen, as he was more than willing to pass down his vast knowledge of performing stunts for the camera. This was not always the case with Jocko. During his own days as an active stuntman he was known for his competitive fire when it came to getting the work. Novice stuntman Jack Young had worked with Jocko on the Durango Kid film *Trail to Laredo* (1948) and found that he was not open to answering questions about the trade. "I'm sorry to report that Mr. Mahoney was not friendly to me," Young recalled. "He was the old pro and I was the new kid. I'm certain he was nicer than that to people he knew, but I guess he didn't like the competition. I kept asking him questions and trying to learn but to no avail. I am sure he was a decent sort and was okay later in years."[1]

Many of Jocko's training sessions with new stuntmen occurred in his own sawdust-covered backyard or in the sandy river bottom of the Los Angeles River near Burbank, where horse falls could be performed with a soft landing. Jocko's backyard was fully equipped with stunt and gymnastic equipment and a huge oak tree with a rope hanging from it. For a small fee Jocko taught his students how to choreograph fights and fall without injury by tucking and rolling. During his stint at Columbia, Jocko had helped break stuntmen Bill Catching and Troy Melton into the business. Fred Krone, Hal Needham, Lenny Dee, and B-western screenwriter Jack Lewis were some of the other young stuntmen Jocko trained, as were actors Robert Dix, James Drury, Jerome Courtland, John Derek, Chris Alcaide, Harry Lauter, George Wallace, Charles Gray, Dee Pollock, John Barrymore, Jr., and Sean Flynn.

Jack Lewis was a few years behind Jocko as a student and swimmer at the University of Iowa, and they first met while serving together in the U.S. Marine Corps in San Diego. Lewis later showed up to interview Jocko at Columbia Pictures while working as a reporter for Iowa's *Cedar Rapids Gazette*. Lewis would submit screenplays to the studios and for a short time in the 1950s did movie and TV stunt work, mostly on jobs Jocko landed him. Lewis figured prominently in Jocko's life some 20 years later. In his book *White Horse, Black Hat* Lewis termed Jocko "one of the better stuntmen around, a successor to Yakima Canutt, and the equal of Dave Sharpe."

Robert Dix found that Jocko's stunt instruction helped him greatly in his acting career. His newly developed physical abilities landed him several roles, especially on low-budget independent films. Producers were always grateful when an actor could do the majority of his own fights and riding. Dix said, "I was a great admirer of Jock's prowess and athletic ability. As you know, he did many, if not all of his own stunts; was a terrific stuntman and stunt coordinator. How to take a punch and deliver a punch, depending on camera angles, was covered. Very useful stuff later in westerns and motorcycle movies and all rough-and-tumble stuff including fight scenes. Fights were choreographed like a dance. Slow at first and then the speed increased. Jock was a great guy!"[2]

James Drury also recalled visiting Jocko's backyard and working out on his gymnastic bars. "I admired his physical prowess," Drury said. "It was phenomenal what he could do. He was an incredible athlete and constantly exercising to stay in shape. He was really handy with everything. I once saw him jump off a horse, knock eight guys over coming off, and land on his feet. I don't know how that's possible, but Jocko did it."[3]

Jocko originally met Drury and Dix on the set of the MGM science fiction film *Forbidden Planet* (1956) where they were playing crewmen of a spacecraft. Jocko was visiting the production, no doubt intrigued by the fantasy aspects. U.S. Navy veteran Drury went on to become the popular star of TV's long-running western *The Virginian* and a lifelong friend of Jocko. They traveled together to many charity functions and publicity junkets. "You couldn't meet a better man to work with or call a friend," Drury said. "Jock Mahoney was the most lovable man in the world. He was a fascinating character and a man of great accomplishments. He generated an intense admiration by everyone who knew and worked with him. He was a pioneer in the stunts we do. He should be remembered by everyone."

Fan magazine *TV People* profiled Jocko and Maggie's new ranch house in Encino, highlighting their backyard activities such as swimming, badminton, and barbecues. Jocko is shown playing with four-year-old Princess Melissa, feeding the dogs, tending to his tropical fish tank, and climbing down from a tree house he built in the mammoth oak tree. Jocko, Maggie, and Princess Melissa are described as a tight and happy threesome. There is no mention at all of Maggie's children Rick and Sally from her previous marriage, an example of the tight publicity control common in that era. Jocko later built a small stable and training ring in the front yard where he kept a 17-hand cinnamon sorrel named Country Fox.

Showdown at Abilene (1956) (originally known as *Gun Shy*) from director Charles Haas was a finely mounted psychological western with Jocko well-cast in the lead as a former Confederate soldier returning to the town where he once served as sheriff. Abilene is now divided by a war between cattlemen and farmers, and Jocko soon has himself embroiled in the center of the action while rekindling an old romance with female lead Martha Hyer. Jocko's character Jim Trask is haunted by his involvement in the war, harboring a dark secret that keeps him from handling a gun. There's enough action to keep things moving, and Jocko has a short street fight with veteran heavy Lane Bradford that features a great leap onto his foe. Jocko also offers a shirtless scene or two for the female audience, showing himself to be super-fit as he entered his late thirties. By the final frame of the film, Jocko has a gun in his hand and takes care of business against bad guy Lyle Bettger.

Upon the film's release Jocko received congratulatory telegrams from John Wayne, Gregory Peck, Randolph Scott, Charles Starrett, Jon Hall, and Errol Flynn in regard to his starring role. *Showdown at Abilene* was typical of Jocko's Universal output and in many ways that is a good thing. It's a fine example of Jocko as a serious western star and offered him another chance to sink his teeth into a character who does more than "smile and not smile."

Variety noted, "Mahoney comes over well as the hero, giving the character a bit more than just the usual strong man handling." According to *The Hollywood Reporter*, "Mahoney, Miss Hyer, and Bettger handle their roles with ease and authority." *The Chicago Tribune* stated, "This western is peopled with characters possessed of some dimension, and its story is told without too much gunfire and galloping. Mahoney, a newcomer, shows promise of being an interesting actor." The review concluded by noting that Jocko displayed "the finest combination of acrobatics and targeting since the days of Doug Fairbanks, Sr."

The Rocky Mountain Evening Telegram was even more ebullient in its praise, commenting: "It is pleasant to report, Mahoney amply confirms the impression he conveyed in his first starring role, that he is an attractive and highly competent actor with a special type of appeal that is somewhat reminiscent of the Gary Cooper of younger days. On the basis of his performance in *Showdown at Abilene* and the original impression he created in *A Day of Fury*, it is fairly safe to predict that it will only be a matter of a year or two before he is recognized as Hollywood's top star in the outdoor action field."

Jocko performs one of his patented leaps on heavy Lane Bradford in *Showdown at Abilene* (1956).

Battle Hymn (1956) was a Douglas Sirk–directed Korean War drama for Universal-International starring Rock Hudson as a trainer of fighter pilots. Jocko, who knew a thing or two about military fly boys, furnished able support as Major Moore. He received sixth billing in the film, shot in Nogales, Arizona. In the finished print Jocko didn't have a lot to do and comes across as square-jawed window dressing. The film concentrated more on Hudson's relationship with a group of orphans than it did on action. The 25 Korean children appearing in the film adopted Jocko as their "American Father" on the set. Jocko spent his spare time with the kids, teaching them to sing songs such as "Marching Through Georgia" and "Home Sweet Home."

Jocko got along well professionally with 6'5" star Hudson, whose portable dressing room he got from the studio due to its oversized furniture. During the filming of one scene Jocko did his own stunt driving of a Jeep while Hudson held on tight in the passenger seat, suppressing a grin as Jocko skidded to a halt directly in front of the camera. Sirk offered that if he were going to drive that fast, the scene really called for a stuntman. Jocko's logical reply to his director was, "In me, you get a package deal."

Variety noted, "Don DeFore, Jock Mahoney, Alan Hale, James Edwards, and other members of the outfit come through strongly, bolstering the entertainment all down the line." Although reviewed at the end of 1956 for the trades, *Battle Hymn* did not have its world premiere until February 1957 in Marietta, Ohio, hometown of the real-life Colonel

Dean Hess that Hudson was portraying. Hudson, Jocko, and Dan Duryea participated in a parade for a crowd of more than 20,000 excited fans. It was said to be the largest event in the history of the small city, even topping a 1938 parade for President Franklin D. Roosevelt. The town loved the interaction with the fan-friendly stars. At one point Jocko grabbed a music baton and led the high school band, assisted by Hudson, to the smiling delight of all involved. Jocko also journeyed to Dallas to promote the film.

One of the programmers Universal assigned Jocko was the prehistoric science fiction film *The Land Unknown* (1957). Jocko stars as Commander Hal Roberts, a man of action accompanying a team of scientists on an expedition to Antarctica. There they stumble on a lost world of dinosaurs. The idea for the story originated from the real-life 1947 South Pole expedition of Admiral Byrd, where they discovered a mysterious area of warm water. The movie was filmed largely on process stages with mock-ups for where the special effects would be added. The entire stage was covered in black velvet with chalk outlines or tape for where objects were intended to be.

Jocko found his first experience working with special effects to be difficult as an actor, reacting appropriately to things such as 18-foot dinosaurs that were not there. Nonetheless, he had a good time making the film. He got to perform plenty of action as the heroic lead, including diving out of a helicopter from 30 feet into six feet of water. "All the good junk I love to do," he told *Starlog* magazine. Some point to the enjoyable popcorn flick as an influence for Steven Spielberg's *Jurassic Park* (1993).

The film's pressbook touted Jocko as "the first full-fledged stuntman to become a motion picture star." It went on to list some of his daring feats in the picture, such as fighting off a giant Tyrannosaurus Rex, leaping 18 feet off a cave to fight an insane caveman, and swimming 150 yards to outdistance an Elasmosaurus. Jocko noted that since he had become a star he was doing five times as many stunts as he normally did in a single picture. Wearing a sweaty, ripped T-shirt and cut-off shorts throughout much of the picture, a tightly muscled Jocko makes a fine square-jawed military hero.

For a scene in which co-star Henry Brandon is floating in a pool of water, two real eight-foot long monitor lizards were placed in the water. The scene called for a strong swimmer who could outdistance the reptiles. Veteran stuntman Sol Gorss served as Brandon's double but apparently became tired in the water and had to call for help. Jocko promptly dove into the water, swam out, and brought Gorss to safety before the lizards could close in on him.

There's a scene in the film where Jocko and co-star William Reynolds have to swim across a lake. Reynolds, a former competitive swimmer, surprised Jocko when he was able to keep pace with him. An out-of-breath Jocko beat Reynolds to the other side, but had some humorous choice words for him when they came out of the water. Reynolds, a Universal contract player, had also worked with Jocko on *Away All Boats* and roomed with him on a stay-over in Texas, where Jocko's *Range Rider* fans continuously called the hotel.

Reynolds told Tom Weaver in *Starlog* that Jocko was "the best big stunt man in the business.... Physically, he was something else; I mean we'd be walkin' down the street, and we'd be talking, and he'd vault over a Volkswagen! He was a startling athlete who could do that with no running start or anything; he could put one hand on the roof and go right over. Just out of exuberance, or just to see if he could do it."

In its review of *The Land Unknown*, *Variety* said, "Mahoney makes the most of oppor-

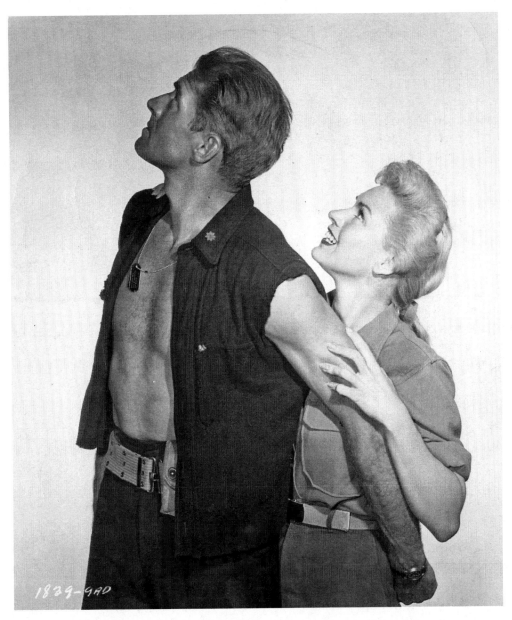

Jocko and Shawn Smith react to an off-screen Tyrannosaurus Rex in *The Land Unknown* (1957).

tunities," while the *San Diego Union* wrote, "Jock Mahoney has the principal role, giving a convincing performance and also taking part in some mild romantics with attractive Shawn Smith." *The Boston Herald* poked fun at the actors being upstaged by the dinosaurs: "Jock Mahoney, Shawn Smith, and Phil Harvey are the prominent actors, though the cards are stacked in favor of the tarsier."

Jocko was more in his element with *Joe Dakota* (1957), a suspenseful modern western filmed in California's Conejo Valley. Director Richard Bartlett's film is a well-made take-off on the recent *Bad Day at Black Rock* (1955) as Jocko plays a mysterious stranger who shows up in a small town looking for an Indian friend. The Indian, known to the town as Joe Dakota, was killed for his land, on which town leader Charles McGraw has begun to drill. It turns out Jocko is the real Joe Dakota, and he butts heads with McGraw and his stooges Lee Van Cleef and Claude Akins. The highlight is Jocko slugging it out with Van Cleef and Akins in a juvenile game of trading punches to see who can be knocked off a barstool. Jocko stays in his seat. He then goes into action against both men and promptly knocks them all over the room. The fight is over in seconds, a shame considering the principals involved. A prolonged Jocko-Akins-Van Cleef fight could have been a tough guy classic. In the climax, Jocko fights McGraw in a black pool of oil as a gusher rains down on them. In real life it took Jocko two full weeks to completely clean his body of the sticky Carbopole material used as an oil substitute.

Six-foot-two, 190-pound Van Cleef originally worked with Jocko on two appearances of *The Range Rider*. Van Cleef had been brought to Hollywood for a villainous role in *High Noon*, and Jocko's show was his first work while he waited for the film to be released. Van Cleef had served with the U.S. Navy during World War II on a sub-chaser and the two men hit it off immediately. Jocko helped Van Cleef with his horsemanship, and both men shared a keen interest in physical fitness and the great outdoors. They remained good friends for the rest of their lives.

Jocko does well as the former cavalry officer who catches the eye of female lead Luana Patten while getting under the skin of the citizens of the town. He may not be Spencer Tracy, but he's in his element here. *Joe Dakota* even gave him the chance to display his pipes, as he sang the Mack David song "The Flower of San Antone" for the film while bathing in a horse trough. In some markets *Joe Dakota* was paired up with *The Land Unknown* for a Jocko double-feature.

Reviews were favorable with Jocko continuing to earn praise. *Variety* noted, "Under Richard Bartlett's direction, Mahoney delivers well." Jocko was especially proud of the fact he was termed "a relaxed, accomplished actor." It helped justify all the hard work he had put into his career thus far. *The Hollywood Reporter* chipped in with, "Mahoney is less laconic than usual and does a good job," while Louisiana's *Times-Picayune* wrote, "Leading roles are played well by Jock Mahoney and pretty Luana Patten."

In *Slim Carter* (1957), also helmed by Bartlett, Jocko played one of his most pleasant leading roles, a self-centered title cowboy star brought down to earth by his interaction with boy Tim Hovey and studio publicist Julie Adams. Jocko even gets to sing a few Jimmy Wakely–written songs, "Ride, Cowboy, Ride," "Gold," and "Cowboy." Jocko acquits himself well with the tunes, with Decca Records releasing a 45 promo containing "Cowboy" and "Gold." There was even some talk of Jocko cutting an entire album of songs for Decca. *Slim Carter* benefits greatly from the presence of likable cowboy actor Ben Johnson, who plays the character of Mahoney's stuntman. Jocko and his lifelong friend Johnson get to stage a short fight scene with one another.

The story has Adams molding the egocentric womanizer Huey Mack (Mahoney) into an old-fashioned cowboy movie star named Slim Carter. One of her promotions is a contest in which a letter-writing fan gets to spend a full month with Slim Carter. Orphan Hovey wins the contest and in the process the hearts of both Mahoney and Adams. Unfortunately, Mahoney realizes that the boy's idealized version of Slim Carter varies greatly from the man he actually is, and he begins attempting to change for the better. Adams likes the change, and she and Mahoney decide that they are meant for one another, and that the boy is meant to be adopted as their son. All ends well as the heartstrings are tugged in the final reel.

Jocko had seen the 11-year-old Hovey in the film *The Private War of Major Benson* (1955) and suggested him for the part to Universal. Life imitated art as Jocko and Hovey took to one another during the course of filming. They became such pals that Hovey would be invited to stay at Jocko's real home, riding horses and swimming with Jocko's kids. He even accompanied them on a hunting trip. Universal was quick to play up the press angle on that story. Hovey appeared again with Jocko in the film *Money, Women, and Guns* (1958). Unfortunately the child actor experienced many personal problems as he grew into adulthood and entered the professional music business. He died of a drug overdose in 1989 at the age of 44. Hovey's problems were a firm reminder to Jocko of the dangers of having children working in the entertainment business.

The highlight of *Slim Carter* is a 47-foot-high dive Jocko makes off a back lot waterfall into less than six feet of water. It's an important plot point as well, as Slim is afraid of heights but does the stunt to impress Hovey. The Falls Lake site at Universal Studios subsequently became known as Mahoney Falls. It was made out of Hydrocal, a combination of cement and plaster. The bottom of the lagoon was made of concrete. The Universal brass was extremely anxious about Jocko doing the dive himself, but Jocko was adamant he would be the one to do the stunt. Tension mounted as director Bartlett was forced to wait for the sun to emerge from behind the clouds and the suits arrived in limousines. Jocko was as calm as could be. He performed the dive perfectly in one continuous take that sees him swim toward the camera and emerge from the water. He had a bit of skin taken off from scraping the bottom but considered the stunt a rather easy one despite the hubbub on the set. The entire cast and crew applauded his effort.

One reason Jocko could be so steadfast about doing his own stunts was that despite all of his minor injuries he had never once filed an insurance claim. He told reporter Vernon Scott on the *Slim Carter* set, "I've taken higher dives into a net. There's always a certain element of fear. But overcoming physical challenges is as important to me as the psychological ones and intellectual ones. I'm the only actor who does his own stunts. It's a matter of pride."

At one point the script called for Jocko to fall from a horse. The studio had assigned a young stuntman to double Jocko, which was common practice even though Jocko typically did everything himself once the cameras were rolling. On most of Jocko's Universal films, Buddy Van Horn was assigned as his double. The young stuntman was noticeably nervous upon arrival to the set, unaware of the Jocko protocol. He felt he was being called to do a life-threatening stunt that the legendary Jocko had refused to do. He was relieved when he realized it was only a simple saddle fall. He did a couple of rehearsals demonstrating different angles for the camera, then collected his paycheck as Jocko did the final fall. The opening credits for the film make it a point to award Jocko a stunt credit in addition to above the title billing.

Jocko's wife Maggie Mahoney cameos in the film as a hatcheck girl, and family friends Bill Williams and Barbara Hale also appear. Iowa-born co-star Julie Adams was one of Jocko's favorite leading ladies, and the feeling was mutual. She wrote in her autobiography *The Lucky Southern Star,* "Jock was a great guy, a very good actor, and a phenomenal stuntman."

Trade reviews were once again positive about Jocko. *Variety* noted, "For Mahoney, part is a change of pace which he nevertheless handles expertly, and he capably warbles three songs." According to *The Hollywood Reporter*, "Mahoney does a surprisingly interesting job, surprising because he has seemed so relentlessly laconic up to now. The stunts are somewhat more spectacular than the singing but the latter is ingratiating and actually more musical

Jocko shows off his unique blend of strength and balance as he holds Julie Adams over a horse trough in *Slim Carter* (1957).

than some stars who have lately crashed the Hit Parade." *The Times-Picayune* wrote, "Lovely Julie Adams and TV-film star Jock Mahoney share the spotlight with Tim Hovey and do a real good job of making the movie well worth seeing."

In 1957 Jocko became the Honorary Sheriff of Encino, California, serving under Honorary Mayor Jack Carson, the veteran character actor. The following year he was again sworn in by new Honorary Mayor Ann Sheridan, the popular actress. It was not uncommon for celebrities to hold such positions in the star-studded San Fernando Valley. Jocko held the ceremonial post for a few years.

Jocko continued making personal appearances, especially for worthy causes. One such event was a Kansas rodeo on behalf of childhood polio inoculations. Another was an athletic demonstration Jocko put on for the Columbia Boys' Clinic in San Francisco in early 1957. In the spring of 1958 he appeared with Rock Hudson, Hugh O'Brian, James Arness, Richard Boone, and Clayton Moore at the Boy Scout Circus in Waco, Texas. It was rare for Jocko to ever turn down children or charities. As proof of his steadily rising popularity, Jocko was named by the National Exhibitors as one of the most promising male stars of the year. Elvis Presley topped the list.

During this period of financial success and professional esteem, Jocko and Maggie tried to realize an acting dream. In May of 1957 they announced the formation of the Comedia Company, a small theatrical group interested in staging productions of the classic satiric plays *Volpone* by Ben Jonson, *Peer Gynt* by Henrik Ibsen, and *The Country Wife* by William Wycherley. Character actor Russell Johnson of *Gilligan's Island* fame and his wife Kay were to be partnered up with Jocko and Maggie. However, this entire project may have been something the wives were behind. No plays were ever produced. When queried, Russell Johnson did not recall the Comedia Company or a partnership with Jocko, saying simply, "No such project is part of my memory."[4]

A curious thing happened to Jocko in May of 1957 at Universal when he visited the set of the film *The Female Animal* (1958). Legendary starlet Hedy Lamarr, often considered "The Most Beautiful Woman in Film," suddenly flew into a rage and demanded that he be barred from the set. A puzzled Jocko reportedly had no idea what the commotion was about. The unstable, oft-married Lamarr was known for her insecurities and one can only guess what it was about Jocko's appearance that set her off. It was not uncommon for Jocko to visit the sets of films in production at Universal. He could often be seen visiting friends such as Errol Flynn on *Istanbul* (1957), Lola Albright on *The Monolith Monsters* (1957), and Julie Adams on *Slaughter on Tenth Avenue* (1957). No doubt his standing and experience in the stunt community gave him an open invite from the stuntmen on the lot to watch or unofficially oversee any number of action scenes in production. He was flummoxed by the Lamarr incident. "I've never spoken to the woman and I don't know why she's mad at me," he told reporter Sheilah Graham. "How can such a friendly, shaggy dog like me barred from somebody's set?"

Director Douglas Sirk once again called upon Jocko to lend support to another military film, the somber World War II drama *A Time to Love and a Time to Die* (1958), from the Erich Maria Remarque novel. John Gavin starred in a story that was unique in that the lead actors played German soldiers on the Russian front. Despite its premise there is little action, mostly melodrama between Gavin and love interest Lilo Pulver. Jocko played the grizzled, disillusioned machine gunner of the outfit, Immerman. He was given third billing behind the leads in what he considered a small but meaty part that concluded with him being blasted to death by artillery fire just as he hoists a beer keg.

The movie was made on location in Munich and Berlin. While on his way to the studio in his character's costume, Jocko ran out of cigarette mixings. As he sauntered about among the Berlin locals in full Nazi regalia, he drew the attention of local lawman Horst Bochert. Initially Jocko was unable to communicate that he was merely an actor and was hauled off to a local jail. Jocko spent an hour there before he was able to convince the authorities that

A black-clad gunslinger in *Last of the Fast Guns* (1958).

he was working on a movie. The predicament garnered a bit of additional press for the picture as Jocko gave autographs to the local law officers.

The film has its admirers, and is considered a classic in some quarters, but was perceived as banal and tripe during its initial release. *The Los Angeles Times* noted, "Jock Mahoney is excellent as a cynic," while the *Oregonian* wrote, "Don DeFore, Keenan Wynn, Jock Mahoney, and Remarque himself are sterling supporting players." Most reviews, however, bypassed any mention of Jocko.

Sirk was the highest profile director that Jocko ever got a chance to work with as an actor. It's interesting that Sirk cast Jocko as a character type in these films despite his leading man looks and status as such on the Universal lot. Sirk made only one more film, *Imitation of Life* (1959), again starring John Gavin opposite Lana Turner. Had his career continued, perhaps Sirk would have cast Jocko as his star. It's a shame that Jocko worked with so many first-time or yeoman helmsmen during his leading man days. Jocko might have been capable of something outstanding as an actor during this period in the hands of a Budd Boetticher or Anthony Mann.

The Last of the Fast Guns (1958) was a routine though nicely mounted picture that was filmed under the title *The Western Story*. There is beautiful location scenery in northern Mexico, and Jocko looks the part of a gunfighter dressed completely in black. The ads proclaimed, "His name was written in bullets!" Universal publicity called it the most vigorous role of Jocko's career, which was a gross overstatement. He does do a few fancy mounts, some hard riding, and performs a fall from a saddle in the climax. However, the story meanders, female lead Linda Cristal barely figures into the plot, and turncoat Gilbert Roland isn't much of a threat to Jocko. All in all, it's a passable film for a rainy day.

Variety noted, "Mahoney makes a sympathetic and interesting character of his role, although his motivations seem somewhat dim, and his romance with Miss Cristal is too thinly prepared." *The Hollywood Reporter* liked the film better, terming it, "a grade A western that goes a long way toward establishing Jock Mahoney as a full-fledged star."

During filming, Jocko had a heroic moment when he saved a stuntman who became caught in his stirrup and was dragged 20 yards. Jocko rushed in and wrestled the horse to a halt, grabbing the animal by the ears and pulling its head down between its legs to prevent it from kicking the stuntman in the head. For his heroism he caught a chastising from the producer and director who fretted over what may have happened to the film had Jocko been seriously injured saving someone they considered a lowly stuntman. The dramatic rescue was captured on film but deemed unusable because so many crew members in modern garb immediately descended upon the scene. While performing another bit of action in the film, Jocko suffered a minor injury when a small weed pierced his eye. It was the kind of injury that even Jocko's notorious preparation couldn't have prevented.

Maggie accompanied Jocko on location, and the two were able to do some sightseeing in his off-hours. They explored Mexico City's historic pyramids of Teotihuacan and relaxed at the Los Flamingos Hotel in Acapulco. While they were in Mexico, Jocko purchased a wedding ring for Maggie. Despite the fact they had been married for over seven years, she hadn't found the perfect ring for their union until that time. Jocko also purchased a fully equipped 24-foot cabin cruiser to sail the ocean.

Money, Women, and Guns (1958) (originally titled *Money, Women, and Dreams*) cast Jocko as dime novel western detective Silver Ward Hogan. He does well in the role investigating the death of a prospector for $50,000 in reward money. Heirs to a gold mine are the likely suspects, and the audience is kept guessing until the final scene. There's not as much action as even a typical Jocko Universal film, but he does get to hold his own acting opposite former Academy Award nominee Kim Hunter and solid character actors Gene Evans, Tom Drake, James Gleason, and Lon Chaney, Jr.

The Richard Bartlett film unfolds at a leisurely pace, once again coming as a disappointment for Jocko's action fans. There's only one brief fight scene with Jeffrey Stone. A lobby card showing a Jocko fight with some Indians suggest an additional action scene that was cut. Jocko was once again battling the producers over doing his own stunt work, so they kept it to a minimum. The film could have used another punch or two, but is well-written and acted. There is scant Lone Pine location photography, and the climactic shootout looks to have been done on a soundstage.

Jocko pushed for realism in the western, particularly when it came to cowboy heroes and their endless supply of shots from their six-shooters. Jocko was well-read on western lore. He knew that real gunfighters only kept five bullets in their gun and left the hammer on an empty chamber for safety. Jocko also made it a point to carry only a single gun slung low. He told *The Long Beach Independent Press Telegram*:

> There were only two top gunfighters who carried two guns. Wild Bill Hickok and Dallas Stoudenmire, the tough marshal of El Paso, and neither of them used a holster. Hickok used his belt and Dallas a leather-lined pocket. All the others carried just one gun. My reading of old accounts of frontier area fights shows that only one gun or a minimum of shots were necessary anyhow. In fact, the five bullets that these guys did carry usually were too many. If you were facing a gunslinger in the old days, one shot would be enough. That's because if you didn't get him with your first shot, you could try to figure out why in a Boot Hill cemetery.

Like so much of his Universal product, *Money, Women, and Guns* is entirely watchable if not particularly memorable. The film was completed in the fall of 1957 but wasn't scheduled for release until a full year later. Perhaps Universal didn't want to flood the market with Jocko films at a time when *Joe Dakota*, *Slim Carter*, and *Last of the Fast Guns* were still in theaters. It's more likely they felt this film wasn't up to the level of the others. In it, Jimmy Wakely sang the song "Lonely Is the Hunter," which may have been a better title for the film.

Variety noted, "Mahoney does a rough-hewn job as the restless detective." According to *The Hollywood Reporter*, "Jock Mahoney continues to look good in cow country costumes, but *Money, Women, and Guns*, which is more of a detective story than an action picture, gives him too much to say and too little to do." *The Monthly Film Bulletin* echoed that assessment: "Jock Mahoney, though given too much to say and too little to do, remains one of the better young cowboy stars."

In three years at the studio, Jocko proved to be a dependable western lead who could carry a routine film on his broad shoulders. In 1958 Universal ran into money problems in the feature film division and suspended film production for the time being. In the meantime their TV production was on the upswing. He was offered a flat salary of $70,000 a year from Universal/Revue to star in the upcoming teleseries *Cimarron City*, but he didn't care for the script. He countered with an offer of $40,000 a year and a share of the profits. Revue promptly turned that down and asked if Jocko wanted his release from the studio. He impulsively said yes. George Montgomery took the *Cimarron City* role. After the first season he sued Revue for alleged financial backhandedness. Montgomery's lawsuit effectively ended his days at the Hollywood studios. Jocko, meanwhile, was weighing his other offers.

7

Jocko Is Yancy Derringer

Jocko made one TV appearance in the spring of 1958, guest starring as a former bare-knuckle fighter on the first season of the fine western *Wagon Train*. The show was attracting quality film talent as guests, and Jocko had the title role in his episode "The Dan Hogan Story." He portrays a former New York City constable who once fought bare-knuckle matches. He is an old friend of scout-master Ward Bond. In a flashback scene, Bond recalls Jocko taking on the huge Buddy Baer with what Bond deems "the fastest fists in the world." Jocko is now a peace-loving family man who resists the local marshal's attempts to deputize him. Nevertheless he runs into trouble with local heavy John Larch. This poses a dilemma for Jocko as he has been ordered to get out of town or be gunned down. A conflicted Jocko intends to take the stagecoach until he learns a friend has been killed by Larch. This leads to Jocko presenting Larch an odd offer: fists versus a gun. Larch agrees and is promptly flattened by a Jocko right before he can completely draw his firearm. Larch even manages to shoot himself in the process.

Directed by Richard Bartlett, it's a superior hour of entertainment from the first season of a classic TV western. A mustached Jocko has one of his best roles as the soft-spoken family man who always tries to do the right thing. With a successful TV performance fresh in his consciousness he began to look for a TV property of his own. In the process he turned down several westerns as well as series as a jet pilot, an athletic schoolteacher, and as a cool explorer of outer space. All these shows, he maintained, lacked integrity. MGM courted him with an offer for a movie and a TV series. Jocko did find a TV project he was interested in with *Yancy Derringer*, a southern western from veteran screenwriters Richard Sale and Mary Loos.

In 1868 post–Civil War New Orleans, Yancy Derringer was a roguish gambler who doubled as a special agent during this wide-open period of Reconstruction. He owned both the riverboat *Sultana* and the Waverly Plantation. Derringer was conceived as a combination of Errol Flynn, Douglas Fairbanks, and Clark Gable's Rhett Butler from *Gone with the Wind* (1939). Some of the *Yancy Derringer* sets were actually from that film. The character was appealing and there was plenty of romance and lots of fighting, ranging everywhere from Mississippi riverboats to Bourbon Street. Much of the action would be set at night and flavorfully shot amidst atmospheric gaslights. In addition to the interesting locale, the storyline would introduce continuity from one episode to another and mix in real historical figures of both lasting and trivial impact. It looked to be a perfect vehicle for Jocko. He agreed to star and be the show's associate producer. He began developing episodes with the husband-and-wife team of Sale and Loos. Sale would direct half the episodes with veteran William F. Claxton handling the rest.

Derringer's name was apt, as he wielded the smallest handgun of any TV cowboy. He kept it hidden in his shirt sleeve or under his hat and could produce the four-shot .22 Sharps derringer in a flash. Coming across as quite a bon vivant, Derringer sported a thin mustache and often dressed all in white. He also carried a cane, which in reality was the sheath for a sword. When not utilizing his many hidden weapons, Derringer could resort to old-fashioned fisticuffs. He had a guardian looking out for him in the form of a silent, shotgun-wielding Pawnee Indian who went by the name Pahoo-Ka-Ta-Wah (Pahoo, for short). Yancy and Pahoo communicated through sign language.

Pahoo was played by stuntman X Brands, whose real name was Jay Brands. Although the actor with the high cheekbones often played Native Americans on TV and films, he was in reality of German descent. When he initially showed up to audition for the role, he wasn't quite sure how he should play the part. Jocko suggested he remain silent during the audition and not say a word.

Brands suspected that Jocko was pulling his leg but didn't open his mouth during the audition, only mimicking sign language as Jocko suggested. To his surprise, he was cast as Pahoo and told that he would use only sign language during the show. That turned out to make the role all the more difficult to play, as Brands now had to pore over Iron Eyes Cody's manual on Indian signs for the sake of authenticity.[1]

Brands worked extremely well with Jocko, and the two became lifelong friends in much the same way Dick Jones had become Jocko's pal. The duo was always looking for new and interesting stunts to bring to the show. Their fluid exchange of weaponry from one to the other is something to behold. Sometimes it's as if the audience is watching two magicians' sleight of hand. They even worked out a stunt where Brands tossed a hunting knife across a room and Jocko caught it on the fly. Jocko also brought in his long-time cohort Fred Krone to work as the show's stunt coordinator, guaranteeing the action would be of the highest caliber.

Brands was quoted on Jocko for *The Westerner*: "[He] was always there when you needed him. We were the greatest of friends. He was the greatest guy in the world. When I came on the show, *he* came up to me. He never stole scenes. Our work together was the greatest. He loved everybody. I never heard this man put another man down. He was so beautiful." Krone commented on Jocko in *Western Clippings*: "He was a fine guy. He could have gone a lot further if he'd quit trying to be Errol Flynn. I loved him like a brother. Maggie, his wife, God, what a sweetheart, good actress. But, Jocko, he had his faults, but don't we all."

Yancy Derringer drew guest stars the likes of Charles Bronson, Claude Akins, Lee Van Cleef, Leo Gordon, Brad Dexter, Ray Danton, Gene Evans, Bill Williams, John Anderson, John Dehner, and Jim Davis. There was an abundance of beautiful women as well: The show featured appealing actresses Frances Bergen, Julie Adams, Lisa Lu, and Beverly Garland. A young Yvette Mimieux had a bit in one episode. Former Jocko girlfriend Peggy Stewart was a guest star, as were Ruta Lee, Marie Windsor, Joan Taylor, Noreen Nash, Patricia Hardy, Karen Sharp, Patricia Barry, and Patricia Blair. Jocko's real-life wife Maggie Mahoney appeared in three episodes as Bridget Malone. Character actor Kevin Hagen portrayed the government man to whom Derringer reported, while Kelly Thordsen, Richard Devon, Bill

X Brands, Frances Bergen, and Jocko in a 1959 *Yancy Derringer* publicity photograph.

Walker, Larry Blake, James Foxx, Woodrow Chambliss, and Richard McCord III also had recurring and colorful parts.

Burly 6'4", 220-pound Thordsen played tobacco-chewing Indian scout Colorado Charlie. Thordsen had been a classmate of Jocko's at Davenport High back when he (Kelly) was known by his legal name Sherman Jess Thordsen. World War II and Korea kept Thordsen occupied for the next decade, and he ended up in Los Angeles working as a motorcycle cop. Jocko had not seen Thordsen for years when he ran into him by chance while dashing back to his car to avoid a parking ticket. It turns out Thordsen had a sideline as an amateur theater actor, so Jocko went to see him with the Tom Daly Players. When Thordsen expressed interest in a professional film career, Jocko steered him into the business with the proper contacts. Thordsen appeared in a supporting role with Jocko in *Money, Women, and Guns* and worked regularly in Hollywood for the next 20 years.

Jocko's main love interest on the show was Frances Bergen, who played Madam Francine, the proprietor of the local gaming establishment. In real life Jocko and Maggie befriended former fashion model Bergen and her husband Edgar, the famous ventriloquist. Their young daughter Candy would go on to a successful film and television career of her own. It's noteworthy that both Candice Bergen and Sally Field were at times likely visiting the *Yancy Derringer* set. On one visit to the Bergen home, Jocko danced the cha-cha with young Candice.

Series guest star Ruta Lee said of Jocko, "Not only was he a star on TV, he was a star in my personal life. He was one of the kindest and most generous of his time, cash, and spirit of any person I ever knew. Also the earthiest. His wife Maggie had the 'good car' so he arrived at my fancy birthday party at LaRue in his pick-up truck filled with manure. In fact, he insisted I drive with him for an after dinner drink to the next ritzy place."[2] Beverly Garland told *Ladies of the Western*, "Jocko was a close friend. I knew him when he was still a stuntman. He was one of my favorite people." Julie Adams recalled in the companion book *Westerns Women*, "Jock Mahoney was such a charming, amiable guy." Noreen Nash told *Screen Sirens Scream* that Jocko was "one of the nicest people I ever worked with." At the 1995 Charlotte Western Film Fair, Kevin Hagen said: "Jock Mahoney was so much bigger than life. He was just a joyous, wonderful, big bear of a man. He used to be and was the greatest stuntman in Hollywood for many years."

By the time Jocko did *Yancy Derringer*, his acting had progressed to the point of competent self-assurance. His portrayal of the flamboyant Yancy is a slick, professional performance, full of subtle nuances for the audience to enjoy. Yancy often presents himself to other characters as something he is not, and Jocko succeeds in offering many different shades to his character. It is quite obvious he has come a long way since the days of *The Range Rider*. Jocko the stuntman is at this point a solid technical actor capable of playing a multitude of complex parts. It should be noted, however, that the show is aimed at the mass audience and no attempt is made by any of the cast to capture an authentic southern accent or French patois. Of his performance, *Variety* commented, "Mahoney is a striking figure and well cast," while the *Boston Herald* wrote, "Jock Mahoney makes a likable hero for these playlets but we wish he'd get along with fewer women."

Behind the scenes, Jocko once again butted heads with the studio over doing his own stunts. The suits fretted over their leading man injuring himself, but Jocko maintained that he knew what he was doing. After all, the publicity department was playing up the fact that Jocko was the only TV star who did his own stunts; it would be false advertising if Jocko were to hand over his action to anyone else. So Jocko could be seen diving off stairwells, through windows, over fire, and into the Mississippi River despite the fact stunt doubles Bob Morgan and Alex Sharp were waiting in the wings.

One notable stunt in the episode "The Belle from Boston" had Jocko swinging 70 feet from an opera box to the stage on a rope. He kicked a bad guy and swung back to the box in one take. Then he delivered the rest of his dialogue to his female companion. Even his friend Richard Sale was insistent he should have used a stuntman for that, pointing out the risk not only to the production but to Jocko's acting career should he be injured. Jocko pulled the stunt off without a problem. On the episode "Nightmare on Bourbon Street" he was dynamited off a second floor balcony.

There are other special action moments. In the episode "Loot from Richmond," Jocko and veteran heavy Lane Bradford set up a short fight on a riverboat staircase. Jocko drops in from the top of the camera frame, landing on the middle of the stairs. His legs immediately bend, and he jettisons himself down the stairs with one of his leaps. As soon as Jocko and Bradford's bodies collide, Jocko has his feet under himself and is hip-tossing Bradford over the side of the boat. It happens quickly and looks simple, but is anything but. Few stuntmen other than Jocko could have pulled this stunt off in one take. Jocko routinely performed stunts that have never been duplicated.

Another standout action scene occurs in the episode "Two Tickets to Promontory." Villain John Larch is on the run, and Jocko cuts his escape off with a great leap over a flatbed wagon. Punches are exchanged as the fight goes up the side of a hill. At the top incline Jocko drops onto his back and flips Larch's double completely down the hill, somersaulting along with him. It's an ingenious bit of action choreography from Jocko and Fred Krone.

Finally, there's a moment in the episode "Game of Chance" where Jocko is chasing an assassin and leaps onto a low stairwell ledge to head the man off. The ledge is about three feet off the ground. He is perpendicular to the stuntman when he flings him backward down the stairs. Jocko follows the man down through the air with his momentum, then upon landing twists his body back the opposite direction onto his feet until he is delivering a fully balanced round of knockout punches. It's all done without a single edit, and the movements defy the way the human body is supposed to move. Although closing in on the age of 40, Jocko still appears to be made of rubber. He told the *Milwaukee Journal*: "I've been blessed with a beautiful sense of coordination and rhythm, and I've kept myself in shape with sensible exercise — not the barbell, bulging muscle type that leaves you unable to scratch your back."

Jocko had some typically outstanding fights on the show with veteran screen punching bags Jim Davis, John Alderson, and John Cliff. He fought 6'5" Mickey Simpson in a bare-knuckle bout on a barge in the episode "Wayward Warrior." In the episode "Thunder on the River" Jocko fights Irish riverboat pilot James Foxx, with both men standing atop a pool table in an interesting bit of choreography. Unlike *Range Rider*, the fights were usually brief and not the focal point of the show. Nevertheless, Jocko performed them expertly. Jocko revealed that unlike most stuntmen he preferred not to use fake breakaway furniture when performing fight scenes. "I like realism," he told Joe Hyams. "I'm not masochistic or sadistic, but if you use real furniture things look real. If you're careful, no one gets hurt."

Veteran stuntman Loren Janes worked *Yancy Derringer* many times through Fred Krone and became friendly with Jocko. A former U.S. Marine, Janes had also been a swimming and diving champion. He grew up in the High Sierras and challenged himself as a youth with adventurous treks into the wilderness armed only with a hunting knife. As an adult he was accomplished in the pentathlon. Janes spent many days at Jocko's house with the two trying to one-up one another with creative dives into the pool. "He was a great guy and a real, real athlete," Janes said. "He was one of my best friends for many, many years. I loved him to death."[3]

At the outset of the show Jocko signed with the personal management firm Clyde Baldschun & Associates for public appearances. They specialized in handling western stars the likes of *Wyatt Earp*'s Hugh O'Brian, *Bat Masterson*'s Gene Barry, and *The Rifleman*'s Chuck Connors. Jocko did his part publicity-wise for the show, including journeying all the way to Mobile, Alabama, for the Greater Gulf State Fair and to Louisiana for riverboat cruises, supermarket appearances, and the New Orleans Horse Show. Jocko was given a key to the city of New Orleans and was made both an honorary police captain and a riverboat pilot. He toured the Midwest with stops in Chicago and Milwaukee but was able to stay in California for the Beverly Hills Easter Seal Society Parade for crippled children, where he rode alongside Fess Parker, Rex Allen, and Hugh O'Brian. In December of 1958 Jocko, Maggie, and Dick Jones were special guests for the Poinsettia Festival Toyland Parade in San Diego.

TV Guide ran a feature on Jocko and included him in a pictorial with other TV cowboy stars. In the photo spread, Jocko, Clint Eastwood, Don Durant, and Steve McQueen worked on their bronco-busting skills on ropes over a swimming pool. Jocko again appeared with other westerners in the June 1959 issue of *TV Radio Mirror* in a feature entitled "Wonderful Western He-Men." In more publicity Jocko and Maggie were featured in a *Look* magazine article on cowboy stars and their wives and appeared together on Ben Alexander's talk show *About Faces.*

Jocko made the rounds of many a society cocktail party with sponsors and network execs. It was during this period that Jocko recollected to his pal Jack Lewis that he took a liking to having a drink in his hand and became in his own words "an instant alcoholic." Lewis was no stranger to booze but had never seen Jocko drink prior to this period. He wrote in his book *White Horse, Black Hat* that the bottle would become an ongoing problem for Jocko over the next decade. In Hollywood, Jocko began spending more time at the La Ronde café on Ventura Boulevard with new TV cowboy drinking buddies Wayde Preston and Peter Breck. However, Jocko remained a firm believer that drinks and stunts did not mesh and was always sober on the set. He never resorted to liquid courage for his stunt work.

Wanted—Dead or Alive star Steve McQueen, a former U.S. Marine, raised Jocko's ire when he spouted to the press that he was the only real he-man among the current crop of cowboy stars. Jocko naturally took exception to that assertion given his own background as an elite athlete, U.S. Marine, fighter pilot, and stuntman extraordinaire. Not to mention that Jocko's favored form of weekend recreation was spear-hunting wild boar on Catalina Island, hooking 200-pound marlin off of Newport Beach, or hunting wild longhorn sheep with his .270 Remington rifle on the rugged volcanic lava rocks of Mauna Kea in Hilo, Hawaii. Jocko suggested to columnist Joe Hyams that he and McQueen should have a survival contest wherein they would each parachute into a wilderness area armed only with a knife and see which man emerged from the wild. Jocko, who taught survival skills in the Marines, intimated that he'd be carrying McQueen out on his back. When put on the spot, McQueen backed off his egotistical boast and deflected the comments with humor. McQueen didn't want any part of an angry Jock Mahoney.

Yancy Derringer was filmed at Desilu Studios. CBS gave the show a Thursday night prime-time slot from 8:30 to 9:00. Midway through the first season, Jocko was told the show was a success and had already been given the go for a full second season by the sponsor Johnson's Wax. It seemed *Yancy Derringer* was bound for a long and profitable run. The Mahoney family purchased a sprawling home appropriate for a well-off television star, and Jocko put some of his earnings into a Montana horse breeding ranch. Upon completion of the first season's 34 episodes Jocko took his family to Hawaii for a month-long vacation. From there he went on a bear hunt in Alaska. Upon his return to California, Jocko was shocked to hear that CBS was demanding a quarter financial interest in the show and a move from Desilu. Jocko and the Sales held firm that they wouldn't be blackmailed by CBS head Jim Aubrey, who later employed the same tactic on the popular detective series *Tightrope*. When neither show would yield to Aubrey's demands, they were suddenly cancelled.

It's a shame that *Yancy Derringer* wasn't given at least another season to grow and expand its audience. Yancy was decidedly different from all the other western characters on the air with the possible exception of Richard Boone's Paladin on *Have Gun—Will Travel*, who could come across as a bit of a dandy when in his plush San Francisco digs. The audiences who watched *Yancy* were faithful and loved it. Decades later there was still clamor for an official DVD release and TV airings were popular with the nostalgia stations. It's also a shame for Jocko's financial and professional sake that the show didn't go another season or two. *Yancy Derringer*'s continued success would have precluded Jocko from taking on arguably his most famous role as Tarzan, which ultimately wound up typecasting him. Three seasons and 100 episodes would have guaranteed profitable syndication for a long time. Jocko claimed he never saw a nickel of his original percentage deal in the show.

Around this time, Jocko's early inspiration turned pal Errol Flynn died of a heart attack at the age of 50. The 6'2", 190-pound Flynn lived a life of high adventure and awesome excess. The Australian-raised Irishman had been a police constable in Papua New Guinea and sailed around the world as a treasure hunter before chancing upon an acting career. In the late 1930s he became Hollywood's most handsome and dashing star, but his penchant for womanizing and love of drink proved his undoing. Flynn was a fine athlete but his hard-living ways aged him prematurely and he was nearly uninsurable in Hollywood by the 1950s. As much as Jocko looked up to the star's swashbuckling two-fisted screen image, it was to his own detriment whenever he emulated Flynn's off-screen lifestyle.

Without a steady Universal or *Yancy Derringer* income, Jocko began having problems financially maintaining the new home due to the excessive property taxes. This was before actors began drawing large residuals off of TV broadcasts, so there was no money being generated for Jocko even though *Range Rider* was still playing heavily around the world in syndication. Only 13 of that show's 78 qualified for residuals. The Mahoney family had to sell their mansion and move to a less expensive abode, a sobering and humbling display of how quickly the tide can turn in Hollywood. Jocko and Maggie were back to being a working-class acting family whose livelihood was dependent on either's next job.

Plans to perform in a motion picture titled *Lazarus Seven*, written by Richard Sale and Mary Loos, did not materialize. The script was based on "Lazarus #7," an Inner Sanctum pulp mystery Sale wrote in the early 1940s. Jocko would have played the globe-hopping infectious disease doctor Steven Mason, a serious character who encounters a fantastic plot involving Hollywood movie stars, a beautiful blonde woman, and regenerated bodies. The nature of the plot sounds as if it would be perfect B-movie material. Sale would have directed Jocko and the regular *Yancy Derringer* performers prior to the start of the second season, but the film died with the demise of the TV show.

In the meantime, Jocko trained and made personal appearances with trick-shooting gun artists Joe Bowman, Rodd Redwing, and Jim Martin. "Straight Shooter" Bowman, who could hit an aspirin at 30 paces, became one of Jocko's closest friends. Performing largely in the California area, a brave Jocko provided the target for the fast-draw sharp-shooters. Redwing was one of the last men to be licensed to shoot live ammo. Jocko would stand against a board and hold a 12-inch balloon over a nickel wafer embedded in the steel backstop. Redwing would stand a distance away, draw his Colt and fire through the balloon into the nickel to the astonishment of the audience. MGM gun coach Jim Martin recalled Jocko as "a real gutsy guy and a hell of an athlete."[4]

Jocko learned a few fancy gun tricks from the gunmen but was more interested in their quick draw prowess. Jocko's favorite trick to perform was a combination of both skills. He could place a poker chip on the back of his outstretched hand, then suddenly withdraw and fire, shooting the flying chip before it hit the floor. Dating back to *The Range Rider*, Jocko's favored gun was a Frontier Colt Single Action with a honed-down spring and a 1.5-pound pull on the trigger for smoother action and quicker speed.

In 1960 Jocko competed in the National Fast Draw Championship at the Sahara Hotel in Las Vegas alongside cowboy actors Clint Eastwood, Robert Fuller, John Russell, Peter Brown, Terry Wilson, and Eric Fleming. Eastwood of TV's *Rawhide* proved the quickest draw and won the celebrity event. When Jocko ran into Rodd Redwing on the Sahara casino floor he let out a loud Indian war whoop. Redwing, working at the time as Paramount Studios' gun coach, replied in kind with his own whoop. The two men jumped onto the roulette table in a boisterous embrace to the delight of the casino patrons. "Jocko had a great sense of humor," Jim Martin said, remembering the moment.[5]

To keep himself in the public eye, Jocko continued to line up personal appearances through Clyde Baldschun, some of them entirely trivial. He and John Russell attended the Native American Tribal Council in Glendora, California, with Redwing, Jay Silverheels, Iron Eyes Cody, and Eddie Little Sky. They dug a pit in the ground to barbecue buffalo and ate cactus as a side dish. In July 1959 he traveled to San Mateo, California, to headline the Redwood Rodeo; then it was on to San Francisco to appear as the special guest star for Dick Stewart's *Dance Party*. In October of 1959 he appeared at the National Peanut Festival in Dothan, Alabama, where he served as the emcee for a beauty pageant. He also served as grand marshal for the International Paddleboard Festival Parade several times, had a horse race named in his honor at Ruidoso Downs, and selected the 1960 Rollerama Queen at a Los Angeles skating rink for the Southwest Pacific Regional Championship of the Roller Skating Rink Operators Association.

Horse trainer Don Burt initially met Jocko at his father's Burbank stables and the two became good friends. He often saw Jocko performing gymnastics with his children in the yard of the home they had rented on Mariposa Street near the River Bottom. The men began riding with one another and Burt was amazed by Jocko's athleticism. Even at the age of 40 Jocko could still perform extraordinary feats. Burt called Jocko "one of the greatest athletes I've ever seen.... He would often cart me with him to the movie set, where he excelled at his craft. I've seen him stand flat-footed and jump up like a coiled spring, clearing one horse and landing astride the one next to it. I was in awe of this great athlete."

Burt related the following story in his book *Horses and Other Heroes*: The duo wanted to train a horse not to spook, so Jocko devised a plan to strengthen its resolve. He told Burt to take the horse out along a narrow trail and he'd surprise them along the way. Burt didn't know what to expect. As he and the horse sauntered along, Jocko suddenly snuck out from behind a huge tree wearing a bearskin rug draped over his head and shoulders. He ran up behind Burt's horse so silently they never heard him. Jocko leaped onto the back of the horse, which immediately took off on a wild ride and bucked both Burt and "the bear" off. Jocko, Burt, and the bearskin flew into the air and landed together atop one another. A laughing Jocko told Burt that if there had been a camera rolling, they could have received a couple of thousand dollars for the outrageous stunt.

On the acting front, Jocko guest starred on episodes of the TV shows *The Christophers*, *The Millionaire*, *77 Sunset Strip*, and *Rawhide*. *The Christophers* was a long-running syndicated religious anthology show that often boasted top guest stars. Jocko appeared in a 1959 episode about Valley Forge and the Revolutionary War. On *The Millionaire* he played a sports car enthusiast-playboy who decides to settle down after receiving a million dollar gift. On the hip, popular Warner Bros. detective series *77 Sunset Strip* he portrayed a nightclub singer who lands a Hollywood movie contract, only to have an oily scandal sheet writer dust off an old story that could ruin him. Jocko makes a threat and the gossip columnist ends up dead. Chief suspect Jocko must rely on series star Richard Long to clear his name. Jocko receives top guest star billing for the episode and turns in a solid performance. However, he is largely absent throughout the latter half of the episode as Long handles the action. Producer Howie Horwitz was with Jocko's Universal films *Slim Carter* and *Money, Women, and Guns,* and he was instrumental in Jocko landing this part.

Jocko did two episodes of the popular western *Rawhide* and did some quality acting on both. In early 1960 he top-lined "Incident of the Sharpshooter" portraying an outlaw who masquerades as an attorney. His character is a cold-blooded conniving killer who charms not only the cattle drovers he encounters but an entire town. He even robs the local bank and puts a bullet in the banker's back. When Clint Eastwood stumbles onto him, Jocko clobbers him over the head and contemplates putting a bullet in him. Instead he decides to frame Eastwood for the murder of the banker and has the audacity to represent him at trial. Series star Eric Fleming finally realizes the truth and outsmarts Jocko in the final reel.

While performing in a scene with Eastwood, Jocko twice missed his cue because he couldn't hear Clint's low volume acting style. Jocko spoke up and offered that if Clint were to pick his nose or scratch his posterior at the appropriate time, it would help Jocko to know when to respond with his own dialogue. The crew applauded Jocko's humorous suggestion, which Eastwood didn't find funny at all.[6] Jocko and Clint had been on friendly terms when both were at Universal Studios, and had even been workout partners for a time at Vince Gironda's famous Studio City gym. They also shared the same talent agent, Lester Salkow. The moment passed without further ado.

In the 1961 *Rawhide* episode "Incident of the Phantom Bugler," Jocko plays a military captain in the employ of a power-hungry judge. The character starts off as a forceful heavy but is humanized by the fact that Jocko has a wife in the story, played by Kathie Browne.

When he feels their relationship is threatened by the presence of Fleming, Jocko has a surprisingly violent fistfight with Fleming. The fight is unique for the era since the heavy beats the hero to a pulp. There's a nice moment where Jocko's ready to land a final crushing blow but reconsiders and relaxes the tension in his balled-up fist. His wife comes to his side, only to have the crooked judge put a bullet in Jocko's back. The final scene has Fleming escorting a recovering Jocko and his wife to a better place for a fresh start. It's another fine special guest job from Jocko.

During *Yancy Derringer* Jocko had paid his own money to get out of a contract with publicist Helen Ferguson. At that time his energies were consumed fulfilling sponsor obligations, and it appeared he no longer needed her services. As it turns out, he had received scant publicity since *Yancy Derringer* went off the air. Given his unsteady financial situation at the time, he was reluctant to take on either Ferguson or another publicist.

In 1960 Jocko was in the running to debut on Broadway with Lucille Ball in the musical *Wildcat*. He had reportedly been cast and was taking daily singing lessons with Lillian Goodman. At some point during rehearsals the famous redhead ultimately decided to go with the more accomplished actor-singer Keith Andes as oil-drilling male lead Joe Dynamite. Considering how many challenges Jocko habitually conquered, it's surprising that Broadway did not become another notch in his professional acting belt. It's doubtful any other TV cowboy would even consider the bright lights of New York City.

Jocko sought to land another TV series of his own, starring in an unsold TV pilot entitled *Simon Lash* in 1960. The show was based on Frank Gruber's cynical ex-soldier turned modern Hollywood detective. Lash preferred to spend time riding horses on his Arizona ranch but could be in Los Angeles in a flash. Produced and directed by veteran Sidney Salkow, it was filmed at the old Republic Studios. Veteran character actor Gregory Walcott co-starred as Jocko's police contact, and Elaine Edwards played his pretty blonde secretary. There is a hint of romance between the two at the end of the pilot, which sees Jocko called into action to thwart a kidnap plot involving gangster Warren Stevens and the Academy Awards. Walcott recalled Jocko as being "very professional and an excellent stuntman."[7]

The 30-minute pilot moves briskly with Jocko kicking in doors and engaging in shootouts and fistfights. The jazzy score by Richard LaSalle keeps the episode moving, as Jocko glides through the story in a variety of costume changes. Fond of western jackets and bolo ties, Simon Lash is so cool and trendy he even changes outfits while interviewing clients. Jocko is solid in the role, and the pilot is as good as most private eye shows of the period. It had plenty of room for interesting stories given the Arizona and Hollywood backdrops. Jocko met with sponsors in the Midwest and was hopeful the show would appear in the fall. However, a Hollywood writers' strike halted the forward progress of the new show. The failure of *Simon Lash* to find a spot in the fall 1960 TV season was a great disappointment to Jocko.

8

Jocko and Tarzan

One of the most popular literary figures of the early twentieth century was Edgar Rice Burroughs' creation Tarzan. Burroughs' first book *Tarzan of the Apes,* published in 1912, told the story of a boy raised in the jungles of Africa by gorillas. The boy grows into a man who can communicate with animals far better than he can his own kind. It is later revealed that he is actually Lord Greystoke by birth, and his self-education through his deceased parents' books lends him many interesting quirks that were explored in each subsequent Tarzan adventure. Fans of the series loved the pulp aspects, especially when Tarzan's primitive nature took over and he turned into a savage warrior beating his chest over a conquest while letting out a guttural yell. Hollywood saw the heroic potential in the character and made the first film *Tarzan of the Apes* in 1918 with a husky Elmo Lincoln as the star.

Burroughs despised Hollywood's handling of his creation, particularly the way they made him into an ignorant hunk of beefcake who grunted only brief lines of dialogue. Nevertheless the Tarzan films proved immensely popular, with Burroughs reaping the significant financial rewards. Six-foot-three, 190-pound former Olympic champion swimmer Johnny Weissmuller was the most identifiable screen Tarzan, playing the character from 1932 to 1948 in 12 films for MGM and RKO beginning with *Tarzan, the Ape Man.* He achieved worldwide recognition with Maureen O'Sullivan playing his romantic mate Jane. Fellow Olympic swimming champ Buster Crabbe also had a crack at the role in *Tarzan the Fearless* (1933) to far less acclaim. Burroughs' own favorite Tarzan was 6'1", 190-pound Herman Brix, an Olympic shot put champ who played the character in *The New Adventures of Tarzan* (1935). With his lean, chiseled physique, Brix was the closest to matching how Burroughs described the character in print. Brix also had the advantage of being the only actor from that era to play Tarzan as a man of superior intellect. His *Tarzan* was filmed in the jungles of Guatemala.

In 1958 producer Sy Weintraub took over the screen rights to Tarzan and set out to enliven the stagnant franchise. Since 1955 the heavily muscled former lifeguard Gordon Scott had been playing the Lord of the Jungle in mostly minor fare for producer Sol Lesser. One film, *Tarzan and the Trappers* (1958), was a failed TV pilot that wound up being released theatrically. Around this time MGM tried to revive the character with a remake of *Tarzan, the Ape Man* (1959), but went the cheap route on all accounts. They initially wanted 6'2", 210-pound contract player William Smith and his streamlined bodybuilder's physique to take on the part. Hoping to build a legitimate acting career, Smith recommended a friend of his, blond, 6'4", 212-pound UCLA basketball player Denny Miller. Ironically, Miller was recommending Smith.

Miller took on the famous role, and his *Tarzan* was shot in Los Angeles' Griffith Park and MGM sound stages. Miller was good-looking and athletic, but the accommodating young actor could do little with the role given the circumstances. To cut costs, MGM color-tinted old black-and-white footage at every opportunity and the public didn't buy it. Miller's Tarzan film was often labeled the worst of the entire series.

Weintraub decided the franchise needed to get off the studio back lots. *Tarzan's Greatest Adventure* (1959) was filmed on location in Africa and provided a huge boost to the series. The 6'3", 230-pound Scott remained in the leading role. Many feel this and its follow-up *Tarzan the Magnificent* (1960) are the best Tarzan films. Future superstar Sean Connery played a supporting role in *Tarzan's Greatest Adventure* and got along well with the film-makers. They wanted to bring him back as the main bad guy for *Tarzan the Magnificent*, but Connery explained some other producers had just taken an option on him for a spy film. This turned out to be *Dr. No* (1962), the first film in the James Bond franchise.

Weintraub set out to find someone else to play his villain and came across the name of Jock Mahoney, who was currently looking for work yet had name recognition in foreign markets due to the popularity of *Range Rider*. Weintraub hired Jocko to play villain Coy Banton, and the cowboy hero excels in the role of the dastardly son of John Carradine. Tarzan manages to apprehend Banton and the bulk of the film consists of the jungle lord attempting to transport him through the African terrain with Banton's father and brothers in hot pursuit. All the while Tarzan is weighed down by a ragtag group making the trip with him, as well as the wily Banton.

Cast almost without fail as a hero for the past decade, Jocko relished the chance to be a cruel rat on the big screen. His Coy Banton is a cunning foil, psychologically pitting the members of Tarzan's expedition against one another. He even creates sexual tension with Betta St. John, to the consternation of her weak husband Lionel Jeffries. The heavily whiskered Jocko is enough of a physical threat to Tarzan to be taken seriously in a fight. Jocko's Banton is arguably the best villain performance in the entire Tarzan franchise. *Variety* noted in its review of the film, "There is good work from Jock Mahoney" while *The Hollywood Reporter* added, "Jock Mahoney and John Carradine are strong help in the more articulate roles." In his book *Kings of the Jungle*, David Fury wrote, "Jock Mahoney is marvelously cast as Coy Banton."

Jocko discussed playing a Tarzan villain with journalist Nancy Newbold: "The heavies are really the most interesting character to develop because of the latitude you have in the role. The leading man is most often a goody two shoes and you can't spit or scratch your knee while playing him. The secret of playing the heavy is to go as far afield as possible in the role and still get the audience to root for you. Everybody knows that Tarzan has to win, but they wondered for awhile."

The film concludes with a memorable fight scene between Jocko and Scott, with both men giving the nearly five-minute battle their all. The fight scene was shot at Kenya's Fourteen Falls. The two men do all their own stunt work and make it one of the all-time great screen fights as they pound one another over the rocks and into the water. The underwater shots were actually filmed later at a swimming pool in Brighton Beach, England. The shot where the two are in the sand after Jocko kicks Scott in the stomach was filmed on a soundstage at Sutherland Studios.

Jocko is leaner than normal due to working in the jungle heat, weighing in at about

195 pounds for the film. He looks almost thin next to the bulky Scott, but is not to be taken lightly. When Scott tried to come on a little strong in the fake fight, Jocko surprised him with his own strength and knowledge of hand-to-hand combat. At one point during the fight, Scott suddenly let out a sharp yell. Jocko thought he might have broken Scott's arm by accident. He looked down to discover that Scott's loincloth had come completely off in front of the crew. It was one of many laughs the two would share together. Jocko and Scott struck up a strong friendship with one another and remained in touch for years.

In an interview for *Starlog*, Scott commented on Jocko: "A great guy. Jock and I had a great time on that, too, and it showed. Even though I was the protagonist and he was the antagonist, we had a lot of giggles on that, because he was a big kid at heart. I really loved the guy. He was a great stuntman, which made it so easy to work with him in the stunt sequences. At 6 feet 5 inches, he was two inches taller than I was, but he made it so easy for me to lift him. He was such a great stuntman that he made me look good."

Jocko did have a bit of fun at Scott's expense. There's a scene where Scott has to carry Jocko out of quicksand, and Jocko intentionally slowed Scott's ascent as much as he could during the rehearsal by wrapping his legs around tree roots under the muck and only giving a little at a time. Scott was so visibly tired when he finally got Jocko out that the director asked if there was a problem. Scott didn't have an answer. They did an additional rehearsal and Scott gave a great heave. Jocko didn't hold him back this time and they both flew out of the quicksand. When they were ready to roll the cameras, Jocko once again latched onto the bottom and made it as difficult as possible for Tarzan. When Scott finally got out, he was totally exhausted.[1]

Scott repaid Jocko's shenanigans by frequently breaking lunch plans as he often allowed himself to become distracted by a pretty lady. Jocko proved to be a bit more adaptable to the jungle and being devoured by tsetse flies than Scott, goading the apprehensive screen Tarzan into swimming in the jungle water. Scott was fearful of a dangerous local parasite called Belhatsa but managed to man up when put on the spot by Jocko. To his credit, Scott had also ridden a rhino and wrestled a live python on his Tarzan films so he was no lily.

Jocko impressed co-star Betta St. John when he jumped out of a Jeep to change a flat tire himself while traveling to the location. During filming, Jocko also managed to save a chimpanzee that fell out of a dugout canoe into a lake. Although Jocko was in handcuffs and wearing boots for the scene, he dove into the water and rescued the chimp. When it came time to stage the fight, Jocko's experience as a stunt coordinator helped immensely. By choreographing the action scenes on location and doing his own stunts, Jocko saved producer Weintraub thousands of dollars. At one point Jocko even doubled Tarzan Gordon Scott when the scene called for both men to take a dive into the water before the climactic fight. It was Jocko who executed both dives. The producer promised Jocko he would repay him with future work, a familiar tune that rarely pans out. When filming ended, Jocko resumed looking for work, not realizing what an impression he had made on the producer of the film.

Jocko was in early contention to play a leading role opposite Gregory Peck in the classic World War II film *The Guns of Navarone* (1961). In Alistair MacLean's original 1957 novel the character of Corporal Dusty Miller is a cynical American demolitions expert. As the film developed, the Allied forces taking on the Germans in the Aegean Sea were switched to a British outfit. This change was facilitated by the much respected British actor David

Jocko kicks off the action with Gordon Scott in *Tarzan the Magnificent* (1960).

Niven agreeing to take on the Miller role if it were changed to a Brit. The producers acquiesced, although star Peck opted to play his role of Mallory without an English accent. Had Jocko co-starred with Peck in this respected hit, the entire arc of his career might have been altered.

Stateside there were little more than black and white B-features offered to the established

TV star without a studio behind him. Jocko carries the low-budget detective story *Three Blondes in His Life* (1961) on his broad shoulders, playing an insurance investigator who is on a case in which a fellow investigator has already gone missing. That man had three blonde women in his life, and the female trio is soon making their own passes at a resilient Jocko for various reasons. Former Miss Denmark Greta Thyssen, a popular pin-up model, plays the main blonde. Valerie Porter and Elaine Edwards, Jocko's secretary on *Simon Lash*, round out the female trio. Jocko, as Duke Wallace, drinks bourbon and lights up cigarettes in the film while offering hard-boiled voiceover narration.

It's odd to see Jocko dressed in modern garb after his many years in cowboy attire, but he's fine in the role. His performance suggests he would not have been out of place playing a TV detective such as Mike Hammer, Peter Gunn, or Michael Shayne. The budgetary limitations make this play like a saucier version of a TV episode anyway, but the performances keep it afloat. There's a surprising lack of action for a Jocko movie until a knockout climactic fistfight with Anthony Dexter that upends a room. Dexter is doubled throughout the fight by Fred Krone. Jocko does a couple of nifty flips into the wall and over furniture. Earlier he performs a face-first fall down a flight of stairs.

Variety noted that Jocko "plays the part with the smirk and swagger technique typical of actors playing private eyes. There is, however, one vicious fight sequence in which he dips into his accomplished bag of stuntman tricks and rises above the norm." *The Hollywood Reporter* concurred: "The plot is routine and highlighted by some action sequences, the latter most strenuously exciting when Mahoney uncorks some handy close contact body work." *Boxoffice* added, "The fact that long-time television cowboy star Jock Mahoney is cast herein as an ace insurance investigator may mean something intriguing indeed to his legion of fans in the nation's living rooms; he provides as forceful a delineation as can be anticipated with a stereotyped script."

There were more guest appearances on TV shows, including his second *Rawhide*, a *Gunslinger*, and two episodes of the western *Laramie*. On the 1961 *Gunslinger* episode "Rampage" Jocko played Halsey Roland, an escaped Confederate major who uses military tactics to rain terror on innocent citizens. It's a great bad guy role for Jocko. Star Tony Young infiltrates Jocko's gang and brings him down by show's end. Unfortunately the Andrew McLaglen–directed episode has not been aired since its initial showing.

Jocko played legendary Robin Hood–like criminal Clay Jackson in the spring 1961 *Laramie* episode "The Man from Kansas." The folksy Jocko robs from the rich and gives to the poor, creating a schism between series stars John Smith and Robert Fuller. His easygoing charm keeps him popular with the citizens of Laramie even after he shoots down deputy Adam West in "self-defense." It's a memorable performance, filled with subtle shades of gray. In the final act he finally reveals himself to be the snake in the grass Smith suspects. Smith and Fuller gun him down in a crossfire, although Jocko manages to graze them both. A trivial highlight of the Joseph Kane–directed episode is seeing Jocko down a mug of beer in one gulp.

Life imitated art on the *Laramie* set: Fuller's character Jess Harper was a believer in Jackson's surface qualities, even to the point of Smith accusing him of buying into a legend. In real life, Fuller was a fan of Jocko. Fuller had entered the film business as a stuntman after serving with the military in Korea and had a great respect for the stunt profession. "I had two cowboy heroes," Fuller said. "Joel McCrea, whom I patterned the way I rode after, and Jock Mahoney. Jocko was quite the acrobat, a great horseman, and a great fighter. I loved the way he fought, and I patterned my fights after Jocko. Fight scenes used to look kind of silly until the 1960s came around. Jocko was ahead of the time. When he threw a punch it looked like it took someone's head off. He was a hero and an idol of mine."[2]

Fuller became very excited when *Laramie* producer John Champion told him Jocko would be guest starring on the show. Jocko arrived on the set in time to see Fuller setting up a fight scene where he is attacked by a group of Indians and bulldogged off a horse. Fuller knew it was the perfect chance to show off what he could do in front of his idol. The fight went perfectly as planned, and Fuller was beaming when Jocko complimented him on putting on a nice brawl, even alluding to the fact that it reminded him of the fights he once did on *Range Rider*. "That made my day," Fuller said.

Fuller was so keen to continue impressing Jocko that his next bit of stunt work involved crashing through a heavy barn door. Feeling too full of himself, he told the effects people not to score the door so it would break easily. He felt confident he could tear right through it and rip it apart. When Fuller attempted the stunt, he rammed into the unyielding wood and was knocked back several feet onto the ground. Fuller had the wind knocked out of him and was in obvious pain as a silent Jocko looked on from a few feet away, shaking his head. "We laughed about it for years," Fuller said.

The two men became solid friends who especially liked hunting, fishing, and shooting together. Fuller often stopped by Jocko's house and watched him do his acrobatics on the parallel and horizontal bars. They would sip coffee, share lunch, or have a drink together and simply enjoy shooting the breeze. Fuller was married to actress Patty Lyon, and their families dined together at home and on the town at classy restaurants such as the Wild Goose in Studio City. Jocko and Fuller did many personal appearances, telethons, and political events together, traveling with fellow screen cowboys James Drury, Doug McClure, and stuntman Chuck Courtney. In the early 1970s Jocko twice appeared on Fuller's series *Emergency*. "We were very, very close friends," Fuller said. "I adored him, and he adored me. He was a fabulous guy. Jocko loved everybody, and everybody loved Jocko. He was a gem."

Jocko's second *Laramie* episode came the following fall in the Lesley Selander–directed "Ladies Day." This time his outlaw Sam Willet is revealed to be a cold-blooded murderer from the opening act. He spends a majority of the storyline masquerading as a bespectacled doctor, a ruse that finds him stuck at the stage relay station run by Smith and Fuller. Jocko has some fun with the part, once again turning on the charm with the ladies and the children for ulterior motives. When circumstances pressure him into revealing his skill as a physician, he goes for the derringer hidden in his jacket. As slick a criminal as he is, Jocko is outsmarted by a child who gives him an unbroken stallion for his getaway. Jocko is ultimately thrown and apprehended. Jocko is fine as the villain, although the episode and the characterization bear a strong resemblance to the *Rawhide* story in which he plays a killer masquerading as a lawyer.

Errol Flynn's 20-year-old son Sean was being courted heavily by movie producers and was signed to follow in his father's footsteps for *The Son of Captain Blood* (1962). Sean's mother Lili Damita was estranged from Flynn since before the boy's birth, and he grew up with only minimal time spent with his father. Nevertheless, the handsome son took after his legendary father in many ways. He was every bit as athletic and a noted ladies' man in his own right. To learn the tools of the stunt trade that he needed for the swashbuckling role, the younger Flynn enlisted the help of his dad's stunt double Jock Mahoney. Jocko set about training Sean in the proper way to fence, fight, and fall for the screen. Some of his training was done alongside Jocko's teenage son Jim, who recalled the two being taught to jump, spin in mid-air, and land backward in the saddle of a 16-hand horse.[3]

Sean Flynn commented on his training in the fan magazine *Modern Screen,* saying: "Most fathers leave their son a business or some other tangible inheritance. Mine left me a name and it's only as good as my first movie. It'll be as good as I can make it, believe me, because it's a challenging, vigorous, swashbuckling part, a new bit of living and I'm especially keen on the stunts. I'm working every day with Jock Mahoney, the stuntman who worked with my dad and this is great. I dig this man, Jock. I respect him. I wouldn't miss a day's workout if I had to steal a car to get there. More than anyone, Jock has given me an enthusiasm for this business and I find myself dreaming up stories. I'd like to have my own producing company someday, to write, direct, produce and act.

Son of Captain Blood was promising enough for 20th Century–Fox to offer him a lengthy motion picture contract. Jocko's work was evident with *Variety* noting that Flynn displayed "agile swordplay and generally graceful moves." Flynn didn't want to be tied down to a movie contract and was determined to live life as fully as his father had. He resided abroad the next few years, starring in the occasional foreign action film while taking on such interesting tasks as safari guide and big game hunter in Africa. Spurred on by the excitement of danger, he took an assignment as a photojournalist covering the war in Vietnam. Flynn became a legend in his own right there, known for his fearlessness as he charged into battle alongside special force Green Berets. Twice Flynn was wounded in action, and on one occasion killed a Vietcong himself in the heat of combat. In 1970 Flynn went missing in Cambodia and was presumed to be captured and killed by the enemy. His body was never recovered. Not yet 30 years old, he no doubt lived his life to the hilt in an effort to establish himself outside the shadow of his larger-than-life father. It should be noted that a little of Jocko Mahoney might have rubbed off on him as well.

Jocko made another B-movie during this period that didn't surface for a few years. *Runaway Girl* (1965) was filmed in 1961 and starred Lili St. Cyr, a notorious burlesque player and striptease artist of the 1940s and 1950s who was said to have influenced Marilyn Monroe's screen image. Jocko had the male lead in the minor Hamil Petroff film playing a vineyard owner named Randy Marelli. Sporting his thin Errol Flynn mustache, Jocko falls for big city girl St. Cyr despite the protests of his girlfriend Laurie Mitchell and his brother Ron Hagerthy. Jocko gets to cut a rug on the dance floor in a couple of scenes with St. Cyr and has a very brief fight scene with Hagerthy. The only other action is toward the end as St. Cyr runs away, and Jocko takes a shortcut to catch her by jumping over a six-foot hedge. Outside of those moments, there's not much to recommend about the cheap black and white film.

It was another attempt by Jocko to be placed in modern garb, but the finished product proved so unremarkable that the independent picture couldn't even find a distributor. It clocked in at barely 60 minutes and simply had no defined marketplace. Jocko cashed his paycheck and quickly forgot all about the little film. Eventually some mildly racy footage of bare bosoms and behinds was added, none of it involving scenes with Jocko. The padded-out film ended up playing in mostly nudie theaters for a number of years due to St. Cyr's audience. It was not pornography, but in hindsight *Runaway Girl* was probably a screen credit Jocko wasn't flaunting. It retains some interest to this day as a novelty item.

Jocko was largely unaffected by ego or his status as a film and TV star. He was always on the lookout for interesting and unusual things and would interact with anyone and everyone who caught his eye. That's how he met John "Bud" Cardos, an actor, stuntman, and exotic animal wrangler who became a legend in the low-budget motorcycle movie arena. Cardos worked in all facets of film production and eventually became a full-fledged director, but in the early 1960s was still an unknown. Jocko noticed Cardos driving a station wagon with a couple of jaguars in the back and hollered to Cardos to pull over so he could check out the wild cats. "He was a great guy," Cardos said. "He was very interested in my baby jag. I only met him a couple of times. I would like to have worked with him, but I never did get the chance. I loved the guy."[4]

In 1961 Gordon Scott decided he was tired of the jungle and skipped out of his Tarzan contract to go to Italy to star in gladiator movies, opening up the role of Tarzan to someone else. Although Olympic pole vaulting champion Don Bragg was under serious consideration, producer Weintraub began to feel that he had a natural successor in Jock Mahoney. After all, Jocko was already a legend for flailing around his backyard like Tarzan. There were stories that Jocko regularly swung on a 40-foot rope to the TV antenna merely to attain better reception. It was not an uncommon sight for his neighbors to see Jocko periodically flying above the roof of his house if he was practicing the trapeze or trampoline. They would also see him take running jumps off the roof into a net he had strung up in the back-yard. He'd be perfect for Tarzan if not for the fact that he was already 42 years old.

Weintraub approached Jocko about taking on the role, selling it as a chance to present Tarzan as an intelligent man of the world. As excited as Jocko was at the prospect of playing Tarzan, he had legitimate concerns about taking on the role. The first was indeed his age. Second, the fact that he was already an established actor, not only as the previous Tarzan film's bad guy but as television's Range Rider and Yancy Derringer. Would audiences accept him as Tarzan? Third, Jocko was concerned that he could become typed as Tarzan by casting directors and studios that were only now seeing him as something other than a stuntman or a cowboy.

Jocko talked the offer over with Maggie as well as family friends Barbara Hale and Bill Williams. He also spoke with his doctor Dwain Travis to ensure that he could take on the strenuous part. All listened to his concerns and gave him clearance if he indeed wished to play Tarzan. Jocko considered the high production values of the last two Tarzan films, and realized it was a great opportunity. Nevertheless, Jocko met with Weintraub and proceeded for 30 minutes to tell Weintraub why he shouldn't hire him. After listening quietly to Jocko's argument, Weintraub asked him point blank if he wanted to be Tarzan or not. Of course he did, Jocko said. What kid wouldn't want to be Tarzan? And so, 42-year-old Jock Mahoney became Tarzan number 13, the oldest beginning screen Tarzan in movie history. Somewhat ironically, Jocko had just bought a new spacious home in the San Fernando Valley community Tarzana, where he was keeping busy installing his own sprinkler system and running stream through the yard.

Jocko immediately went on a workout and diet regimen to beef himself up for the role. His normal 200 pounds was deemed too lean for the part. Jocko began to lift heavier weights and increase his time on the parallel bars and the rings. He swam more laps in the pool, pushing himself harder. In a matter of months he distributed 20 more pounds of symmetrical muscle across his frame, adding five inches to his chest until it expanded to 50 inches. At the same time he managed to keep his waist measurement near 31 inches.

Jocko's long frame could easily add and subtract weight. He had broad shoulders and strong back muscles with a wide flat chest. Depending on the camera angle, Jocko had the unique ability to look lean or muscular within the same shot. A slight shift of his body made the muscles jump to life as did the outline of his pectoral muscles. His waist was trim and his abdominals rock-hard. He had long muscle attachments (especially in his arms and legs) that prevented him from ever appearing muscle-bound. The back of his legs were especially well-developed for the era. A clean-limbed Jocko would never be labeled as having bulging biceps or thick triceps, but he was deceptively strong to all those who were willing to test him. In terms of height and weight he was actually a bit heavier than many of his fellow Tarzans were when playing the role. What was most important to Jocko was that his physique was functional and agile.

In further preparation Jocko grew his hair shoulder-length in the back and tanned his body to a golden brown. He set about reading all of Burroughs' Tarzan books, where the Tarzan character is a literate man who chooses to live among the animals of the wild rather than the self-serving two-legged variety of modern society. That is how Jocko would play the character, as an educated and articulate man whose home is with the animals. It was a decision that would have made the late Burroughs proud. Burroughs always disliked the monosyllabic Tarzan that the movies presented to audiences. Jocko was ready to become Tarzan. "Action is my business," he told columnist Bob Thomas, and there was no way in Jocko's mind that he would disappoint.

Weintraub had achieved success taking the franchise off the Hollywood back lot and filming on location in Africa with his last two films. He began to see Tarzan traveling to other jungles of the world to explore different cultures, and Jocko was perfectly willing to go along with that idea. Left in Africa would be the characters of Jane, Boy, and the chimpanzee Cheetah. Their first globe-trotting foray would be to India for the appropriately titled *Tarzan Goes to India* (1962). Jocko began to research India and the Hindu religion prior to leaving the States. Mindful of his friend Gordon Scott's loincloth troubles, Jocko packed plenty of nylon briefs in his luggage to wear under his Tarzan trunks.

Filmed in Bangalore, Bombay, Mysore, and Madras, *Tarzan Goes to India* concerns Tarzan coming to the rescue of an endangered herd of elephants whose stomping ground is near a newly constructed dam. Jocko rides an elephant, faces down a deadly cobra, crosses paths with a leopard, swings from vines 40 feet above the ground, dives from rocks and airplanes, and treks barefoot over all kinds of rugged terrain. Despite his advancing age, he is a fine Tarzan, representing the character with uncommon grace, poise, and dignity. Unlike many of his predecessors, Jocko did all of his own stunts and refused to use a foot loop when swinging from the jungle vines. He would have it no other way. He even did his own jump off the wing of a biplane into the waters of the Aswan Dam despite the fact the camera was so far away no one could tell it was him. As was his intention, he comes across as much more educated and erudite than his predecessors. *Tarzan Goes to India* successfully appeals to children and adults alike.

There is some discrepancy on whether Jocko performed the jump from the plane or if a dummy was used. The Indian government forbade the performance of the stunt, claiming it was too dangerous. Film publicity downplayed the jump, never claiming it was Jocko, but at least some of Jocko's friends claim he did it. Jim Martin remembers Rodd Redwing calling him on the phone to tell him what their crazy friend had done.[5] Tarzan authority Phil Petras

Fighting a leopard in *Tarzan Goes to India* (1962).

confirms that Jocko made the jump, writing, "Jocko was always proud to state that as an actor he never needed a stuntman. It was he who jumped out of the plane. I believe he said they were rolling camera at the practice stunts just in case they got it right the first time."[6]

Jocko discussed the Tarzan part with *The Burroughs Bulletin*: "It's one of the roughest roles I've ever played. Of course, I do all my own stunt work, but from a dramatic standpoint too. Tarzan is a difficult role, you know he's going to win, so the difficulty is to play this great character in such a way that you keep him within the realm of reality and simplicity.

A fabulous man; he spoke seven languages and was really a British nobleman — Lord Greystoke. The kind of man every man would love to be. A gentleman, as well as a savage. A man who asked nothing, took nothing, but was utterly happy in the simplicity of his surroundings."

There were plenty of problems on location in India, especially involving safe food and water. Jocko arrived in Bangalore in early 1962, two months before a camera ever rolled due to licensing and permit entanglements. One of the greatest challenges for the filmmakers was problems with the generators that affected the sound. The audio ended up out of sync, and the entire film ultimately needed to be post-dubbed after filming in London, England. Another major problem involved communication, as there were different languages being spoken and in different dialects. Throw in a large cast of wild animals and scenes that contained hundreds of extras, and one can imagine the headaches that ensued.

Despite the difficulties during filming, Jocko loved the people and the experience. He was particularly moved by a crude birthday cake the locals made him. He had hoped to save the cake for a visiting Maggie to see, but large rats crawled in his bedroom window at night and ravaged it. The windows of Jocko's accommodations had bars on them, and he slept in mosquito netting. There was no air conditioning in his room, only an overhead fan. Temperatures were often sweltering. Such is the life of a movie star on location.

Jocko developed a close friendship during filming with local child actor Jai the Elephant Boy, and that translated to the screen in both of their performances. Unfortunately, Jai wasn't there under the best of circumstances. His father was gambling away his earnings as fast as the boy could make it. Jocko became his big buddy and looked out for the little boy. Despite the hefty demands on Jocko's time as the star of the picture, he gave Jai horseback riding lessons in his free hours. When the film ended, Jai became very emotional because his friend Jocko would be leaving for the States. Their goodbye at the film's close is touching and was heartfelt for both. "He was a great action actor," James Drury said of Jocko. "But he also had a great sensitivity in a scene. He acted right from the heart. Everything he did was believable."[7]

Jocko did have a conflict on the set with director John Guillermin, who was suffering from an illness and took out his anger on Jocko. Jocko was struggling with the unpredictability of the jungle animals he was working with and wasn't always able to hit his spots for the camera. The elephants proved especially difficult for Jocko to move on cue. An impatient Guillermin took to calling Jocko names. Jocko calmly told him the last man who called him "a yellow son of a bitch" ended up a bloody pulp, and Jocko was in a mood to quit the part. He had never had a problem with a director before and did not suffer fools gladly. Weintraub offered up an apology, and Jocko agreed to finish the movie despite the rudeness of Guillermin.

A major argument between the director and star stemmed over a scene in which Jocko was to take on a tiger. Jocko watched as the locals sewed up the tiger's mouth. He offered that the claws of a tiger's massive paw were much more dangerous for someone hoping to wrestle it. The man could be slashed to ribbons and ripped apart with ease due to the tiger's great strength. As it was late in the shooting day, the handlers assured Jocko that they would declaw the animal, but Jocko noted that the tiger was fixating on him as the reason for its misery. Having its claws pulled would make it even angrier. Jocko refused to fight the tiger, much to Guillermin's dismay.

The next day the crew produced a smaller leopard in the tiger's place, but it was of little difference to Jocko. He knew leopards could be deadly as well. He agreed to do two-shots with the animal but would not fight it. British bodybuilder turned stuntman Gerry Crampton stepped in for Jocko in the scene and fights off the leopard. Even though the animal had been declawed and slightly sedated, it still left permanent scars on Crampton's body. Jocko, a fan of stuntmen in general, was always quick to point out that he was doubled in this instance. Considering the injuries incurred by Crampton, Jocko was correct in refusing to fight the animal despite director Guillermin's taunts.

Perhaps scarier than fighting either a tiger or a leopard was his fight scene with villain Leo Gordon. Tough guy Gordon had served time in prison and was one of the most feared men in the movie industry. He could work "stiff" in fight scenes, and many an opponent wound up feeling the brunt of Gordon's fists. Jocko, however, had no problem with Gordon, and their brief fight is one of many highlights in the top-line film. It's only a shame they didn't have an extended fight for the ages. The battles Gordon put on with Clint Walker on TV's *Cheyenne* and the film *Night of the Grizzly* (1965) are legend. To amuse themselves during down time at the hotel, Jocko and Gordon strung bananas around their necks and played with the local monkeys. The two remained good friends for a number of years.

Jocko did incur a painful injury on the set when he was swiped up by the tusk of a massive elephant and thrown 18 feet into the air. Jocko was able to right himself in flight to prevent a major injury, but did strike the side of his foot on a rock. This resulted in a painful cut that somehow did not become infected even though Jocko was running around the disease-ridden country barefoot. For the most part, working with the elephants was a highlight experience. Jocko would mount the 11-foot-tall pachyderms by stepping on their toe, grasping a floppy ear, and pulling himself up astride the massive back much to the dismay of the traditional mahout locals who preferred to let the elephants raise them up with their tusks.

Jocko got to ride atop elephants named Rajendra, Gajendra, and Mahaveda in the picture, leading a 60-elephant stampede at speeds over 35 miles per hour. It made for some spectacular and thrilling footage. The locals would beat drums and make noise at the call of action to initiate the stampede. Mahaveda suddenly became frightened and took off into the forest with Jocko on its back. Jocko managed to stay on for the wild ride through the thick branches and scrub. As a result he ended up with over 200 scrapes and cuts. Only his legs escaped damage as they were protected by Mahaveda's huge ears. Jocko was finally able to calm the berserk creature, despite the fact it knew only Indian dialect commands and Jocko's curses were coming in English. In an article Jocko penned for *Bow and Arrow* magazine, he said of the experience: "Riding a skate board on the Los Angeles freeway on a wet Saturday night is a piece of cake compared to an elephant stampede."

Jocko's adventure with the bow and arrow provided whimsy. The crude arrows furnished for the film were all bent to varying degrees. Jocko was able to compensate and stick three of them in a targeted area for the camera. Jocko did an amazing thing with an arrow in the film's climax that was actually captured by the cameras but was deemed unusable for the film. While riding atop an elephant he shot an arrow with a stick of dynamite on it into the air and turned to look back at the elephants rumbling behind him. When he looked up to locate the arrow, he realized it was now coming down at his present location. Jocko reached out with his hand, snared the arrow in flight, nocked it, and let it fly again.

MGM publicity touted Jocko as "the world's greatest stuntman" for its ad campaign.

Still from *Tarzan Goes to India* (1962).

To promote the film Jocko covered 51 cities in 60 days on a publicity tour that he admitted to Hedda Hopper left him "a little crazy in the head." The personal appearances helped immensely as Jocko proved to be a fine ambassador for the Tarzan franchise. In Dallas, Jocko visited the Crippled Children's Center and donated time to the Cerebral Palsy Easter Seal drive. In Fort Worth, he held an orangutan for photos taken at the local zoo. While

Jocko was in Louisiana, Governor Jimmie Davis made him an honorary colonel. *Tarzan Goes to India* met with critical and commercial approval, doing fantastic business for MGM, which was in dire straits at the time due to their over-budget Marlon Brando flop *Mutiny on the Bounty* (1962). Mahoney's Tarzan became the biggest moneymaker in the entire history of the Tarzan franchise.

Jocko's Tarzan tour resonated with the many dedicated Burroughs fans around the country, known amongst themselves as Burroughs Bibliophiles. Harry Habblitz, an artist and writer, approved of Jocko in the role, penning in *Erbania*, "His portrayal of the ape-man was of a real flesh and blood person, intelligent, articulate, caring. He was physically tall and rangy, adroit and agile. Gone was the beefcake weight-lifter and the grunting noble savage. For the Burroughs fan, his was the nearest approximation to the book Tarzan since Herman Brix." Burroughs Bibliophile John Szuch wrote in *The Gridley Wave* upon meeting Jocko in 1962, "I could not help but be impressed by his physical appearance. It was as if Tarzan had stepped out of one of J. Allen St. John's paintings. Here truly was a man who resembled the Tarzan that Edgar Rice Burroughs wrote about!"

Noted Tarzan authority Phil Petras said, "I certainly consider Jocko to be one of the best actors to have played the role of Tarzan. He had the role down, having read all the Burroughs novels, and he seemed to inhabit the character. Take a close look at some of his scenes when he is threatened, with that smirk of a smile and confidence; that was right from the novels. And when everyone else is kneeling before the new king, Jocko/Tarzan remains standing. Pure Tarzan."[8]

David Fury wrote in his book *Kings of the Jungle*: "Mahoney turned out to be one of the best Tarzan actors, and it's a shame he didn't get to play the role until reaching his middle forties. A 30-year-old Mahoney as Tarzan, with his great skills as a stuntman, and the intelligent fire of Greystoke in his eyes, might truly have been the answer to Edgar Rice Burroughs' quest to film his fictional hero as he had created him."

Camille "Caz" Cazedessus, the editor and publisher of the Burroughs fanzine *ERBdom*, shared his memories of meeting Jocko: "He was really a good guy, a tall, tanned, strong looking, very alive and very alert individual, quite the gentleman and easy to talk to. I was at the local Baton Rouge airport when he landed and got off the plane with a copy of the ACE edition of *Land That Time Forgot* in his hand, a smile on his face. It's all a bit foggy from there. We chatted, visited, he spoke at the theater, and was soon gone. It was only several years later that I realized that I had met one of the great TV actors of all time, as Yancy Derringer, and finally an excellent movie Tarzan."[9]

One of Jocko's concerns before taking the role was that critics would not take him seriously as an actor. This fear was somewhat alleviated by the positive reviews, with the influential *Variety* noting that Jocko "has graduated to the title character, a role he endows with admirable physique, dexterity, and personality. A longtime film stuntman, Mahoney is the best Tarzan in years." *A Los Angeles Herald Examiner* critic wrote, "Juvenile action fans are in for a treat as they watch tree-swinging Jock Mahoney go to work. Mahoney lives up to the Tarzan tradition in an entertaining movie." *The New York Mirror* said of Jocko, "He's capable in the role, which asks little in the way of dramatic ability." *The Dallas Morning News* wrote, "Mahoney makes an excellent addition to the long list of actors who have portrayed the jungle hero, certainly one of the best of the recent list." Despite the successful notices, taking on the role was a great risk for Jocko's career. When syndicated columnist Bob Thomas asked Jocko point blank what playing Tarzan could possibly do for his career, Jocko responded somewhat fortuitously, "Probably get me 12 pictures in Italy."

Immediately prior to the first Tarzan picture, Jocko starred as a daredevil soldier of fortune in a western entitled *California* (originally *Don Mike*) (1963). Set in the 1840s, the modestly budgeted movie dealt with the early statehood of California and the animosity between America and Mexico. It was filmed on the old Republic Studios lot with Faith Domergue and Susan Seaforth appearing as Jocko's leading ladies. *Boxoffice* said of *California*, "Jock Mahoney, whose multi-faceted emotive qualities have included TV's top-rated *Yancy Derringer* series as well as the big-screen Tarzan epics, is teamed with some spirited thespians in this latest adventure yarn."

Jocko got along well with Australian co-star Michael Pate, the villain of the picture. Both men were surprised when they were told that they were about to film a swordfight for the movie's climax. There was no swordfight in the script, but evidently it was a late brainstorm from director Hamil Petroff. Jocko and Pate immediately went to work and quickly blocked out a sword duel with coordinator Fred Krone while the production crew waited. The men dueled up and down a staircase with rapiers. Jocko emerged triumphant and the crew applauded the men's effort.

Pate wrote of Jocko in his *Western Clippings* column, "Jock and I hit it off right away and we had a great time making the film.... I never did get to see Jocko again, but I thought of him from time to time. How can anyone forget him in the many westerns and TV series he made and in that swatch of Tarzan films wherein he handled himself with such aplomb and derring-do!"

A highlight of *California* was the work of Jocko's favored stunt partner Fred Krone. The men engaged in two rousing fistfights in the film, completely demolishing a saloon in the opening bout. It recalled the furniture-busting glory days of *Range Rider*. Krone also doubles for Pate during the climax, which sees Jocko jumping off rooftops and performing a superb leap into the saddle. *TV Guide* ran a short feature in their February 23, 1963, issue entitled "The Stuntman" with Jocko and Krone putting on a special fight scene for the cameras. In 1961 Krone, Loren Janes, and other veteran elite stuntmen formed the Stuntmen's Association of Motion Pictures to help regulate the profession. Although Jocko was no longer an active stuntman, he was made an Honorary Member of the fraternal organization.

Publicity-wise Jocko did a fashion spread with Susan Seaforth for *Cavalier* magazine, graced the cover of *Screen Thrills Illustrated* in a Tarzan shot, and was profiled in the November 1964 Joe Weider muscle magazine *Young Mr. America*. Mention was made of Jocko's healthy lifestyle and dedication to a lifetime of fitness. Jocko noted that his goal was not to pile on muscle like a bodybuilder through heavy lifting. He favored long lean muscles that would aid his athletic abilities and trained accordingly with lighter weights and higher repetitions. Most of his workouts remained built around free-hand exercise such as chin-ups, dips, and push-ups utilizing his own body weight. Jocko remained a proponent of the Dynamic Tension isometric exercises made popular by Charles Atlas. He simply did more of them when playing Tarzan. He even admitted to doing these exercises while he was driving. When not playing the ape man, it was important for him to stay a trim 200 pounds as the cameras often gave the appearance of adding 10 to 15 pounds. At 6' 4", Jocko didn't want to limit his acting opportunities by dwarfing his potential co-stars.

The summer of 1962 saw Jocko and Maggie take a two-week vacation to Mexico in their new Dreamer pickup camper. Jocko had the top of the line trailer mounted to his three-quarter–ton 1961 Dodge pickup truck, giving them a home on wheels. The couple stayed on the beaches of the Bay of San Carlos with Jocko indulging in his love of scuba diving and snorkeling in the Sea of Cortez. Many of their meals were caught by Jocko, who was armed to the hilt for any kind of interesting game action. He took with him four rifles, three Colt bows, three spear guns, a hunting knife, a hatchet, a machete, and a lariat. He also armed himself with plenty of bubblegum, balloons, and harmonicas to hand out to the local children.

Jocko's pal Walt Wiggins, a writer and photographer from New Mexico, accompanied the couple in his own camper and documented the trip for a cover profile in the September 1963 issue of *Mobile Home Journal*. The association with the Dreamer led to an endorsement deal for Jocko, who appeared in print ads for the trailer in sporting magazines. The pictures of the trip do reveal Jocko looking a bit huskier in his swim trunks. There was plenty of physical activity for Jocko on the trip and the Mexican sun maintained his Tarzan tan. However, the evening cocktails on the beach were adding a slight thickness around his once taut waistline. His training for the next film was further hindered when he accidentally sliced a finger in September while cutting a steak at Sasso Restaurant in New York City. It was a minor injury but one that affected his grip on the variety of exercises he habitually performed. Nevertheless, Jocko felt he was ready to once again play Tarzan of the Apes come the New Year.

Based on the success of his first starring role as Tarzan, Jocko was enthusiastic about journeying to Thailand in early 1963 to star in the second film of the series *Tarzan's Three Challenges*. (He even planned to take his own camera equipment to document the filming.) The majority of the footage would be shot in the village of Chiang Mai outside of Bangkok, with some location work in mountainous regions that were mere miles from the border of Red China. There would also be unprecedented filming inside the ancient Temple of Wat-saunddock. The plot had Tarzan summoned from Africa to escort young spiritual heir Ricky Der across the Thai jungle to take his place at the throne of Sun Mai. Along the way they are besieged by rival interests.

The director this time around was Robert Day, who had successfully helmed *Tarzan the Magnificent* and had a sunnier disposition than John Guillermin. Day was quite open to Jocko's suggestions on script changes to insure that the Tarzan character remained true to Burroughs' books. Jocko's co-star was former UCLA track sensation and professional football player turned pro wrestler Woody Strode, a 6'4", 210-pound mountain of sinewy muscle who memorably opposed Kirk Douglas in the gladiatorial arena in *Spartacus* (1960). The script called for a climactic battle between Jocko and Strode and both men looked forward to the clash. Jocko had several hundred pounds of iron weights shipped to the location and once again began to add muscle to his frame to match up with Strode. In *Every Step a Struggle* Woody Strode called Jocko "a physical actor who can do anything."

At the outset of the picture, the 220 pounds Jocko was carrying wasn't the same hardened weight he had carried for the first picture. By his own admission, he was a little softer going into the picture than he was in the first film. Still, given his age he'd have been the envy of most men ten years younger during this era. Jocko rightly figured that he'd shed a few pounds given all the action in the film and the strenuous location. He had no idea how much he would actually lose during the course of the filming. In fact, *Tarzan's Three Chal-*

lenges is infamous for nearly killing Jocko. "The biggest challenge was my finishing the movie alive," he told *The Salisbury Post*.

It all started early in the filming when the script called for the movie villains to attempt running Tarzan over with a speedboat in the Klong River. Jocko naturally was ready to do his own stunts. His friend Strode cautioned him, however, on the wisdom of swimming in the waters of a Third World nation. The Klong River was notorious for being one of the most polluted in the world with sewage and human waste. Jocko instinctively knew better but also didn't want to put a stuntman at risk. The script called for Tarzan to swim in the Klong, and Jocko was Tarzan. He would swim in the Klong. Jocko inadvertently took in some water while swimming.

At first, it seemed that Jocko had escaped any harm and filming continued as scheduled. In one memorable sequence he was strung between a pair of water buffaloes pulling in opposite directions. The scene showcased Jocko's strength, but the demands on his body were great. Jocko's arms were so tired from the scene that he needed to be spoonfed afterward as he literally could not lift his hands to his mouth for days. Another problem was the wear and tear the physical role took on Jocko's feet. He had to resort to wearing flesh-colored pads on his soles. He told the *Advocate*: "You start barefooted, but by the time you're two weeks in the picture you're wearing flesh-colored sneakers. You wouldn't be able to walk otherwise."

Gradually, an amoebic bug began to wear Jocko down. It would take a full month of strenuous location work in 100-degree heat before the seemingly superhuman Jocko's immune system became all too human. He became sick with Dengue fever, ptomaine poisoning, and amoebic dysentery but stubbornly soldiered on with the filming. The only time he held up filming was when he felt that his friend Strode had been racially slighted by a member of the production crew. Jocko demanded Strode be given an apology, which he promptly received. Not until then did Jocko step back in front of the camera.

Jocko became terribly ill. The dysentery and Dengue fever was soon accompanied by tertiary malaria and pneumonia. Any one of these diseases would have knocked a normal man off his feet. Within a 10-day period Jocko dropped over 40 pounds of muscle in the oppressive humidity. He couldn't eat and hold down anything of substance. He couldn't sleep more than a few winks at a time. Somehow, he miraculously continued to film against medical advice in an effort to get the picture completed. The pneumonia became interstitial in his lungs, which could have turned into a death sentence. In the final days of filming he was passing out from weakness dozens of time a day and there were crew members standing by to catch him should he collapse in front of the cameras. Between takes he was in an oxygen tank or wrapped in ice.

"My biggest fear was roasting my brain," he told *The Salisbury Post*. Yet time and time again he rose from his sick bed to answer the camera's call. This was the man who was so proud of being able to save *Range Rider* a few thousand dollars an episode, and now an entire expensive feature film was riding on his back. Strode recalled in his autobiography *Goal Dust*, "Anybody else would have died but Jock Mahoney.... He was one of the strongest men in the world."

Although Jocko should have been dead, he still had the biggest action scenes of the movie to film: the climactic race across the terrain, a 120-foot dive off the Begor Bridge, and a sword battle with Strode atop a net suspended over vats of boiling oil. Jocko and Strode did the first 30 feet of the bungee jump off the bridge into a net. They also did the

The test of strength in *Tarzan's Three Challenges* (1963).

last portion of the shot where the two dangle upside down over the water by a rope as they struggle with one another. Dummies were used for the long portion of the jump and were ripped apart at the end of the line. It is surprising Jocko has any memory at all of the experience given his weakened condition. By the time of the fight scene on the net, he was down to 175 pounds. "I was so skinny," he told interviewer David Rothel, "that my diaper kept falling off."

The net battle was extremely tricky due to the balance required and the bounce of the rope. Several of stunt coordinator Ray Austin's stuntmen were thrown off during preparation for the scene. With every movement it would quiver and shake and threaten to dislodge Jocko and Strode. There was little chance of extended rehearsal with the principals on account of Jocko's feverish condition. During the fight on the rope his temperature hovered between 104 and 105 degrees, a deathly ill state. But Jocko never fell off the rope. This was a point of pride in light of the struggles of the other stuntmen.

When the fight scene was finally in the can, Jocko literally passed out. Strode and others rushed him in a Land Rover to the hotel. Strode carried Jocko to the bathtub and filled it with ice while a doctor was summoned. They gave Jocko strong antibiotics in an attempt to save his life. Jocko pulled through but the near-death experience had a dramatic impact on his health and acting career. In the long run, it likely took ten years off his life. Strode wrote that the film sadly "made an old man out of him."

The film was shot largely in sequence. Although the change in Jocko's appearance during the course of filming is shocking, most viewers were too caught up in the excellent action and exotic location to realize how haggard and ashen-looking the leading man had become. Despite the difficulties in completing the picture, the final product is another superior Tarzan movie. The locale is interesting and gorgeously filmed in rich colors. Thai tem-

Jocko (left) and Woody Strode hang over a river in *Tarzan's Three Challenges* (1963) (11 × 14 lobby card).

A 175-pound Jocko battles Woody Strode with machetes on a bamboo net in *Tarzan's Three Challenges* (1963).

ples, Buddha statues, and jeweled elephants are only a small sampling of elements audiences were unaccustomed to seeing on an average day at the theater. Strode, playing two roles in the film, makes for a fearsome opponent, and there is a well-done sequence with Jocko running through a burning jungle. The foliage was so green that gasoline had to be poured to get it to burn, and Jocko was almost caught by the flames a couple of times. Reviews were positive and box office receipts solid, topping those of *Tarzan Goes to India*.

Variety noted, "Mahoney, with his natural athletic prowess, is able to make a gymnasium out of the jungle in the best Tarzan tradition." *The Motion Picture Herald* commented, "Although he seems to lack something of the weight and heft of the earlier Tarzans, he is certainly sufficiently active, strong, and ruggedly handsome to satisfy." *Boxoffice* noted, "Jock Mahoney, the tall muscle-man, is one of the better of the thirteen Tarzans to date." *The Hollywood Reporter* added, "Mahoney is a lean, strong type, but the biceps don't bulge like balloons. [He was] a real person, not a stereotype, faithful to Edgar Rice Burroughs' durable creation." *The Los Angeles Citizen News* claimed Jocko and Strode turned in "top performances." *Film Daily* cited Jocko's "rugged appeal," but *Films and Filming* found him "too old for the part" and "not savage enough."

Jocko ultimately became known in the history books as the skinny Tarzan. Sandwiched between the portrayals of bodybuilder Gordon Scott and rugged 6'3", 210-pound football player Mike Henry, the word "thin" is an apt description of the sick Jocko who appeared on screen at the end of the second film. Most audiences forget the robust portrayal of a healthy Jocko in the first film, where only knowledge of his advanced age kept him from perfection. After seeing *Tarzan's Three Challenges* Johnny Weissmuller commented to the *San Diego Union*, "Jock's a good stuntman but he's skinny — a long drink of water — and he's got no build on him."

It's interesting to note that after Mike Henry's three films were made, Weintraub cast Ron Ely for the TV series (Henry refused to carry on in the role due to the rigors of the jungle). Ely's lanky physique was a near match for Jocko's midway through *Tarzan's Three Challenges*. The strenuous location work was tough on all three men, a burden that Weissmuller and Lex Barker never had to endure during their back lot studio days.

Jocko told John Hagner, "I refused to take my own advice — know your own limitations and fight the urge to do the stunt just one more time." U.S. Navy veteran Hagner was one of the up-and-coming stuntmen Jocko had befriended. He was also an aspiring writer and artist who put out a newsletter honoring stuntmen and published a book in 1964 entitled *Falling for Stars*. Jocko assisted Hagner in the project by writing an eloquent introduction in which he likened stuntmen to the great risk takers of the past: "Men among men who have sought to persevere in areas of excitement and danger where the minute exactness of coordination between mind and body can mean the difference between life and death."

Still in a weakened physical state, Jocko was summoned to London two months later to redub the picture as the location sound had problems similar to those of his first Tarzan film. He had managed to put some of his weight back on but was still suffering. While in London Jocko met the Royal Family and engaged them in discourse on UFOs, a subject Jocko had a great interest in. He also met actor David Niven, whose part in *The Guns of Navarone* (1961) Jocko had been up for before it was rewritten to accommodate the Brit. He also learned that he was very popular in England. *The Range Rider* had been running there continuously for the past ten years under the titles *Rex Rider* and *King Rider*. The sprockets on the film were nearly worn out from use. *Range Rider* was also a big hit in Rome.

Jocko embarked on an extensive publicity tour for MGM, covering more than 100 cities in the United States using gimmick luggage covered in leopard skin. In cities like Dallas he visited as many as eight different theaters in a single day. Sometimes he barely had the strength or time to walk across the stage and say a few words to audiences, but as was Jocko's style he soldiered on. Tarzan authority Phil Petras called him "the ultimate professional."[10] Some days were better than others. When feeling up to it, Jocko could still be coaxed to a local pool to execute a perfect dive off the high board. He couldn't resume his daily workouts for several months, but through normal consumption of food was able to get his weight back up to what he felt was a soft 200 pounds.

In July of 1963 he had his first swimming workout since the sickness while making a public appearance in El Paso, Texas. According to witness Dale Walker's account in *The Burroughs Bulletin*, it was as if Jocko had never missed a day: "Bouncing as much as six feet above the board, the sinewy athlete clove the water perfectly with enough momentum to carry him underwater the length of the enormous Hilton pool. His diving and swimming styles were Olympic, beautifully coordinated and without ornamentation."

In Dallas, he put on another diving exhibition in late July at the Holiday Inn pool. In August, still on the Tarzan publicity tour, Jocko was accepting pre-arranged swimming and diving challenges against champion athletes over 20 years his junior at the Aquatic Club in Baton Rouge, Louisiana. Although he remained in a less than healthy state, Jocko would not shy away from performing a triple twisting forward one-and-one-half somersault dive when put on the spot by high school SAAU diving champion Keen Day. Jocko repeated his impressive swimming and diving exhibitions a few days later at the New Orleans Athletic Club.

Life magazine featured an article on the making of *Tarzan's Three Challenges* and the physical toll it took on Jocko in 1963, noting how Jocko "manfully finished the role." The accompanying photos showed a shockingly worn and haggard Jocko taking a break between scenes. Despite his late summer rebound it was painfully obvious that Jocko would be unable to continue in the role, but while on the publicity junket he still held out hope that he would be playing Tarzan in further adventures taking place in Cambodia and Brazil. "As long as I can hold together," he told *The Burroughs Bulletin*. Eventually, he and Weintraub reached a mutual decision to dissolve his Tarzan contract and split on amicable terms.

Jocko was 44 years old and suddenly feeling his age. It took him over 18 months to regain the strength he had lost on location, but eventually he was able to get back into his daily exercise regimen and resume acting work. He still managed to keep busy, even outside of the exhausting Tarzan tour. He attended a cerebral palsy charity event for the Hillside House, promoted the unrealized Nevada fun park Vegas Land, and crowned Edy Williams Miss Tarzana in a beauty pageant. Jocko was also elected to serve on the Screen Actors Guild Board of Directors, a post he carried for several years. He was instrumental in setting up a one-stop permit office for the motion picture studios in Los Angeles City Hall for Mayor Sam Yorty.

Professionally he had been married to the Tarzan character for nearly two full years. Jocko spent so much time touring and promoting Tarzan that he was unable to make any other films during this period, parts that might have helped him avoid the pitfalls of type-casting within the industry. Considering that he had top-lined the two biggest moneymakers of the Tarzan franchise and went to great lengths to assist MGM in publicizing the films, Jocko was disappointed that there were no further offers from the studio for other roles. He had hoped to garner some quality acting assignments from the grand studio.

9

The Parent

The overwhelming majority of Jocko's co-workers in the film industry up to this point all came away with a great deal of respect and awe. While not considered a superstar, he was generally known the world over and was a hit when interacting with a large fan base. Jocko was a tough guy and may have had an occasional drink, but the gossip columns were not filled with accounts of him being drunk or disorderly and engaging in any real-life fisticuffs. His female co-stars all spoke highly of him, and he was not known as a philanderer outside of his marriage to Maggie. If there were any on-set romances, Jocko remained discreet about them.

However, there was one aspect of Jocko's life where his deficiencies have dogged him with a lasting impact. He was not considered a particularly good father by those who would know the best: some of his own kids. This is ironic considering how well Jocko interacted with children on screen and on publicity junkets. Unfortunately, children inevitably grow up. It's a part of life, and it was the part of Jocko's life where he occasionally struggled. As it so happened, one of his children would reach superstar status, thereby putting family history out in a public forum for the world to see as the media psychoanalyzed all aspects of Sally Field's life story.

Over the years Jocko had continued to keep his body fit with a stringent workout routine executed in his pool, his backyard, and his home gym. He also devised workouts for his children, who were expected to keep up with his nearly Olympian performance. When Jocko was home the kids were in the pool, on a trampoline, or on the back of a horse. Sometimes he literally had them jumping through hoops he held up into the pool. It was not uncommon for Jocko to throw them into the air and catch them as they fell, preaching the importance of gymnastics and learning the capabilities of one's body. Jocko's intention was pure in that he knew the benefits of exercise were healthy for his children, but sometimes he could become more hard-lined coach than sensitive father. While they may have worshiped him as tots as so many children did, by the mid–1960s they were all reaching adult age or the formative teenage years. As they began to assert themselves in their own lives, they began to clash with Jocko, none more so than his stepdaughter Sally Field.

In a 1986 interview with *Playboy* magazine and a 1991 follow-up with *Movieline*, Field spoke of the difficult times she had growing up under the roof of Jock Mahoney, a man who never revealed himself to his children and often remained a larger-than-life character even at home. She likened the intense daily exercise to being a form of physical child abuse. Sally had an especially hard time because of her eagerness to please him, a goal she met neither athletically nor emotionally. Jocko represented and expected strength. He didn't want his daughter to be considered a sissy, but the truth was Jocko's jungle gym of stunt equipment, 16-hand high 50-gallon drum with a saddle on it, and double high bars in the family's backyard intimidated Sally tremendously. She retreated into a world of her own imagination with acting becoming her passion.

As Sally reached her teenage years she experienced a sudden shift in her personality. By her own admission to *Playboy*, the once helpless, frightened little girl turned into an aggressor as she began confronting her stepfather. The 5'2", 100-pound Sally stood on the coffee table so she could scream at Jocko eye to eye. She felt the only way she could be heard was to be as big and loud as he was. At times an exasperated Jocko ended an argument by "throwing her into the backyard" to cool off. Her words ended up twisted around in translation between different sources to the point where some now believe Jocko physically hit his children. In reality, Jocko didn't even spank his kids. He and Maggie both believed in grounding them over raising a hand. Some people even confuse him with fellow screen Tarzan Lex Barker, who was alleged to have sexually abused his wife Lana Turner's teenage daughter. This, of course, is a gross error in regard to Jocko.

According to Sally, Jocko's actual abuse was of a purely psychological nature. As the children reached their teenage years, a "tyrannical" Jocko began to aggressively pick and needle them for their deficiencies. In a 2008 interview with *The Academy of Achievement* website, she described him as "charismatic" and "terrorizing" in the same breath. "He destroyed a lot of good things about his children," she said, searching for a reason why Jocko became such a bullying parent. Perhaps it was his U.S. Marine drill instructor background coming into play, systematically tearing down the troops before building them up to attain solidarity. Jocko liked to boast he was extremely perceptive about people and often proclaimed he could find anyone's secret weakness. This made Sally very insecure growing up in his omnipotent presence. She was always afraid he would reveal her deepest personal flaw and she'd be destroyed forever as a result.

On the other hand, it also strengthened her in the long run. She began to channel her anger into her acting. The grit and determination she displayed throughout her career in roles such as *Norma Rae* (1979) could be attributed in large part to Jocko developing a fighting spirit in her. Sally's eagerness to attain his approval thus shaped a large part of her being. It's not a coincidence that one of her defining moments came in her 1985 Oscar acceptance speech for *Places in the Heart* (1984) when she proclaimed, "You like me!"

Certainly her boyfriends had to pass muster with Jocko, and many wound up terrified of his booming voice and physical presence when they met him at the front door. From an early age Jocko warned Sally that many boys would pursue her for sex alone and would likely break her heart if she dropped her guard with them. In defiance she would apply lipstick and mascara prior to a date, which he did not approve of on a young lady. On one occasion Jocko wiped the mascara off a humiliated Sally in front of her date. Jocko's assessment might have been on the money, but it no doubt left Sally with a cold detachment when it came to boys. It's interesting that years later one of her most significant relationships came with actor Burt Reynolds, a macho former college athlete and stuntman cut from the same cloth as Jocko.

The open-minded Mahoney household could at times border on the mildly eccentric. Jocko and Maggie were both into UFOs and the family experimented with ESP. According to an early 1970s Sally Field interview for *The Morning Record,* Maggie and the kids would band together and try to contact Jocko telepathically if he was late coming home. However, that line of communication never seemed to work. Jocko did sometimes act on odd intuitions that he felt strongly about. Sally recalled, "We would be going somewhere, the whole family, like once we were on a boat going to Catalina. And he suddenly had a vision or something that things were going to go wrong. He turned the boat around and headed for home. That kind of thing happened often."

Sally described her stepfather to Oprah Winfrey, saying: "He was a colorful character.... He was really big and handsome. I was both terrified of him and madly in love with him. Unfortunately, that stayed with me as I grew up. I was attracted only to men I simultaneously feared and loved. My stepfather was both cruel and loving, and therefore our relationship was very confusing." For *The New York Times* Sally remarked, "I was a thorn in his side because I was a fighter. I decided if you can't beat 'em, join 'em. I decided to be as big and bold and ugly as he was."

Jocko most often clashed philosophically with Sally due to her desire to be an actress. Both Jocko and Maggie maintained that they didn't want Sally to begin acting professionally while still a child, but it was Jocko who took the hard line. The feisty Sally saw this as a stifling of her creativity and sought outlets in school. At Birmingham High she was heavily involved in the drama department and was a cheerleader. At home she studied Shakespeare and other classics. Upon Sally's graduation from Birmingham, Jocko finally encouraged her to enroll at the Columbia Pictures Workshop to study acting for film. He put her in touch with Eddie Foy III, a casting director who auditioned Sally for the leading role in the surfer girl sitcom *Gidget* (1965–1966). She won the part and was soon on her way to a long career that included multiple Oscar and Emmy wins. While she and Jocko rarely saw eye to eye, a strong difference of opinion is common among teenagers and their parents. This was especially true during the turbulent decade of the 1960s. Jocko and Sally would speak highly of one another in later years and with at least a certain degree of professional fondness and respect.

Due to the nature of his occupation, Jocko was frequently away from home for long periods of time. He was on the road as the Range Rider and Tarzan, or he was filming in faroff regions of Central America, Africa, Europe, and Asia. Jocko undoubtedly missed many important events in the lives of his children. These absences, when added up, took their toll. His biological children Kathleen and Jim had been largely raised under a different roof, with Jocko seeing them sporadically. All Jocko's children were beginning to move in different directions. Kathleen, Jocko's grown daughter from his first marriage, maintained the lowest profile. After attending California State College at Long Beach she married Allen Kaye in 1964 and settled in Pomona, California, to raise a family.

Her brother Jim was a chip off the old block and took after his old man in many ways. By the early 1960s Jim had already traveled the world numerous times courtesy of his grandparents the O'Donnells, including two month-long safaris in Kenya where the 12-year-old lassoed an angry rhino and shot a lion with a pellet gun. At the age of nine he had survived a Mau-Mau uprising while on safari and was racing rickshaws in Hong Kong. With special instruction from his dad, Jim was an All-City diver by the age of ten and an All-City track star for Wilson High specializing in the pole vault where he cleared 13 feet. By the age of 15 he had accumulated his father's entire repertoire of physical skills although he was short-changed a few inches in height at 6'1".

Sports were the only thing that kept Jim in school and away from the beach or the ski slopes. At 17 he was the youngest ski instructor in the history of Mammoth Mountain. His summers were spent surfing in Malibu, Mexico, and Tahiti while his winters were generally occupied as a ski instructor in Aspen, Colorado. Jim began to surf and skateboard competitively in the early 1960s, winning a number of trophies in those sports. For recreation he pursued hang gliding, piloting, and race car driving, setting a straightaway speed record at Long Beach. Twice he broke both his legs in hang-gliding accidents. "O" (as he was known amongst his friends) was one of the first adrenaline junkies and a forefather of the extreme sports generation.

Jim was far from a slacker though. He found interesting work as an award-winning photographer and writer for surfing magazines. His photos appeared in publications such as *Newsweek, Time, Life,* and *Sports Illustrated* and he worked assignments for CBS Sports. Jim started *Skateboard* magazine in 1975 and later served as the features editor for the surf and skate magazine *Juice.* He wrote and published the books *Freestyle Handbook* and *Skateboard Handbook,* which both became instant collector's items. Jim became infamous in the skating community for being the first person to submit the word "skateboard" to *Webster's Dictionary.*

Jim O'Mahoney even followed in his old man's footsteps, appearing as a stuntman surfer on TV's *Gidget* and stunt doubling the character Ronald McDonald for a skateboarding segment in a mid–1970s TV commercial. He also performed hang-gliding and skateboard stunts for a few minor films. Jim was the creator of the legendary Signal Hill skateboarding speed event and invented a number of skating aids and devices. In 1977 he won the World Pro Skateboarding Slalom Championship. He then relocated to Mammoth Mountain with his wife and children and became one of the first snowboarders.

Jim had long been a collector of relics and artifacts, opening the store Cowboy Star Antiques in the late 1960s. In 1992 he became the curator of the Santa Barbara Surfing Museum, an eclectic building full of interesting artifacts the self-described treasure hunter collected over the years. He returned to surfing the senior circuit with first place finishes in the 1988 Rincon Classic, the 1993 USSA WSA West Coast Championships, and the Malibu Oxbow World Championship in 1994, where he represented the country of Ireland through some creative maneuvering. His win made him the number one ranked surfer in Europe and the fortieth in the world at the age of 52. He later handed over much of his surfing memorabilia to singer Jimmy Buffet for the Honolulu Surfing Museum, an offshoot of Buffet's Beachcomber Restaurant in Waikiki.

"My dad was one of the best stuntmen in the history of the world." Jim O'Mahoney told *Juice* magazine. He has been interviewed by a number of publications in regard to his surfing and skateboarding careers. Brief mention is usually made of the fact that his father was Tarzan, but he has not talked at length about Jocko during any of his interviews. When queried, he admits that it was somewhat tough growing up as the son of Tarzan, with athletic expectations coming from a number of areas since Jocko did just about everything.[1] As a result, Jim did just about everything athletically and did it well.

Jocko's stepson Rick Field often trained in the backyard and the home gym with Jocko, but the two had a highly competitive relationship. Much of Sally's anger toward Jocko stemmed from his treatment of her brother, which often revolved around athletic contests between the two in which Rick seldom if ever came out on top. Rick remembered in a 1986 interview with the *Orlando-Sentinel* that Jocko would arm-wrestle and always beat him. As Rick grew older he began lifting weights in order to beat Jocko. Once he could put Jocko's arm down, Jocko lost interest in continuing to arm-wrestle Rick. Perhaps it was a rite of passage the young man had conquered in Jocko's eyes, or the simple fact that Jocko didn't like to lose. Rick described the often absent Jocko by saying, "He wasn't exactly the world's best dad."

The competitions between Jocko and Rick ultimately paid dividends for the young man. Rick became a champion gymnast, winning the CIF Side Horse title while a student at Birmingham High. He also won the 1962 Los Angeles City Championship in rope climbing. His athletic skill, forged in the backyard by Jocko, garnered him a college gymnastic scholarship to the University of California at Berkeley. He specialized in the rings for the Golden Bears and became an All-American gymnast. In 1965 he won the NCAA Western Regional All-Around title. Nationally he ranked second in the still rings, third on the parallel bars, and sixth overall. Despite his Olympic potential, UC Coach Hal Frey admitted to *The Hayward Daily Review*, "He isn't the easiest boy to coach. He's a strong personality and has a mind of his own."

In 1966 Rick was awarded the Jake Gimball Award for his combined excellence in athletics and academics. Unfortunately, elbow surgery derailed his athletic career. More importantly, the athletics gave Rick access to one of the country's top science and math programs. A Regent's Scholar with near perfect grades, Rick graduated with his Bachelor Degree from Cal Berkeley in 1966 and completed his PhD at the school in 1971. He went on to become a top particle scientist and assisted Nobel Prize–winning physicist Dick Feinman at Cal-Tech. In later years Rick became a noted theoretical physicist at the University of Florida in Gainesville, where he taught and lectured.

Jocko's youngest biological daughter Princess loved the backyard full of stunt equipment and followed after her father's athleticism. As an adult, she did some acting in the 1970s as Augusta Mahoney, Melissa O'Mahoney, or Princess O'Mahoney in the films *Coma* (1978), *The End* (1978), and *Hooper* (1978) and TV fare such as *The Partridge Family* and *Beach Patrol* (1979). She eventually found work behind the scenes in the film industry as a production assistant and assistant director on motion pictures such as *Maverick* (1994), sometimes credited as Princess McLean. She also worked on several Burt Reynolds films and many TV shows, including the likes of *ER* and *Dexter*. In a notoriously tough industry, she managed to find a lasting foothold.

The combination of Jocko's extended illness post–*Tarzan's Three Challenges*, troubling financial investments, and his difficulties in relating to his growing children led to a strain in his relationship with Maggie. One common misconception, often brought up in articles on Sally Field, is that an old-fashioned Jocko demanded Maggie give up her career when they were married. This is not true, and the evidence is in the fact that Maggie continued to act regularly on TV throughout the 1950s and early 1960s. She even appeared on numerous occasions with Jocko. It wasn't until the kids reached their difficult teen years that her acting credits slowed down, as did Jocko's. Maggie did not completely give up her acting career until Sally got married and had a baby while starring in the TV series *The Flying Nun*. The new grandmother opted to spend her time caring for her grandchild rather than chasing acting roles. Jocko had little bearing on her decision to give up acting at that point.

In the book *Screen Sirens Scream* Margaret Field said: "By the '60s, my children were growing up and Sally had become a teenager. I had always felt that I was going against the grain, against the way that women were supposed to be. During this period it became hard for me to continue acting. Women were supposed to stay at home and take care of their children, and I was a renegade for my time. I decided to stay at home and be with my children and just quit acting. Sally was about 13, and she was having a tough time, as most teenagers do during this time, with normal teenage situations. I had always felt guilty about having worked steadily for nearly 20 years and also felt that I was neglecting my home matters. I had to take care of these things now to the fullest."

The TV series *The Flying Nun* (1967–1970) was another point of friction between Jocko and Sally. The show had a ridiculous concept, and Sally initially didn't want to do it. She felt her serious acting ambitions could survive the teenage *Gidget*, but that something called *The Flying Nun* would be too dumb to overcome. Jocko, on the other hand, told her that a young actor or actress should never turn down work. The industry was tough on up-and-coming talent. One needed to take work when it was offered, and things would eventually fall into place in terms of a career. After losing out on auditions for the films *The Graduate* (1967) and *Valley of the Dolls* (1967), Sally reluctantly agreed to accept the role.

As luck would have it, *The Flying Nun* wound up being a hit and ran for three seasons. In addition to hating the concept of the show, Sally was typed in the industry, and her serious acting ambitions were nearly squashed. She second-guessed heeding Jocko's advice for a long time. In *Screen Sirens Scream* Margaret Field said, "Jocko and I always helped her when she was young. We did not always stand over her with advice, but instead told her what to expect. Sally was always a fighter, and she wasn't going to let anyone walk over her."

Overall, the influence of Jocko's genetics and parental guidance produced a group of offspring who were overwhelmingly successful. The odds of even one achieving marked success in any field of endeavor would be minuscule, but so many of Jocko's brood rising to the top of their chosen professions has to be considered uncanny. It says something about the man presiding over them, even if his rigid methods were at times questionable. Jocko pushed them hard to be the best that they could be, and the results speak for themselves.

10

The Falling Star

While things may have been changing at home with his children, the status of Jocko's film career was also in a state of flux. The man who so recently had above the title billing for a big MGM moneymaker was now having difficulty finding acting work because of that very role. His initial fears regarding the character were being realized. Jocko had fought hard not to be labeled as merely a cowboy actor. He had played heroes and villains with skill. He presented the most articulate Tarzan the screen had ever seen, but the powers-that-be in Hollywood were narrow-minded regarding the ape man. Jocko now had to overcome being a former Tarzan, and a graying, middle-aged one at that.

Johnny Weissmuller was never able to get out of the jungle. After one Tarzan film Buster Crabbe became a low-budget serial star in *Flash Gordon* and *Buck Rogers*. Crabbe moved to the East Coast when his career sputtered in the 1950s. Herman Brix was forced to change his professional name to Bruce Bennett and pretend he never played Tarzan. Lex Barker had to go to Europe to find work. Gordon Scott made his Italian peplum films then disappeared. Only Denny Miller, with one Tarzan film to his credit, subsequently found a legitimate home in Hollywood as trail scout Duke Shannon on TV's *Wagon Train*. Although Jocko had a variety of acting roles to his credit, he was now finding himself being lumped into the same category as many of his ape man predecessors.

This would probably have been a ripe time for Jocko to return to the land of the TV western and star in another series. There were rumblings on the long-running *Rawhide* that star Eric Fleming would be replaced, and eventually he was, in the final season, by veteran character lead John Ireland. The trail boss role didn't do much for Ireland's career, but might have been a boon to Jocko's. A western that ran a couple of seasons may have secured Jocko's financial future and cemented his legacy as one of the great TV western stars. Something along the lines of the Chuck Connors series *Cowboy in Africa* (1967–1968) could have been a perfect vehicle for Jocko during this period. No doubt the negative experience with *Yancy Derringer* and CBS made him hesitant to return to TV at this time, although he had long harbored dreams of playing a globe-hopping adventurer in a series that could be filmed around the world. The logistics and cost of that endeavor proved prohibitive, but the Robert Culp-Bill Cosby series *I Spy* (1965–1968) became a great success following just such a format.

Looking for work and not finding it stateside at his now accustomed financial rate of $5,000 a week, Jocko accepted an offer to star in two Filipino-made action films in late 1963. Due to his Tarzan association, Jocko had a great fan base in the western hemisphere.

Jocko gets his kicks in the Filipino-made _Moro Witch Doctor_ (1964).

Even though Asia had nearly killed him, Jocko would once again brave the jungles. Having survived _Tarzan's Three Challenges_, Jocko took the Friedrich Nietzsche phrase "That which does not kill us, makes us stronger" to heart. He actually began to seek out challenging and interesting locales.

Moro Witch Doctor (aka _Amok_) (1964) was a bare-bones low-budgeter with Jocko top-lining as CIA agent Jefferson Stark. In the film he takes on religious fanatics and an opium smuggling ring on the island of Mindanao. The movie, made by prolific Filipino filmmaker Eddie Romero, gave Jocko ample opportunity to fight gunmen and machete-wielding mani-acs using fists and karate kicks. It received limited release from Lippert Pictures and 20th Century–Fox as a drive-in second-feature, clocking in at barely 62 minutes.

The making of the film and the location were difficult as the film's plotline apparently wasn't that far from the reality of the situation. Moro Muslims believed that killing a white Christian guaranteed them 100 servants in Heaven, so Jocko and co-star Margia Dean's lives were literally on the line. The film crew employed guards with machine guns to keep the actors safe. The critical reception was not kind, with most making mention of Jocko's action prowess over his acting abilities. _Boxoffice_ opined, "Mahoney gives his customary two-fisted portrayal," while _Film Daily_ noted, "Mahoney lets his fists bear the brunt of the acting." _Variety_ said succinctly, "Mahoney has no chance at all with his role."

Dean became one of the first of Jocko's co-stars to come away with anything less than superlatives to say about him. In an interview with Michael Fitzgerald for *Western Clippings* she commented: "Jock Mahoney was not very pleasant to work with. He wasn't gracious or warm or anything. He didn't do anything wrong, he was tall and nice-looking with sex appeal for some people. But he was a pompous ass, and pardon me for saying that, but he just wasn't friendly or pleasant. But we were out in the jungle, where you pottied behind bushes. You could get malaria. It was hundreds of miles even from Manila, in the Philippines."

It should be noted that in the same interview Dean used words such as cocky, rude, lousy, and vile to describe actor Scott Brady. She called Jocko ungracious and a bit pompous but he got off light considering the adjectives that could have been thrown in his direction. Still, this was the first of Jocko's female co-stars to come away unimpressed. Perhaps the rigors of the location and completing the film affected Jocko's disposition. He was still recovering from his near-death illness, and the demanding workload could have been too much too soon. The growing problems at home exasperated by Jocko being halfway around the world could have been weighing on his mind. *Moro Witch Doctor* isn't worth delving into further. It has been unavailable for viewing for years.

The following year's *The Walls of Hell* (aka *Intramuros*) fared much better than *Moro Witch Doctor*. The film is about the fabled walled city of Intramuros and the 10,000 Japanese soldiers who held up there at the end of World War II. Jocko, as Lt. Jim Sorensen, leads a group of soldiers on a rescue mission to free hostages in the city before the climactic siege in which all the Japanese soldiers perished. The $65,000 budget was slightly higher than *Moro Witch Doctor* and the result was a gritty black and white war film that has its admirers. Jocko is appropriately tough in the lead, and a highlight of the film is a short fight with Filipino action star Fernando Poe, Jr.; it takes ten men to break it up. Jocko later labeled this as a typical Filipino-made film but *Walls of Hell*, co-directed by Eddie Romero and Gerry DeLeon, actually aspired to be something better and largely succeeds.

Reviews were mixed. *Boxoffice* noted Jocko's "marquee value" and that "the scenes between Mahoney and Cecilia Lopez are touching." *The Motion Picture Herald* praised the film's action and Jocko's "first-rate performance." *The New York Times* commented somewhat neutrally on "the erstwhile screen Tarzan," saying Jocko is "laconic, serious, and muscular." *Variety* noted "a stolidity of facial expression among most of the cast, even spreading to Jock Mahoney and the other professionals." They called Jocko "efficient without being particularly impressive."

While Jocko was staying in the Philippines, another film was in production in Manila. Former actor John Derek was producing and directing a World War II movie starring his statuesque blonde wife Ursula Andress, *Once Before I Die* (aka *No Toys for Christmas*). Among the cast were he-men co-stars Richard Jaeckel and 6'4", 210-pound Ron Ely, whom Jocko got along well with. Jocko and the athletic Ely often swam laps together in the Manila Hotel pool. The Texas-born Ely, whose career was on the upswing, continuously teased Jocko about playing Tarzan. The former oilfield roughneck suggested Jocko would never get over the typecasting, and he himself would never stoop to portray the jungle lord. A few years later Ely ended up doing just that on TV, to Jocko's delight.

The casting director of *Once Before I Die* was lamenting that he needed to find three American military types to handle some dialogue for the next day's shooting. Jocko suggested they simply condense the dialogue into one part and Jocko would play the role. When the casting director commented that they couldn't afford Jocko, the ever-obliging Jocko said he'd work for hamburgers. Jocko performed the unbilled cameo role of a military major and set about to have lunch. Considering the low budget of the film, John Derek drew a laugh when he told Jocko he didn't know he was going to eat three hamburgers for lunch and the film's budget was now compromised.

Jocko's lone scene in a crowded military bar is memorable as he drinks beer and carves a wooden dart while conversing with a very effective Richard Jaeckel. The latter plays a war-loving soldier who claims that he has just single-handedly killed 16 Japanese soldiers. Jocko doesn't believe him until Jaeckel returns and dumps a dead soldier's body onto Jocko's table. Derek's film is beautifully shot but was heavily edited prior to its 1965 release and suffers because of that. It's worth another look.

Jocko next traveled to South Korea to tackle the starring role of war correspondent Nick Rawlins in *Marine Battleground* (aka *The Marines Who Never Returned*) (1965), set at the outset of the Vietnam War. Jocko's part is largely stationary. He spends the film interviewing Korean nurse Pat Yi at an American medical unit in Vietnam. She recounts through flashback the effect of the Korean conflict and the Battle of Inchon on her life. The parallels to the brewing troubles in Vietnam are obvious and intentional. *Marine Battleground*, directed by Manli Lee, found only a limited release in the States through the independent Manson Distributing. It's another Jocko title that has gone missing in action over the years.

Armed and ready for action in *Walls of Hell* (1964).

Career-wise the Asian films seemed to do little for Jocko other than provide him with a paycheck. However, Jocko continued to be enamored with the Asian way of life. Errol Flynn had owned the 80-acre Navy Island in Jamaica where he moored his yacht, and Marlon Brando purchased a Tahitian island for his own indulgence. John Wayne had recently bought the island of Taborcilla off the coast of Panama. Taking a page out of these superstar's books, Jocko purchased a small island for himself 20 miles off the northern tip of Luzon in the Philippines. On it he intended to build an A-frame house which would become his refuge to get away from it all, suggesting he was beginning to become disillusioned with the Hollywood lifestyle. He still hoped to fulfill his childhood dream of building an 80-foot schooner and sailing the South Seas.

Jocko set about making his own films in the Philippines as star and director, beginning with a western entitled *Blood in the Sky* with Pancho Magalona. Jocko had secured a number of contracts for this film while making *Moro Witch Doctor* and *Walls of Hell*. He intended to follow *Blood in the Sky* with *West of West*, a film he wrote; it would co-star Fernando Poe, Jr., and Jocko's pal Bill Williams. Westerns were surprisingly popular in the islands where they were known as Pinoy Cowboys. They were never released in the U.S., and it's not apparent if *West of West* was ever begun let alone finished. It's rather telling that Jocko wasn't able to get these westerns made stateside. Unfortunately, Jocko's getaway house never made it past the initial stages either. In the summer of 1964 he found himself back in Hollywood looking for work.

Around this time Jocko revealed his political affiliation as a staunch conservative as he stumped around the country for Republican presidential candidate Barry Goldwater, whom Jocko liked because he "shoots from the hip." Jocko's extensive time spent overseas had made him acutely aware of how America's money was being spent abroad, and he felt Goldwater was a solid choice to get the country back on track. Jocko spoke to the Young Conservatives Group at Louisiana's Loyola University in October of 1964. With his standing as a sportsman and antique firearms collector well known, Jocko became further politically involved with a controversial gun bill that was drawing heated debate in Congress.

The Dodd Bill was an effort to outlaw the cheaply made "Saturday Night Special" handguns that often fell into the hands of criminals. Jocko and pal Robert Fuller were all for this. However, National Shooting Sports Foundation (NSSF) executive director Charles Dickey had Jocko and Fuller read the complete bill, which included in the fine print many of the Colt and Smith & Wesson handguns that sportsmen favored. Jocko and Fuller decided to fight the bill at Dickey's urging with the support of the firearm industry. They were sent to Washington, D.C. where they spent a full week doing ads and interviews on radio and television in opposition of the Dodd Bill. They even spoke in front of Congress against Senator Thomas Dodd and Teddy Kennedy and were ultimately successful in beating the bill. "We had a great time," Fuller said of the week in the nation's capital.[1]

The legislation morphed into the Gun Control Act of 1968 signed by President Lyndon B. Johnson. Provisions were made for the importation of firearms for sporting purposes, including hunting and organized competition. Jocko's pro-gun stance couldn't have been a popular move in Hollywood in the wake of the November 1963 Kennedy assassination, but Jocko was firm in his beliefs. He began to take an interest in writing for sports and outdoor magazines to voice his opinions. He also began to pen the beginnings of an autobiography to be entitled *This Will Kill You*, a phrase he heard numerous times throughout his career before undertaking a challenging stunt. No doubt reflecting on his life's many successes drew attention to the career crossroads where he now found himself.

Jocko's former mother-in-law Gladys O'Donnell had rose to prominence in the Republican Party, and by 1966 Jocko was actively campaigning for his friend Ronald Reagan's bid for governor of California. Jocko knew Reagan well from the Screen Actors Guild and liked his chances in government. Interviewed by Hayward, California's *Daily Review*, Jocko said,

> I'm worried about the direction our government is headed, and I hope that my efforts for Reagan will help in some way to restore ethics and morality to government. I know Ronnie's record as President of the Screen Actors Guild, and it's an enviable record. I like the way he handles business matters. I like the way he deports himself, and I like the way he deals with people. Most of all, I like his belief in the rights of individuals. And I think he'll be more for the people of this state and I know he won't take his directions from Lyndon Johnson like the present Governor.

It's possible that Jocko's outspokenness on pro–Republican matters did slight damage to his hiring potential in the heavily Democratic Hollywood. However, Jocko's friend Robert Fuller felt that politics didn't play into Jocko's lack of domestic film work in the mid–1960s, pointing instead to the lingering effects of the jungle sickness. "He never really recovered," Fuller said. "That knocked the crap out of him. He was so sick and worked on top of it. It took him forever to get back to the Jocko I knew."[2]

Another factor affecting Jocko's hiring potential was that in his leading man days he had unnerved any number of executives at Columbia, Universal, CBS, and MGM with his insistence on doing all his own stunts. It's likely that by 1964 he was deemed not worth the risk, the $5,000 a week cost, or the headaches he could create. Why hire Jocko as star when an injury could endanger an entire production? Rory Calhoun and Dale Robertson came with their own stuntmen. If one of those doubles became hurt a replacement could soon be on the set with little production time lost. There is little doubt that the association with Tarzan was now hurting Jocko career-wise, but he remained steadfast that the role had been a great opportunity and he had no regrets.

In the 1980s he told *Favorite Westerns*, "I was over 40 years old when I played Tarzan, and what man that age doesn't want to put on a diaper and go swinging through the trees? I thoroughly enjoyed it. And if I wasn't so fat and too damn old, I'd go back and do it again." He later told *Starlog* magazine, "I loved the role of Tarzan because it was such a distinct challenge. I remember being 40 feet up in a tree, sunburned as hell. And I thought to myself, 'What is a 42-year-old man doing 40 feet up in a tree, getting ready to swing out over a bunch of thorn bushes that if you ever fell into you would be cut to ribbons and damned near killing myself to get up there?' So I laughed and thought, 'Well now, who wouldn't want to play Tarzan?'"

Jocko wasn't the only one of his generation who was struggling career-wise. His contemporaries George Montgomery, Rod Cameron, Scott Brady, John Russell, Lex Barker, Guy Madison, Willard Parker, Rory Calhoun, and Audie Murphy were all having difficulty finding legitimate film work in Hollywood. In hindsight it would have been nice if Jocko could have become one of the stock supporting players in the films of his friend John Wayne. Even a recurring supporting part in a television series would have been a welcome gig. He would have been well-cast as the beleaguered Texas Ranger Captain Parmalee on the television western *Laredo* (1965–1967), a role that Phil Carey played.

There were still a few leading roles that he was well-suited for. Writer John D. Mac-Donald's popular Florida salvage expert Travis McGee could have been a most interesting character for Jocko. MacDonald's books were action-packed and right up Jocko's alley. MacDonald's literary description of McGee had Jocko written all over it: McGee's "knight in slightly tarnished armor" was a 40-something ex-football player who stood 6'4." The much-shorter Rod Taylor ended up playing McGee in the film *Darker Than Amber* (1970), which contained one of the screen's all-time great fight scenes between Taylor and William Smith. Jocko's name has also been mentioned as ideal casting for the secret agent Matt Helm that Dean Martin played broadly in four goofy films at the end of the decade. No doubt a Matt Helm played by Jocko would have been closer to the serious tough guy seen in the Donald Hamilton books.

Jocko still had his popularity with the public to fall back on in the form of personal appearances. One venue where he was always welcome as a celebrity guest star was Corriganville Movie Ranch, which in 1965 was in the last year of its existence as a public tourist attraction. Former movie cowboy Ray Corrigan sold the ranch to Bob Hope that year. In the spring of 1965 Jocko served as host for Long Beach's annual Festival of Fun and Fashion for the United Way and Red Cross. He then journeyed to Hershey, Pennsylvania, to serve as master of ceremonies at the Dreamer Pickup Camper Rally for 1200 camper enthusiasts and their more than 200 truck-mounted trailers. In June it was Hollywood Palladium's Night of Stars celebration for Senator George Murphy. In July, Jocko and Robert Fuller served as judges for the Miss Salute to America beauty pageant.

In August of 1965, Jocko, Maggie, and Princess traveled to Ocala, Florida, for a month-long visit with Jocko serving as the guest of honor at the western theme park Six Gun Territory for the duration of the visit. At the two-year-old park he interacted with the public and participated in the staged gunfights and stunt shows. After scouting the surrounding area, he also began to lay down the groundwork for more permanent Florida roots. He liked not only the climate and the sporting Florida wildlife but also the opportunity to realize some of his ambitious ideas.

Jocko revealed his serious plans for a Marion County stunt school to the local newspaper *The Ocala Star Banner* and began meeting with the Ocala Chamber of Commerce. He envisioned a summer youth camp to be located on 200 acres at the edge of the Ocala National Forest. The $200,000 camp would be the temporary home to 200 boys and girls age 9 to 15. The children would rotate through four two-week sessions each summer at a cost of $100 a week for each child. Jocko would be on the grounds as the head instructor, leading the children in classes devoted to physical fitness, tumbling, swimming, and horseback riding. Assistant instructors would be college students majoring in physical education who would receive credits for their summer work.

Jocko's goal was not only to promote an active lifestyle for the kids but also to train them as prospective stunt people for an industry which he saw was in need of new, well-trained talent. Jocko had nearly unleashed his idea a few years prior in Las Vegas but was concerned about the effect of the desert heat on the youth. The Florida weather would be more accommodating. The grounds would also feature boats, animals, archery, and a rifle range. During the fall and winter months the camp's buildings would serve as a huntsman's lodge for adults. In these months Jocko would return to acting in Hollywood before resuming his summer duties at what he was calling Camp Derringer.

Armchair psychiatrists could theorize that Jocko was replacing his own growing kids with a never-ending stream of fresh Jocko worshipers. Being so far removed from Hollywood, the presence of a genuine cowboy movie and television star would always be a draw to the kids and their parents. Jocko could not only interact with them as a teacher, but also revel in the hero worship of the young hearts and minds. It seemed like a reasonable excursion for Jocko at this point in his life.

While thoroughly exploring the Florida environs to indulge in his favorite pastimes, Jocko became a familiar face at Ocala's Silver Springs Airport. There he made the acquaintance of Jack McGowan, owner of Guided Tours, Inc. McGowan was also a professional videographer and producer of training films. Through their budding friendship the two came up with the idea for a television series to be made locally. The show began to take precedence over the stunt school as Jocko opted to remain in Ocala longer than his paid commitment to Six Gun Territory.

It was decided that Jocko would co-produce and star in *Charter Pilot*, an action-packed weekly series about the adventures of an aircraft pilot. Local singer Billy Sandlin was cast as Jocko's son and actress Carol Wise as his daughter. McGowan and Jocko secured the donation of a Piper Aircraft for the show as well as two six passenger Cherokees. Production of the pilot episode would start as early as the beginning of December. Jocko's plans for Camp Derringer took a backseat as production of the new TV series dominated his Florida days.

Charter Pilot was filmed in December of 1965 and deemed successful enough by its makers to warrant approaching the networks. In March of 1966 the show was put under option by Hollywood Television Productions and was expected to be aired by CBS as a new series in the fall of 1966. Plans were made to film 25 episodes during the summer months. The episodes would take advantage of the local terrain and Jocko's standing as an action star and aircraft pilot. Each episode would feature a name guest star from Hollywood with the majority of the remaining casting done locally.

By the summer of 1966 CBS apparently had a change of mind, and production on the series was cancelled. The practice of pulling the rug out from underneath a new series is commonplace within the industry. Jocko could recall his own experiences with *Yancy Derringer* and *Simon Lash* for quick reference. Perhaps CBS wanted more control over production and opted for a Hollywood-based series instead. Jocko's continued insistence on doing his own stunts and flying likely came into play as well. The aborted series plans were no doubt a blow to Jocko's psyche as well as his bankbook. He hadn't had an acting gig paid for by someone else for nearly a year. Jocko's ambitious and costly Camp Derringer idea was jettisoned with the death of *Charter Pilot*. He returned to California and once again set about finding acting work, but the horizons seemed as bleak as the year before. For the second time in less than 10 years, the family lost the comfort of their home and had many of their items repossessed. The best horseman in Hollywood suddenly didn't have a horse.

Back in Hollywood in 1966, Jocko tried to get another TV pilot for a western aimed at kids on the air but the project fizzled. Screenwriter Jack Lewis had plans to make a film starring Jocko, but that never materialized. Jocko did film a pair of Kool Cigarette spots to rival the famous Marlboro Man ads, but that was not a lasting or well-known association. He then did a one-minute commercial for RCA Victor where he raced a quarter-horse with a camera strapped to his chest during an exhibition race at Ruidoso Downs in New Mexico.

Jocko rode at full gallop on a straightaway to get close-ups of the jockeys and horses in action. Halfway through the race, Jocko pulled out of the middle of the pack and surged ahead to win.

Although it was needed work and potentially profitable, the commercials did nothing to get his film career back on track. Hollywood columnist Hedda Hopper, godmother to Jocko's children and always ready to mention Jocko in her syndicated column, passed away in early 1966, and Jocko's presence in fan magazines completely vanished. *Range Rider* finally went out of syndication and was locked in film vaults for the next 30 years. The only film of Jocko's that was still in theaters was *Runaway Girl*, and that was regrettably showing up most often in nudie markets with spliced-in footage of nude girls showering, dancing, and cat-fighting in a swimming pool. Jocko couldn't have been happy about this development. In a cutthroat business known for the question "What have you done lately?" Jocko hadn't done anything other than campaign for the staunch conservative Ronald Reagan.

Part of the problem was that Jocko had become a living legend, and no doubt with age was bordering on becoming a caricature. He was, after all, a middle-aged man still expected not only by audiences but also by himself to perform great athletic feats on a larger-than-life pedestal. This was the man who swung around a rope in his backyard, took running dives off balconies into swimming pools, and fired off blanks in the home of publicist Jack Mullen. However, with age and inactivity Jocko's standing as the best stuntman in Hollywood was no longer valid. A daring man named Hal Needham was the new top dog in the stunt pack, with Loren Janes, Ronnie Rondell, and Dean Smith nipping at his heels.

The effect that drink was having on Jocko at this point also has to be taken into consideration. Jocko was a bourbon and water man, or took his whiskey neat with a beer back. While he never missed work or was a drunk by outward appearances, he had been imbibing alcohol regularly now for a number of years. By Jocko's own admission to friends Gene Ryals and Jack Lewis, he could put it away. Intake of such magnitude will ultimately catch up with anyone, even a Jocko Mahoney or an Errol Flynn. Cameraman Richard Kline, who worked on the Durango Kid films, thought Jocko was a terrific guy but commented to *Western Clippings* that Jocko "abused himself pretty well."

Jocko liked to say that his oft-performed fight routines in the days of *Range Rider* and *Yancy Derringer* were great for him psychologically because he was able to work out all of his aggressions in that manner. It was perfect therapy. After throwing punches all day, there was nothing left to be upset about. His exercise obsession burned off whatever other negative energy there may have been. However, with no current fight scene outlet and a backing-off on the exercise routine due to his health concerns, Jocko's pent-up aggressions no doubt began to manifest themselves in his personal character. This was magnified by his increased down-time, consumption of drink, and his increasing bitterness over the raw deal he felt he was getting from Hollywood casting directors and producers. He was a lifelong workaholic suddenly without work. The brass ring he had worked so hard to attain was slipping from his grasp.

In the summer of 1966 Jocko's career did get a boost from ... Tarzan. Sy Weintraub, the producer of the new *Tarzan* television series being shot in Brazil, called with an offer for Jocko to guest star in an episode. Jocko readily agreed. He casually asked who the new Tarzan was and got a big laugh out of the fact it was Ron Ely, his old buddy who used to delight in razzing him about being the ape man while the two made *Once Before I Die* in the Philippines. Jocko commented that he would have done the series for free to get a chance to tease Ely. Upon Jocko's arrival in Brazil, Ely initially sought to avoid Jocko as much as possible. The new Tarzan finally accepted that Jocko had him dead to rights and the two had a great time together. Ely has said that Jocko was his favorite guest star.

All was not well with the new Tarzan show. The series was running desperately behind schedule due mainly to torrential rains. In over five months of shooting through the spring and summer, the production crew managed to complete only five episodes for the fall 1966 season. They had some great footage though, particularly of Ely at the magnificent Iguazu Falls. Ely was a lanky Tarzan in the tradition of Jocko, who played a game warden in the series second aired episode "The Ultimate Weapon." Jocko's first scene sees him shot in the back by an elephant poacher. He spends the remainder of the episode recovering in a bed or walking around in a bathrobe while trying to avoid the wrath of the son of the now-dead poacher. It's largely an undemanding role, but one that Jocko puts some realistic sweat and grimaces into.

Jocko has several shirtless scenes in the episode, and it is to his credit that he stands next to the current Tarzan without shame. His shoulders remain broad; however, the muscles that Jocko sported only four years earlier while playing Tarzan have largely disappeared. Granted, his character is recovering from a horrendous gunshot wound, but it is easy to see how much his own real-life portrayal of the ape man took out of him. His face especially is beginning to show the strain of age. The tough conditions on cast and crew in Brazil weren't easy on anyone, but Jocko had experience and expertise in such matters. He never was the kind of actor who looked comfortable being confined to a cushy studio setting anyway. Jocko was all for new experiences, and the Brazil location and nearby city of Rio were that and more.

With Jocko's episode completed, the production company moved to Mexico to complete the rest of the first season. Jocko was asked to make another episode as a different character, this time a lead heavy. This role Jocko could sink his teeth into. The two-part episode "The Deadly Silence" is one of the best of the series. Jocko took special delight in playing a nasty villain known only as the Colonel, a whip-wielding veteran of two wars who plans to build his own empire in the jungle. He raises Tarzan's ire when he burns native villages to the ground. The two are at one another's throats from the beginning of the episode, with Jocko boasting he knows "a thousand ways to kill a man." He attempts to intimidate Tarzan by telling a tale of killing a giant sumo wrestler with only two fingers, but Tarzan is unfazed. The jungle lord points out that the Colonel now hides behind his whip. Jocko laughs and says the whip is only a toy that amuses him. The audience doesn't have to wait long for the two to engage in the first of their big fights.

Woody Strode shows up as Jocko's second-in-command, and the two throw grenades into a pond that causes a submerged Tarzan to become temporarily deaf. Jocko is soon at Strode's throat, and the two have a giant three-minute fight that manages to surpass their battle in *Tarzan's Three Challenges* when Jocko was near death with fever. In 1970 the two-part endeavor was released theatrically as *Tarzan's Deadly Silence*, and it's a fine showcase for Jocko. He excelled at the required villainy and this should have opened up a new phase of his career as a lead villain on TV fare.

Strode's son Kalai accompanied his father on the shoot and recalls meeting Jocko: "I only met Jock once…. In Mexico City Jock seemed fairly subdued. He spoke about his daughter who was doing *The Flying Nun* and seemed very proud of her. My father and Jock didn't hit the town after work. They didn't keep in touch much, as far as I know."[3]

Sensing the chance for great publicity, Weintraub arranged for a Tarzan reunion at Churubusco Studios in Mexico to coincide with the first season's premier episode in September 1966. Weintraub hoped to get ten Tarzans but managed only Ely, Jocko, Johnny Weissmuller, and Jim Pierce, a former All-American center for Indiana University's football squad who played Tarzan back in 1926. The reunion garnered plenty of national press, with the four shirtless Tarzan climbing onto a tree and posing with vines in hand. A crew-cut Jocko showed up for the event with a huge bruise on his forehead, the apparent result of filming his fight scene with Ely.

The TV series guest shot offer was actually two-fold. The producers were hoping that Jocko could serve as an unofficial mentor and stunt coordinator to Ely as well, teaching him the tricks of the jungle such as swinging on vines and diving off cliffs. The athletic Ely was determined to do all his own Tarzan stunts and was spending a significant portion of production time on the mend for various injuries. Ely had garnered a reputation for being unable to hold back in fight scenes, unintentionally clobbering more than one opponent. The bruise on Jocko's head attested to this. Jocko was expected to school Ely in the proper way to film screen fights, which he was glad to do.

Jocko discussed his Ely fight scenes with David Rothel in *Opened Time Capsules*: "Ron

Taking a fall for Ron Ely on the TV series *Tarzan* (1966).

did all his own action, and I did all my own action, so we loved to get together and beat the hell out of each other. I loved playing baddies, which I always did with Ron. You get rid of all your aggressions; you get to hit him, spit on him, get to do all the things a dirty little kid would do, and then you get paid for it."

Jocko guest starred in the *Tarzan* series one more time in the first season. He was another bad guy in the episode "Mask of Rona," a mercenary in the employ of an eccentric art collector. Jocko sports a white beard for this character, giving three totally different looks to his trio of guest appearances. The highlight of the episode is another fight with Ely. This time the two fall off a boat into a river and struggle beneath the surface while wrapped in a rope. It's an extremely well-done fight and appears to be quite dangerous. This is no studio tank but a real river, and the men are submerged at least ten feet at times. Jocko is wearing clothes and heavy boots, which had to make it more difficult for him to fight. Both men repeatedly try rising to the surface only to have the other one pull him back down. Ely finally breaks the water's surface alive. The great fight lasts a minute and a half underwater. "Mask of Rona" aired in the winter of 1967.

The two Tarzans turned out to be real-life heroes when Diana Ross and the Supremes were guest stars in the 1968 episode "The Convert." Ross and her fellow singers Mary Wilson and Cindy Birdsong were playing nuns and were in a canoe that tipped over. The girls immediately had trouble in the river wearing their heavy habits and began to sink. Ely quickly dove in and pulled up one girl. Jocko was on the set that day, likely working as the show's stunt coordinator. He dove in from the dock and helped Ely rescue the others. The event could have been a publicist's dream, but its mention was never acknowledged until some 30 years later when Ely recalled it in an interview. For Tarzans like Ely and Jocko, rescuing a trio of pop singers was all in a day's work.

Despite its popularity the Tarzan series folded by 1968 due to the physical toll it had taken on its star. Ely discussed the rigors of the filming with the magazine *Fighting Stars*: "It was the challenge of my physical career. Just managing to stay alive and survive was a challenge. 'Bring 'em back alive' was the call that went up when we'd leave for location. And that didn't refer to the wild animals, it referred to the actors ... I couldn't do any more, it was just too difficult a show to do. We did 64 shows or something like that and that really stretched us to the limit of our capacity—all of us. It was like shooting a major motion picture for every episode because there was a lot of action in it with wild animals and all sorts of things that made it uncontrollable and difficult to shoot. As a result, it wasn't the standard form of television in any regard."

Jocko made two appearances on the popular TV series *Batman* for producer Howie Horwitz. On the campy hit, he was a henchman in the 1966 two-part episode "The Purrfect Crime" and "Better Luck Next Time." He portrayed the simple-minded Leo, muscle for Julie Newmar's Catwoman. Jocko has some fun with the role and gets to take part in some robust action as he engages Batman and Robin in fisticuffs. Jocko even does one of his patented leaps, which Batman (Adam West) evades. In his 1968 appearance, "I'll Be a Mummy's Uncle," he played a mining foreman in the employ of Victor Buono's villain King Tut. This role is nothing more than a cameo, and Jocko plays it broadly. The *Batman* roles did little to provide his career with any type of boost.

Jocko guest starred on a 1967 episode of the TV western *Daniel Boone* opposite 6'5" Fess Parker, playing a good guy in the episode "Secret Code." Jocko portrays a baker friend of Boone who helps him fight the British. It's a bit odd to see someone standing over Jocko, but he and Fess Parker play off one another nicely. Jocko even gets to spring into action to bail Parker out of a jam in the final reel. It's the kind of role that could have become a recurring one in the popular series. However, Jocko never again appeared on the show despite the series running a couple more seasons.

The motorcycle genre was a brand new field, and Jocko became attached to an early entry entitled *The Glory Stompers* (originally *The Fate Race*) (1967). Joel McCrea's son Jody was the star with Dennis Hopper playing the crazed bad guy. Jocko was on hand to play an older cyclist named Smiley, the mentor of young McCrea, and he arrives to help save the day in the climax. Jocko was enticed to make the drive-in–targeted film by the offer of ten percent of the gross. The opening film of the biker genre, *The Wild Angels* (1966), was in the midst of making filmmaker Roger Corman a ton of money. Jocko realized a backend deal lending his participation into the product could amount to a hefty payday in his case. However, that was not meant to be.

As so often happens in the case of low-budget films, the $100,000 budgeted *Glory Stompers* ran out of money in mid-production. McCrea and Hopper begged Jocko to give up his end of the production money so the film could be finished. For the sake of finishing the movie, Jocko agreed to forego his 10 percent deal. The movie was finished and ultimately released, becoming notable for Hopper's charismatic performance and an early appearance by muscular villain and real-life tough guy Robert Tessier. The crude movie did robust business (in the neighborhood of $6 million) and made somebody a lot of money. That somebody was not named Jocko Mahoney.

The Los Angeles Times wrote upon the movie's release, "Dennis Hopper and Jock Mahoney perform well." Outside of that praise, however, most of the reviews of the exploitative film were overwhelmingly negative. One reviewer noted that Jocko was apparently playing the oldest biker in the world. That wasn't a fair shot at Jocko as the original outlaw motorcyclists were indeed World War II vets exactly like Jocko. Despite the pair of ridiculous sunglasses he hides behind, Jocko was convincing in his grizzled portrayal and got to putt around on an iron horse, an enjoyable activity for the former stuntman.

Interestingly, *The Glory Stompers* was originally written as a western with Jocko's character an old gunfighter. The story was drastically updated to accommodate the burgeoning cycle field. In hindsight Jocko realized he should have stuck to his guns in regard to the money deal. The movie offered him a chance to have fun riding motorcycles for the camera and little else. He had few other memories of the film outside of the many funny cigarettes Hopper was constantly smoking. Jocko took to calling him "Grass" Hopper.

According to an Apacheland Movie Studio press release Jocko was set to headline another action-packed western TV series for the fall 1967 TV season. In April he made a weekend autograph signing appearance at Apacheland outside of Phoenix to promote the new show. The trip also gave him the opportunity to visit his old friend Charlie Aldrich, the former ranch foreman and entertainment organizer at Corriganville. Jocko huddled with the Apacheland executives to discuss shooting a feature film at the location in the near future. Neither the TV series nor the Apacheland movie were heard from again.

There was a bit of negative publicity, no doubt trivial in the land of Hollywood, concerning a summer 1967 charity appearance Jocko made at Apacheland for the United Cerebral Palsy Association. Jocko, Robert Fuller, and Doug McClure headlined the two-day western-themed show, along with approximately 20 other guests from Hollywood. Local factions complained in the *Arizona Republic* that the event turned into a "drunken shambles" and leveled charges at the organizers that they were promoting their own interests in the form of the film location. There were also complaints about $2,700 in funds that were spent inappropriately on gifts of Winchester Rifles and whiskey for Jocko, Fuller, and McClure, who were otherwise unpaid for the event. Jocko did leave his boot imprint in concrete at the movie studio.

On the personal front, Jocko and Margaret Field's marriage had run its course. They were divorced in 1968 after 15 years of marriage. Maggie commented on an *A&E Biography* about Sally Field that Jocko could be a very erratic husband. At times he would be sweet and loving, at other times mean and ugly. She grew to feel that there was no pleasing him. No doubt the troubles they were having with the children growing up as well as Jocko's health scare and alcohol-clouded judgment during this period put a tremendous strain on the union. The last three years of the marriage had seen them financially upended as Jocko literally attempted to relocate them around the world while maintaining the upkeep and housing of horses, boats, and aircraft on a rapidly diminishing income.

Later that year Jocko wed his third wife, actress Autumn Russell, a 1950s model and film starlet who had made minor appearances in *Sweet Smell of Success* (1957) and *Spartacus* (1960). Once tapped by Paramount Studios as the next Carole Lombard, her biggest role was the female lead in the low-budget cult film *Zombies of Mora Tau* (1957). She was perhaps best known as NBC's "Color Test Girl." The Oklahoma-born Russell's real name was Patricia Rice. She had wed Charles Russell in the early 1950s and put raising their three children ahead of advancing her own career. The beautiful Autumn O'Mahoney remained with Jocko until his death some 20 years later.

Jocko's acting career had reached such an impasse that he began to look for another way to earn a living. He temporarily found that selling boats at Newport Beach, a vocation that kept him in the fresh sea air near his pal John Wayne. Jocko was commonly seen wearing faded Levis and a battered commodore's cap during this period. He still managed to train stuntmen and aspiring actors in how to do their own fight scenes at the Film Industry Workshop, most notably Chad Everett, James Brolin, Sam Elliott, and Lloyd Haynes. He also assisted his old friend Jay Silverheels at the Indian Actors Workshop, teaching Native American actors and stuntmen such as Robert Potter the finer points of the film business at the old Spahn Movie Ranch.[4]

Jocko still made the occasional personal appearance. He served as grand marshal for the 1967 International Outdoor Archery Championship at Brookside Park in Pasadena and took part in the inaugural Grand National Quail Hunt in Oklahoma. Jocko wrote an article about the latter event in his friend Jack Lewis' magazine *Gun World*. In June of 1968 Jocko was the guest of honor at Ruidoso Downs, where he was a familiar horse race figure for the past decade. Jocko also traveled to Guaymas, Mexico, to make a short advertisement for the opening of a plush resort on the Sea of Cortez.

Jocko did a cameo in the 20th Century–Fox western *Bandolero!* (1968) for director Andrew V. McLaglen. The entertaining film stars stalwarts Jimmy Stewart, Dean Martin, and George Kennedy and holds up well. Jocko, playing the husband of Raquel Welch, is gunned down during a bank robbery in the film's opening minutes shot in Brackettville, Texas. It's a blink-and-you-miss-him one-line part and could have been played by nearly anyone, although Jocko was paid $5,000 for his one week's work on the film. It's another curious appearance for the man who was top-lining MGM films only five years prior. (Additional footage of Jocko didn't make it into the final print.) It did suggest that Jocko might have made similar token appearances in McLaglen's subsequent John Wayne films *Hellfighters* (1968), *The Undefeated* (1969), *Chisum* (1970), and *Big Jake* (1971), which no doubt would have endeared him to the huge Wayne fan base over the years. Jocko, however, could see the writing on the wall and began to formulate a new plan.

In the meantime, he did some stunt driving on the Disney classic *The Love Bug* (1968). It was no doubt fun for Jocko to keep the juices flowing, but it was once again indicative of where his career was at. He might have been able to move into further jobs as a stunt coordinator, but there was a crackdown on television violence in 1968 that put many stuntmen out of work for the next two years. As it was, the ambitious young Turks in the industry were clashing with the old guard of the Stuntmen's Association, breaking away to form a new group called Stunts Unlimited that created temporary bad blood as they all fought to get what few stunt jobs were out there. It was an ugly scene and Jocko did not want to be a part of it.

Jocko's own acting career continued to flounder, with the theatrical agency Goldstone-Tobias doing little to land him legitimate work as they concentrated on the rising careers of other talent such as Steve McQueen and Ryan O'Neal. In the spring of 1968 Jocko was

Jocko gunned down in front of Raquel Welch in the opening reel of *Bandolero!* (1968).

announced to co-star with Scott Brady, Melody Patterson, and Maray Ayres in a film titled *Portrait of Violence* for producer Maurice Smith, the man behind *The Glory Stompers*. The project became the motorcycle movie *Cycle Savages* (1969) with Bruce Dern playing one of his nuttier creeps, out to get artist Chris Robinson for sketching him. Jocko is nowhere to be found in the finished film. He likely dropped out prior to filming due to the gratuitous violence and sleaze that dominate the drive-in film. Veteran actor Steve Brodie appears unbilled as Brady's detective partner, the role Jocko was likely tabbed for.

Jocko was in the midst of turning 50 years old and his days of being a leading man were done. In the eyes of casting directors he was either a cowboy relic of the *Range Rider* era or a past-his-prime Tarzan. Most of the public now referred to him as the stepfather of Sally Field, the star of *Gidget* and the gimmick TV show *The Flying Nun*. His Hollywood life consisted of daily stressors and bad influences. What income he was generating was being divided now by another ex-wife. Jocko had reached that familiar crossroads in life yet again. The old Irish restlessness returned, and Jocko set his mind upon doing something completely different from acting. He was done with Hollywood for the time being. As so often happened, whenever Jocko jumped, he managed to land on his feet.

11

The Vagabond

Jocko liked to consider life a series of opportunities either taken or not taken. When he decided to quit acting, an interesting vocation loomed on his immediate horizon. There was a solid offer to take on a position at a Colorado dude ranch, where Jocko's presence and stature in the world of cinematic cowboys would no doubt lure in potential customers. Other past-their-prime athlete-actors had already or would be taking similar positions. Jocko's friend Buster Crabbe, a former Olympic champion swimmer and screen Tarzan who shared Jocko's birthday, became the director of water activities at the Concord Hotel in the Adirondacks. Johnny Weissmuller became a greeter at Caesar's Palace in Las Vegas. So, Jocko decided to enter the leisure industry. In addition to a steady paycheck, it was a chance for him to get away from everything with his new wife and once again enjoy nature.

From 1968 to 1970 Jocko served as the general manager and public relations director at the Vickers Lodge, a working dude ranch in Lake City, Colorado. He handled daily operations and promotions for the business. Jocko was no doubt in his element among the horses and livestock, and his engaging smile and personality worked well with the clientele. At Lake City, a beautiful area situated in the San Juan Mountains of Southwestern Colorado near Lake San Cristobal, there was plenty of opportunity for hunting, fishing, hiking, skiing, and riding among the mountain peaks, streams, and clear blue skies. The community consisted of only a few hundred people, which provided a nice change of pace for Jocko from the hustle and bustle of Hollywood. He became a member of the Colorado Guide and Outfitters Association and even served as the president of the Lake City community's chamber of commerce.

During this time Jocko managed to return to Davenport, Iowa, for his 30-year class reunion and reconnect with old school friends. Davenport held a Jock Mahoney Day to honor their favorite son. He enjoyed driving around his old haunts and reminiscing about his youth. He'd come a long way since then. His face was known around the world, but he'd learned how fleeting fame can be. Although Jocko enjoyed Colorado, he soon began to look for other opportunities that might appeal to him—in particular, an opportunity that removed him from the cold winters that caused his stunt-battered bones to ache. He longed to get back to the Pacific Ocean.

He found what he was looking for in Hawaii. In 1970 Jocko and Autumn moved to Honolulu, on the island of Oahu. There Jocko worked for well over a year as the vice-president and general manager of Paradise Park, a resort located near the scenic Manoa Falls. Jocko oversaw all functions in relation to the daily operation of the largest collection of

Citicene parrots in the United States. Among the rare birds on the preserve were a black palm cockatoo and blue and gold macaws. Jocko was also in charge of a 250-seat restaurant, 15 acres of tropical flora, a gift shop, and a fleet of trams and buses. Paradise Park (now defunct) was at the time a popular tourist attraction, and the novelty of having Tarzan among the staff was no doubt enticing to the tourists. Jocko also became a member of the Hawaii Visitors Bureau Special Events Committee.

Hawaii gave Jocko and Autumn plenty of opportunity to bask in the sunshine and enjoy the local shows and luaus. There was time spent at the beach and in the Pacific Ocean swimming, snorkeling, scuba diving, sailing, and sport fishing. There was one other activity going on in Hawaii at the time that piqued Jocko's interest: production of the highly rated TV crime series *Hawaii Five-O*. Jocko touched base with the filmmakers, led by the influential star Jack Lord, and brought an episode into the park. In January of 1971 he joined *Five-O* co-star James MacArthur and stuntman Beau Van Den Ecker as members of the Board of Directors for a local video production unit named Hawaiian Video Industries. Conceived to make educational films, the firm had a full studio center with sound stages, cutting rooms, and mobile equipment. The privately financed company was the city of Honolulu's first video production outfit.

Jocko was soon in line for a guest starring shot on the *Five-O* series. In the two-part episode "The Grandstand Play," aired in the spring of 1971, Jocko played former major league baseball player Coley Bennett, now manager of the minor league team the Islanders. Pernell Roberts is the main guest star, a former Jocko teammate and big league star who has returned to the minors thinking it might be easier to care for his simple-minded son away from the mainland. However, the boy is witness to a murder at the ballpark, and Roberts' sense of protectiveness is soon hindering Lord's investigation. Jocko appears in a number of scenes, in baseball uniform no less, but never manages to become a catalyst to the action. He's usually there to fill in Roberts' history for Lord. Still, it was a chance for Jocko to get back in front of the cameras and sink his teeth into a character part, however small.

The experience got Jocko's creative juices flowing, and he began to make plans to return to the States and take on this new arc of his acting career. Before that happened, Jocko went back stateside for three TV talk show appearances. The first was a TV reunion of the surviving Tarzans on *The Mike Douglas Show* with Johnny Weissmuller, Buster Crabbe, Gordon Scott, Jim Pierce, and Denny Miller. In March of 1971 Jocko appeared with Weissmuller, Crabbe, Pierce, Ron Ely, and Lex Barker for a Tarzan segment on *The Merv Griffin Show*. In July of 1971 he returned as a guest on *The Merv Griffin Show* in a special entitled "The World of the Athlete" that also featured sports figures such as football player Fred Williamson.

To Jocko's credit, even though the Tarzan role might have hampered his acting career, he always embraced the part and enjoyed engaging Tarzan fans and interacting with his fellow actors. The Tarzans reunited the following year in July of 1972 at the Westercon Science Fiction convention in Long Beach. That same week they appeared on *The Tonight Show* with Johnny Carson to promote the show. Jocko and Weissmuller stirred things up at the Edgewater Hyatt Hotel bar with Weissmuller breaking out his signature Tarzan yell. No doubt these two stalwarts of the jungle left plenty of admirers in their spirited wake.

In late 1971 Jocko and Autumn moved back to California so that Jocko could resume his acting career. Initially they lived with Ron Ely. Like Jocko, Ely had struggled to find acting work in Hollywood upon hanging up his loincloth. The only initial offers were low-budget films in Europe, although Ely was on the cusp of landing the big screen role of Doc Savage. When placing calls to the homestead, Jocko would on occasion reach Ely's answering service. When asked to leave a message, Jocko would jokingly say, "This is the real Tarzan speaking." Jocko and Autumn eventually moved into an apartment of their own. Fifty-two-year-old Jocko kept himself fit and strong by walking up two flights of stairs on his hands every time he arrived home.[1]

In November of 1971 Jocko and Autumn attended the Annual Stuntman's Ball at the Hollywood Palladium put on by the Stuntmen's Association. Jocko appeared in the Studio City Christmas Parade and began to reconnect with past Hollywood acquaintances. He formed the B.S. and Grub Club with Jack Iversen, Slim Pickens, and stuntman Big Al Fleming specifically for old cowboy actors to reminisce about the good old days over weekly breakfasts. They routinely met on Saturday mornings at the Smokehouse Café in Sherman Oaks, only a few blocks from where Jocko lived. The informal group eventually grew in number and moved to the Coral Café in Burbank. Jocko had befriended Fleming back in 1965 during a guest appearance at the Corriganville Movie Ranch.[2]

Another hangout was the Backstage Lounge, a bar near the old Republic Studios lot that had become CBS Studio Center. The Backstage was a favorite watering hole for stuntmen. The cowboy cast and crew of shows such as *The Big Valley, The Wild Wild West,* and *Gunsmoke* could often be found wetting their whistles. Jocko's old pal Charles Horvath tended bar there, and the stuntmen clientele such as Dick Durock, Dar Robinson, Jesse Wayne, and Wild Bill Mock were known to break into fake fights to impress outsiders. In addition to Jocko and the stuntmen, character actors Charlie McGraw and John Mitchum were regulars.

In 1972 Jocko and Robert Fuller made guest appearances for stuntman Rick Arnold at the Kern County Fish and Game Protective Association's annual barbecue in Bakersfield, California, and at a rodeo in Yuma, Arizona, that benefitted youth summer sport leagues. Part of Jocko and Fuller's contribution involved partaking in donkey softball games. Fuller recalled the humor involved in the men hitting a softball with a bat, then jumping on the back of a donkey while trying to get it to move to first base. If the donkey was too stubborn to move, a trainer was there to pop it with a hot shot at which point it would either take off or buck. "Jocko and I spent a lot of time on our backs," Fuller said. "Jocko was so tall that one time he just stood up and walked out from underneath the donkey."[3]

In 1972 Jocko served as a judge for the World Fast Draw Matches, meeting up with his old friend Jim Martin, the single action gunsmith and California Fast Draw and World Fancy Gun Handling Champion. Jocko would judge many gunfight competitions in the ensuing years. In September of 1972 he journeyed to Window Rock, Arizona, for the Navajo Tribal Fair. He participated in the fair with fellow screen cowboys John Wayne and Rory Calhoun. Jocko wasn't afraid to stand up for his beliefs, politically lending his presence to the Republican Party for the 1972 election campaign trail for the Richard Nixon Presidency. Early 1973 saw Jocko and Terry Wilson headline a stuntman's fundraising event with John Hagner in Escondido, California.

Jocko and Dave Sharpe were instrumental in helping Hagner get the Hollywood Stuntman's Hall of Fame off the ground. Jocko, one of Hagner's first inductees, served as the organization's vice-president. He helped bring such Hollywood heavyweights as John Wayne, Charlton Heston, Randolph Scott, and Chuck Connors onto the Advisory Board. Jocko also designed the Dusty Award, which was like a stuntman's Oscar. The faceless statue held a can of film in one hand and a stunt bag in the other. Initially Hagner envisioned a stunt-themed amusement park accompanying his Hall of Fame but that never came to pass. Hagner's museum moved often throughout many states but remained a functioning entity for decades. During this period Jocko lived near silent movie stuntman Richard Talmadge (the double for Douglas Fairbanks) and attempted to document the pioneering legend's life story for posterity.

Jocko resumed helping actor Tony Miller and his wife Patricia George at the Film Industry Workshop in Studio City, teaching young actors and directors the importance of putting safety first. He also showed how to incorporate martial arts successfully for the film cameras. Jocko was not a karate black belt, but he had basic skill sets in the martial arts and knew what worked well for the camera. He had been teaching aspiring actors and stunt-men for as far back as one could remember. Jocko trained more than 100 aspiring actors through the workshop, with producers and directors calling him for his appraisal on would-be hires. During this period, Jocko hosted an industry-aimed training film for actors and stuntmen detailing preparation and safety standards. Mention was made of Jocko's safety film in *The Filmmakers Newsletter*.

Assisting Jocko at the Film Industry Workshop's Physical Action Lab was stuntman Clarke Lindsley, who recalled that Jocko liked to make the classes fun as well as informative. For their very first class they devised a surprise stunt for the students during a demonstration on how to jerk a prone person from the floor to his feet. Jocko jerked Lindsley with such force that the stuntman flew over the set's wall to a secretly concealed stunt pad on the opposite side. The stunt drew a large gasp from the shocked students and a mighty laugh from Jocko. "Jock's laugh was the most infectious thing in captivity," Lindsley said. "Jock was one of the greatest people and friend that I had the privilege to know."[4]

In May of 1973 the non-profit Film Industry Workshop put on a movie studio carnival at CBS Studio Center for the CBS affiliates. A number of celebrities (including Charlton Heston, Glenn Ford, Chad Everett, John Russell, and Rod Taylor) showed up for the festivities as Jocko and a group of stuntmen including Clarke Lindsley staged horse falls, gunfights, and motorcycle-riding through the western street that normally served as the set for the long-running TV series *Gunsmoke*. All proceeds went toward scholarships for the workshop. Clarke Lindsley remembered the CBS affiliates got a big kick out of meeting Jocko.

Since Jocko's heyday, the hierarchy in Hollywood had changed considerably due to the success of Peter Fonda and Dennis Hopper's biker film *Easy Rider* (1969), which ironically may not have been possible had it not been for *The Glory Stompers* coming before it. The power of the studios yielded to independent productions, and the days of actors being under studio contracts were coming to an end. Television remained a productive machine, but the shooting pace was fast and the pay generally minuscule compared to what Jocko had once earned on films. The days of the western dominating the airwaves had vanished. Cop shows were the new thing, and few studios turned them out like Universal. Character actors of the day generally earned a living going from show to show during a TV season. If they had a built-in familiarity with TV audiences from success of days gone by, then it was likely they would get more work. A role could be attained, filmed, and on the air in a matter of weeks with immediate feedback. It was to this new climate that Jocko returned from paradise.

Jocko landed a bad guy part on George Peppard's superior mystery TV series *Banacek*, in an episode about a kidnapped football player entitled "Let's Hear It for a Living Legend." Jocko lent his forceful presence to one scene near the episode's conclusion, tussling with Peppard over a shotgun. Stuntman Hal Needham played Jocko's cohort in crime. Jocko's good in the role, but it's a small part that he likely landed due to his friendship with producer Howie Horwitz. It aired in the fall of 1972.

Jocko and writer pal Jack Lewis encountered Dave Sharpe on the Universal lot during this period. Jocko asked the 62-year-old Sharpe if it was true he could still do a standing back-flip and land on his feet. Sharpe did just that and replied without missing a beat there was no truth to the rumor at all. It was a routine Jocko and Sharpe had no doubt been doing for years.

Jocko made minor guest appearances on episodes of *Emergency* and *The Streets of San Francisco* from 1972 to 1974. The latter show's episode "Blockade" was indicative of how far Jocko needed to go to get back into the mainstream. Jocko was not included among the episode's guest stars that are audibly announced in the opening credits. Instead he shows up with low nondescript billing in the final credits. It's quite a comedown for a man who had his own TV series and once graced the cover of *TV Guide*.

The *Streets* role itself is a one-scene cameo, with Jocko playing the grieving father of a daughter slain by vicious hoodlum Don Stroud. Acting opposite series star Karl Malden, Jocko quietly vows to avenge his daughter's death if he gets his hands on her murderer. The scene is effective but comes across as filler. It doesn't advance the plot, and Jocko never figures into the story again. The director Virgil Vogel had worked with Jocko on *The Land Unknown* and might have included the part as a way to get Jocko back into the public eye. Future *Charlie's Angels* star Cheryl Ladd plays Jocko's daughter using her maiden name Cheryl Jean Stopplemoor.

It's probably somewhat prophetic that on *Emergency* Jocko was repeatedly cast as the victim of a medical event. In the January 1972 episode "Mascot" he's an actor who has a heart attack during a boozy party where all the guests believe he is faking. It's a short part in which Jocko looks effectively pasty and diaphoretic. In the March 1973 episode "Boot" he plays an athletic man described as a tower of strength. He jogs every morning with his son and regularly plays handball and tennis. However, he self-medicates an old football injury by popping aspirin which contraindicates the blood thinner he is on. He develops internal bleeding and lands on his back in Rampart Hospital as a patient of Robert Fuller. Although he was warned not to take aspirin by his doctor, Jocko continued to do so in order to keep up with his exercise. It's the kind of character that could be described as being very close to home for Jocko.

Outside of episodic television, Jocko played a racist cop alongside Aldo Ray in the low-budget black action film *The Bad Bunch* (1973). The Greydon Clark movie was filmed under the working title *Tom* and at one point was even known by the highly volatile title *Nigger Lover*, a phrase uttered by Jocko in the film. It may be hard to fathom how Jocko ended up in this bare-bones film other than the fact that the writer, director, and star Clark was a fan of *Range Rider* when he was a kid. In reality the multi-talented Clark had a friend who knew Aldo Ray, the thick-necked 1950s leading man who had fallen on hard times due to an alcohol problem. When Ray came on board it nevertheless lent the film a veneer of professionalism. Clark began submitting the script to various agents to find a name actor to complement Ray. Most turned the part down either due to the subject matter or the film's low budget. Clark received a maybe from Jocko's agent and sent him the script. In an effort to kick start his acting career after returning from Hawaii, Jocko agreed to take the part despite reservations about the subject matter.

Greydon Clark commented: "I met with Jock the week before we began filming. He was full of questions, most of which involved the racist dialogue in the film. We agreed that if we were going to make an explosive film about race in America we should go all the way and make it as real as possible. Jock was very helpful on the set, especially with the stunts. He was a legendary stuntman. I learned a great deal about stunts from him."[5]

Despite an earnest attempt to address racial tensions and the effect Vietnam has on the homeland, the film contains harsh language and an abundance of full frontal nudity for the exploitation crowd. Due to the high cost of film and the unit's overall lack of it, the first take was a print on virtually every scene. The movie is actually far better than it should be in light of this. Clark recalled on the film's DVD commentary that both Aldo Ray and Jocko were professional and great to work with. They stuck to the script and nailed their dialogue despite the rushed nature of the production. It had to be interesting for the old pros. They only worked a couple of days on the film, but make a memorably nasty team.

Filmed in the fall of 1972 the entire movie was completed in two weeks time for only $15,000. Many of the location shots in Watts were done with a hidden camera as the production couldn't afford to get the proper filming permits. During the scene in the alley where Jocko and Ray confront Tom Johnigarn, the skeleton crew were stopped by a pair of motorcycle cops who demanded to see a valid permit. Clark said they were making a student film and quickly finished the shots of Jocko beating up Johnigarn with brass knuckles before the police returned. There were no stuntmen on the film, so Jocko coordinated the fights and the action for the climactic scene where he and Ray confront the gang. Jocko is hit by a shovel and takes a fall over a sofa chair. The action is captured from multiple angles and in slow motion. It's the best sequence in the film.

In retrospect *The Bad Bunch* was one more instance of Jocko playing a menacing bad guy to the hilt and having some fun with the part. He looks trim in his sport jacket and captures the character's cruelty well. He no doubt could have continued playing villains in the black action genre had he so desired, but this was a firm case of "once is enough." The film did its business in the grindhouses and drive-ins and had little impact on Jocko's career. Only over time would it emerge as something of a curio or cult item.

Jocko picked up some uncredited stunt coordinator work on a couple of low-budget films around 1972. Stuntman Rodd Wolff recalls one of the titles was a martial arts action film.[6] It's not known if these films ever made it into release. For comparison's sake, Al Wyatt was coordinating the famous comic western street brawl seen in *Blazing Saddles* (1974) for Mel Brooks. As he had so often done in the past, Jocko looked to take control of his career himself. With friend George Willson he formed the independent film banner Enchanted Filmarts, Inc., in 1973. According to the trades, Willson would serve as the production company's president and Jocko the vice-president. They planned to make four films a year with Jocko working in front of as well as behind the camera. History shows the company as a film distributor for the 1973 releases *Warlock Moon* and *The Chinese Boxer* (aka *The Hammer of God*), a U.S. release of a Jimmy Wang Yu film made in Hong Kong.

Enchanted Filmarts is also linked as the production company for a movie entitled *Outlaw Legacy* (1973), co-produced by the husband-and-wife team of Betty Ann and Lester Fritz of New Mexico and directed by film editor Danford Greene. *Outlaw Legacy* was announced as filming in Arizona at Old Tucson Studios in the late spring of 1973 on a 24-day shooting schedule. Guy Madison, William Smith, Mark Miller, and Antoinette Bower were the stars. It's not known if the film was ever completed or if Jocko was playing a role as well or coordinating stunts. Enchanted Filmarts seemed like a good idea at the time. However, as his recent casting on *Emergency* would forebode, Jocko had been playing a dangerous game of Russian roulette with his health for quite a while.

12

Jocko's Toughest Fight

While working a guest shot as a heavy on the popular TV western series *Kung Fu* in the late summer of 1973, Jocko suffered a stroke on the Warner Ranch set at 10:30 A.M. Given his pre-med background and lifelong devotion to physical fitness, he knew immediately what had happened. However, he had never held up a production in his life and vowed even this would not fall him as he underestimated the severity of the stroke. His wife was on the set with him and he swore her to secrecy despite her protests. The crew broke for lunch at noon and Jocko was growing worse. He literally couldn't swallow his food. The stroke had critically affected his entire right side and the left side of his face. Still, he waited it out for the one scene he was scheduled to shoot that day. He leaned on his wife for support and climbed aboard a horse at 1:30 P.M., which gave him steadiness.

With the crew readying the shot, Jocko prepared to throw a rope around a fellow actor. The cameras rolled, but Jocko could not make his trusted body cooperate. He threw the loop five times and repeatedly hit the man in the face. He was throwing not by feel but by memory. His entire right side had abandoned him. Finally, he lost his temper in front of the stunned crew. No one had seen Jocko fail before. The director, Robert Totten, encouraged him to try one more time. Jocko nailed the scene and then let the cat out of the bag as Autumn motioned to the crew that he wasn't well. As his complexion grew gray, he was immediately taken to the emergency ward. It was the first time he had made a trip from a movie set to the hospital and actually been admitted in his entire career.

What brought on Jocko's stroke at the age of 54? Jocko was, after all, the super-fit Tarzan of the movies. The major risk factor for a stroke is hypertension, or high blood pressure. Jocko could have been building up stress trying to get his acting career going. Long-time friend Jack Lewis recalled in his memoir *White Horse, Black Hat* that for as long as he knew Jocko, his friend never revealed anything of a private nature to him. Lewis never felt like he actually got close to Jocko, or that anyone could for that matter. Jocko was not one to call out for help or reveal his emotions. This internalization without release can be unhealthy in the long run.

Contributing factors to a stroke are smoking and alcohol consumption, both actions Jocko was guilty of in abundance for a number of years. He later acknowledged that he suffered from serious blood sugar abnormalities, although it's not known if his hypoglycemia was hereditary or diet-related. The high sugar content in alcohol may have been messing with Jocko's blood glucose levels. Another risk factor for stroke is trauma, something that Jocko had endured plenty of through decades of horse falls, high falls, and tumbles over tables and chairs. One has to wonder if the extremes Jocko put his body through as Tarzan a decade earlier in Thailand and his subsequent weakened condition played a part in his stroke.

Jocko's stubborn stoicism in the face of a medical emergency could have caused him severe harm, but that was Jocko's way: to will his body through adversity. The stroke was a major one and required years of rehabilitation. Jocko spent the first few days in a local hospital, then a week at UCLA Medical Center. This was followed by another week at the Motion Picture Country Home before Autumn checked him out. Jocko spent a significant period of his early rehab at the Motion Picture Home, where he reconnected with his Three Stooges friend Larry Fine, also a stroke victim. The Stooge never made it out and died there in 1975. Initially Jocko was confined to a wheelchair until he was able to walk, which amounted to a mere matter of weeks due to Jocko's tremendous willpower.

Jocko literally taught himself to walk again by taking daily laps around the indoor track at the Hollywood YMCA. When he'd lose his balance he'd merely bounce off the wall and right himself, gradually strengthening his coordination until he was able to walk a straight line under his own power. Jocko quit smoking and drinking cold turkey to get his health back in line. He gave up eating red meat and changed his diet for the better to manage his hypoglycemia. Jocko was determined this was a battle he would win. "He was a fighter," fellow stuntman Stephen Burnette said. "You couldn't tell he'd had a stroke at all, except his agility was gone."[1]

Jocko was soon out in society, but reconnecting with the acting and producing career he was trying to jumpstart at the time of the stroke would now be extremely difficult. Jocko managed to get back in front of the cameras within a year for another small part on a fall 1974 episode of *The Streets of San Francisco* entitled "One Last Shot." Again relegated to the end credits, this time Jocko is killed off before the first commercial break. Playing the partner of alcoholic cop Leslie Nielsen, Jocko is accidentally shot by his friend. Jocko looks older and slightly heavier here, sporting a gray mustache. There is little action for his character other than to slump to the ground after taking Nielsen's errant bullet. An astute viewer will notice his movements are a bit hesitant, but there is little other evidence to suggest he was the victim of a recent stroke. He handles his dialogue well.

The Streets of San Francisco appearance served notice that Jocko was once again available for acting work. However, the stroke altered Jocko's mindset about a Hollywood comeback at this point in time. Jocko took note of the need to slow down and relax, telling *Saturday Morning TV* that the stroke was "a bitch of a warning." There seemed to be little on the horizon but hustling for more bit TV parts, and Jocko became especially concerned about he and Autumn's financial future. In regard to Jocko's acting career, his good friend Dick Jones said, "The stroke hurt him the worst."[2]

Jocko and Autumn decided to move to the San Diego area to get away from the film business and the smog of Los Angeles. Oceanside, Carlsbad, Del Mar, and La Jolla were seaside areas Jocko knew from his time in the U.S. Marines. In an attempt to keep his mind occupied and a paycheck coming in, Jocko accepted a job offer as a tourist greeter for the Winner's Circle Lodge, a resort across from the horse track in Del Mar. In addition to the job, he and Autumn were able to live on the premises. Although Jocko put on a professional front, he found the work to be a little demeaning.

Trying to stay creative, Jocko directed three original musical stage productions at the

Winner's Circle Lodge, beginning with Donald Carl Eugster's one-act play *The Primrose Path* in June of 1974. The other abbreviated Eugster plays done throughout the summer were *Escape with Me* and *Three Men on a Horse*. *The Primrose Path* was a comedic melodrama that parodied and turned the usual theatrical clichés inside out. Its highlight was an exciting duel with canes that was coordinated by Jocko. The melodramatic score was composed by Eugster, who had a long background as a professional musician having written songs for Frankie Laine. *The Primrose Path* was well-received by audiences and garnered a positive review in the local Del Mar paper.

Eugster only knew Jocko for the three months they worked together on the shows but recalled: "He was a real delight and a wonderful man. I became very fond of him. He was smart; very interested in metaphysics and esoteric occult subjects. Jock was not a director by any means, but he was great at physical business. He came up with great physical bits for the show. *The Primrose Path* was a very exciting, fun little show."[3]

Due to his lack of strenuous exercise (and because he'd stopped smoking), Jocko added weight to his midsection, leveling off at about 225 pounds. He grew a grayish-white beard to hide the beginning of jowls and the changing color of the thinning hair on his head.

A 1975 publicity photograph signed for a fan.

Jocko wasn't one to feel sorry for himself, but it would be hard for him to make lemonade out of this lemon life had dealt him. He could still ride and swim moderately but his activity level was now a far cry from his youthful vigor. On occasion he'd visit his old friend Charles Starrett, who lived in nearby Laguna Beach.

Longtime pal Jack Lewis could tell Jocko was unhappy and came up with a new and more interesting job for him. In 1975 Jocko went to work for Lewis, now a magazine publisher for Gallant/Charger Publications whose offices were based in Capistrano Beach. Jocko's position was as advertising manager and he sold and placed advertising for Lewis' magazines *Gun World, Horse and Horsemen, Bow and Arrow,* and

Performance. He also handled public relations, saving a number of accounts with his tact and diplomacy. The work was good for Jocko and got him out and about, often times to gun shows or trade events such as the National Sporting Goods Association. He became a national representative for John Williams, importer of Fontaine telescopic sights for hunting rifles. He told the *Santa Ana Register,* "If I make the right deals, I can spend the rest of my life making a living hunting, fishing, and going to outdoor shows."

Bow and Arrow magazine did a nice feature article in its December 1975 issue on Jocko teaching his daughter Princess O'Mahoney to draw a bow properly and hit a target. Jocko started the six-foot Princess with a 25-pound bow, explaining that the majority of new students begin with bows that are far too heavy for them and become discouraged. Jocko himself used a bow with a 60-pound pull and a 28-inch draw length. "You build a whole new set of muscles when you take up archery," Jocko explained in the article. "And it's not just brute strength that puts an arrow in the center of the target. It's a knowledge of how to pull and hold, among other things." The article concluded with Princess hitting her target after heeding Jocko's instruction.

At an NSGA trade show in Chicago, Jocko met archery champion Diane Miller, who interviewed him for the magazine *American Archer.* Jocko struck up a friendship with Miller and stayed in contact with her. Miller wrote, "He used to call me at my business once in a while and I still have a postcard he sent telling me about being on *BJ and the Bear* in the 1970s some time. One of the girls that worked for me would answer the phone and she was so excited to think she had talked to Jock Mahoney that she could barely contain herself. He knew my husband and I were great fans of John Wayne and I remember once he asked if we would like to come to California and he would introduce us. At the time we were just getting started in our business and really didn't have the time or the money to go. I have kicked myself 100 times ever since."[4]

In 1975 Jocko was a judge for a Tarzan Yell Contest held in Burbank. One of the competitors was Gene Ryals, who was at the time working security at the studios. Ryals didn't win, but he had a lengthy conversation with Jocko about *Range Rider* and old cowboy stars. A few months later Jocko and Ryals were on the same plane together going to Memphis. They had a layover in Dallas where Jocko bought Ryals breakfast and the two solidified their friendship. Jocko later invited Ryals and his two sons down to Oceanside to visit. Ryals and Jocko enjoyed activities such as swimming, horseback riding, dinner, movies, and political talk. Ryals called Jocko "an exceptional man.... The Range Rider belt buckle and the two fringe jackets he gave me are treasured possessions."[5]

Most of Jocko's free time was spent meditating, writing poetry, painting, sketching, and reading. Jocko's favorite books were the Bible and Kahlil Gibran's *The Prophet.* He owned several books and charts from the metaphysical writer Manly Palmer Hall. Jocko's favorite fiction author was Alexander Dumas of *The Three Musketeers* fame. He also enjoyed reading Louis L'Amour westerns and the science fiction novels of Jules Verne and Edgar Rice Burroughs. His favorite film was *Patton* with George C. Scott, and his favorite actor was John Wayne. Jocko kept an open mind about many subjects and was particularly fascinated by Eastern religions, philosophy, and Native American Indian lore. For years he wore a gold chain around his neck with a symbolic mustard seed centered within a small crystal ball. He also wore a ring with a 4,500-year-old scarab gem taken from the tomb of an Egyptian mummy. He listed the five greatest human beings as Jesus Christ, Buddha,

Greek philosopher and mathematician Pythagoras, the Chinese messiah Chenny, and Hermes, the Greek athlete and "Messenger of the Gods."

One of Jocko's more interesting pastimes was journeying into the desert to look for UFOs in the star-filled skies. This interest dated back to his marriage with Maggie. Jocko had been friends with writer George Adamski, author of several extraterrestrial-oriented books such as *The Flying Saucers Have Landed* and *Inside the Space Ships*. The controversial author claimed to have seen several UFOs and even communicated with alien life forms. Prior to his 1965 passing Adamski, a cavalry soldier during the hunt for Pancho Villa along the Mexican border, publicly announced that he wanted Jocko to portray him in *The George Adamski Story*. The movie was never made.

Jocko's other hobbies included collecting antique art, knives, and firearms. He was a rock hound who enjoyed cutting and polishing stones in addition to woodworking and fashioning clothing. He often designed his own moccasins and buckskin jackets, a skill he learned from top Hollywood leather crafter Bob Brown. Some of his antiques were acquired from his world travels. He owned a huge Rosewood table from India that took five men six months to hand-carve. Another interesting piece of furniture was an elephant statue from Thailand, the world's largest figure ever carved out of a single piece of teakwood. A mounted antelope head was a trophy from a one-shot hunt in Wyoming. Jocko had a sailor's trunk full of his Hollywood memorabilia and collected curios that he began distributing to interested friends and fans during this period.

Jocko was surprisingly skilled in the kitchen and enjoyed coming up with a variety of intuitive dinners for himself and Autumn. Jocko's recipes for Sea Ranch Scallops and Chile Chicken Lemon Soup are in Ken Beck and Jim Clark's *All-American Cowboy Cookbook*. Mindful of his health and well-being, Autumn paid close attention to Jocko's food intake and made sure he was eating well. He regularly consumed raw fruits and nuts to keep his blood sugar at an even keel.

In November of 1975 Jocko appeared at the San Diego Comic-Con International as the event's special guest alongside fantasy filmmaker George Pal. The three-day event was held at the El Cortez Hotel. Actor Patrick Culliton was performing on stage in a show about magician Harry Houdini and took in the convention as he had been a fan of Jocko's since *The Range Rider*. He later met Jocko poolside and enjoyed a one-on-one conversation. The 6'1" Culliton was especially impressed by Jocko's sheer physical stature. "I felt like a jockey next to him," he said.[6]

Jocko accepted a film offer to make a special guest appearance in a low-budget independent entitled *Their Only Chance* (aka *Spirits of the Wild* and *To Speak as Brothers*), a 1975 movie capitalizing on the recent success of *The Life and Times of Grizzly Adams* (1974) and similar family-themed wilderness films. The J. David Sidon–directed movie was shot in picturesque Oregon locations around Grant's Pass and the Rogue River such as Dutchman's Flat and Bachelor's Butte. Portions were also shot in the states of Washington and Idaho with Jocko portraying dual roles as both a rancher and a mountain man known as Grizzly Bill. It's a testament to Jocko's growing acting skill that he is convincing in both roles and nearly unrecognizable as the same actor playing two characters.

Jocko worked closely with animal trainer George Toth and co-star Steve Hoddy to interact with a pair of timber wolves, an eagle, and a cougar integral to the plot. The $250,000 film was shot in fits and starts between the spring of 1974 and the snowy winter of 1975, allowing the generous use of a photo double for Jocko's heavily bundled character when the script called for him to carry Hoddy on his back. Jocko would have loved to have been able to do all the action himself, but in reality was simply happy to be working on a film set again. "My legs aren't up to par now," he told the *Bend Bulletin*. He did get to ride a horse on screen, impressive for someone only a year removed from a stroke. The movie had a limited release and later became somewhat of a collector's item on videocassette.

Jocko's own pride in not asking others for work kept him from taking on many potential acting parts during this period. He would gladly lobby to obtain work for his friends, but when it came to asking for himself he was tight-lipped. It would have been nice to see Jocko acting in other independent films, but this was the only job he felt up to tackling. Part of that had to do with what was being made. Jocko discussed his newest film with the *Bend Bulletin*: "It's a good clean picture. I used to go see [Errol] Flynn and I felt ten feet tall, like I could whip the world. Today movies deal too much with pornography and psychology. It's time we get back to what made the U.S. great—pioneer spirit. And to hell with the anti-hero. Let's get back to the hero."

There was one person Jocko wanted to work with during this period while they both had their health intact, and he personally let him know. It was the man he once nearly doubled on screen in the late 1940s: John Wayne. Although they were good friends, somehow they had managed not to share the screen together. Jocko told Wayne he would be willing to do a walk-on bit to appear in a scene with The Duke. Wayne agreed that they would find an appropriate role for Jocko in an upcoming Wayne project, but Jocko wasn't able to make it into what turned out to be The Duke's final film *The Shootist* (1976). "Like many of us," Jocko told *Campfire Embers,* "he got busy with a lot of things and then his health declined, and unfortunately, I never had the pleasure."

One activity that kept Jocko busy was the film festival circuit. In the summer of 1974 Jocko appeared at a nostalgia convention in Houston along with former Superman serial star Kirk Alyn and stuntmen Dave Sharpe and Tom Steele. The year 1975 saw Jocko accept an invitation to the Dum Dum North American Science Fiction Convention for a centennial Edgar Rice Burroughs Tarzan reunion. He was a guest of honor along with fellow screen Tarzans Buster Crabbe, Johnny Weissmuller, James Pierce, and Denny Miller. The August gathering merited write-ups and photos in *Life, Time,* and *Newsweek*, with Jocko and Weissmuller mugging for the cameras with a gorilla and a hoisted-up Jane.

While Jocko had been the oldest Tarzan, Denny Miller had been the youngest. After playing Tarzan he landed a solid part on *Wagon Train* where he was able to observe a number of fine guest stars working on their craft. After *Wagon Train* Miller discovered a flair for both comedy and TV villainy and worked often. He made memorable appearances on *Gilligan's Island* and utilized his size and developing acting skill to good advantage to play a number of forceful bad guys on episodic television. He and Jocko got on well, with Miller describing Jocko as "an overgrown kid" who was always laughing and playing practical jokes on his pals. Miller called Jocko "a gifted athlete" and "one of the best stuntmen ever."[7]

In November of 1975 Jocko, Miller, Weissmuller, Crabbe, Pierce, and Gordon Scott appeared on *The Mike Douglas Show* before a live audience at the San Diego Wild Animal Park. Miller related the following Jocko story. Each Tarzan was introduced one at a time to the audience. Upon Jocko's introduction he promptly took a pratfall that got a big laugh

Five Tarzans get together: (left to right) James Pierce, Johnny Weissmuller, Buster Crabbe, Jock Mahoney and Denny Miller (photograph courtesy of Denny Miller).

from the audience and the host. However, Autumn was in the stands and Jocko had neglected to tell her he was going to take a stunt fall. Coming on the heels of his stroke, she feared another attack and rushed down the steps to the stage. By the time she reached Jocko, he was on his feet and laughing with the other Tarzans. Seeing Autumn next to him a sheepish Jocko suddenly realized his error in not informing her of his plans. Miller wrote, "Jocko was always fun to be around."

Tarzans Jocko, Weissmuller, Crabbe, Pierce, and Miller appeared on *The Tonight Show* in 1975 with guest host McLean Stevenson filling in for Johnny Carson. A medley of action scenes was run for the Tarzans and the audience. When the guest host noticed that Jocko was sporting an accessory in his earlobe, he made a sly on-air comment that one of the Tarzans seemed to be wearing an earring. Jocko turned to Stevenson with a hard stare and said simply, "Yes, this Tarzan does." After an uncomfortable pause on Stevenson's part, the subject was changed.

At the 1976 Dum Dum Mid America Con in Kansas City, Missouri, Jocko was the lone guest of honor and received the Golden Lion Award, the highest honor in the world of Tarzan. Burroughs Bibliophile D. Peter Ogden, the editor and publisher of *Erbania*, recalled Jocko: "I only met him once. He was very friendly and personable and gave an interesting speech. I enjoyed his performance as Tarzan and admired his guts for taking on the role when he was the same age as Weissmuller, when Johnny quit the role. He is one of the top four actors to play Tarzan."[8]

Jocko began traveling to all sorts of functions such as the Dallas Western Film Convention, the Memphis Film Festival, the Charlotte Film Festival, the Houston-Con Film Festival, and the San Diego Western Film Festival. In the summer of 1976 he took part in the Giant Indian Parade through the streets of Santa Monica with Iron Eyes Cody, made a return visit to the Navajo Nation Fair in Arizona, was foot-printed in cement for the Stuntmen's Hall of Fame, attended a Salk Institute benefit, and was the grand marshal of the Swallows Day Parade in downtown San Juan Capistrano, California. He continued to fit these appearances around his magazine work for Jack Lewis.

In 1977 Jocko traveled to a nostalgia convention in New York City as a late substitute for featured guest Johnny Weissmuller, who was forced to miss the event due to illness. The promoter continued to advertise Weissmuller as appearing until the paying customers were in the door. Needless to say, there were several disappointed and justifiably angry members of the public who were forced to argue for refunds. Nevertheless, Jocko set about winning over the crowd with his entertaining stories and thoughtful responses to all manner of questions. He signed many autographs and posed for a number of pictures with fans. Jocko emerged as a hero to both the promoter and the customers.

Jocko enjoyed meeting his fans and proved to be a popular raconteur in these settings. Audiences loved the gregarious bear of a man who could bring down the house with his hearty laugh and mischievous grin. Jocko was always happy to talk about his favorite roles as Range Rider and Tarzan. Some of Jocko's tales grew increasingly tall with the passage of time. A foot or two was added to a jump here or there; an extra horse was vaulted over. Jocko had fun spinning the yarns. None of it made much difference because the stunts themselves were so visually astounding. Jocko also began to take on assignments as a motivational speaker. Jocko's friend Marty Rendleman recalled in her memoir that Jocko had a favorite phrase: "The answer is 'no,' till you ask."

Jocko rarely turned down any request for his time or presence during these years. He personally answered his fan mail, habitually sending autographed photo requests at his own cost. He was known to handwrite apologies if he felt he wasn't timely enough in his return. For some lucky fans whose letters touched Jocko, he sent Christmas cards every year. These traits continued to endear him to all those who had contact with him. Imagine the surprise and delight of Tarzan fan Phil Petras of Hellertown, Pennsylvania, when he wrote Jocko a 20-page letter of appreciation and received a personal reply that turned into a friendly correspondence. Petras eventually turned his Tarzan memorabilia collection into the Petras Museum of Tarzanography, with some of the material donated by the thirteenth screen Tarzan himself. Jocko always made time for his fans, especially the devoted ones.

Petras first had the opportunity to meet Jocko in person at the 1975 Dum Dum Edgar Rice Burroughs convention. The following year he presented a Tarzan slide show at the San Diego Con. After the show, Jocko invited him home to meet Autumn, and another strong friendship developed. Jocko even visited Petras when he was in Pennsylvania and had dinner with his family. Jocko always greeted Petras with a friendly bear hug at conventions and allowed him to visit his home as a guest whenever he was in California. Jocko once hosted a celebrity tennis tournament and surprised Petras with an unannounced meeting with Ron Ely. The TV Tarzan often shied away from discussing the ape man with fans but made an exception for Jocko's friend. Petras noted of Jocko: "A friendlier giant of a man, you could never have met."[9]

The trend toward nostalgia among the citizens of the United States continued as the population met and reconnected with their childhood heroes. Jocko proved to be a leading figure among the cowboy stars. The movie memorabilia magazine *Film Collector's Registry* had Jocko on the cover for the April 1977 edition with a photo tribute inside. The July 15, 1977, edition of the similar *Film Collector's World* sported a Jocko cover. A 15-page Tarzan souvenir booklet entitled *Jocko Jungle Lord* was published by Vern Coriell and proved a popular item for Jocko to sign. Thirty years later, Internet auctions would ask for more than $100 for a signed Jocko copy. The continued interest in his career convinced him it was time to return to Hollywood and resurrect his acting career.

After years of being cast aside professionally as the cute beach girl Gidget or the silly Flying Nun, Sally Field resurrected her career with an Emmy-winning performance as a schizophrenic in the TV movie *Sybil* (1976). It was bravura acting work and confirmed her as a major talent. She followed that playing the female lead in the immensely popular good old boy movie *Smokey and the Bandit* (1977). This movie starred Burt Reynolds and was directed by stunt ace Hal Needham. Reynolds, a former football player at Florida State, received his own start in the business as a stuntman on live television in New York. Sally quickly became America's sweetheart and the apple of Reynolds' eye. The two were an item for nearly five years.

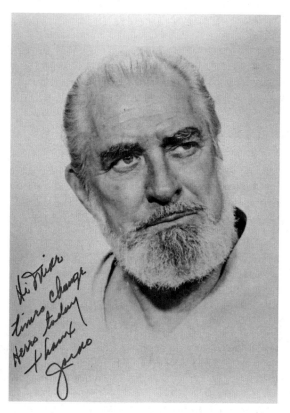

A late 1970s publicity photograph signed for a fan.

One of the decade's biggest stars, Reynolds attempted to branch out in other directions. One ambition was to direct his own film, and he chose an offbeat movie about a man who thinks he is dying. There was plenty of slapstick comedy in *The End* (1978), chiefly involving Reynolds and co-star Dom DeLuise. For his female lead Reynolds again chose Sally Field. To surprise his girlfriend he hired for the production her mother Maggie and her stepsister Princess O'Mahoney for small acting roles. Reynolds also hired her former stepfather Jocko, a man he looked up to in more ways than one. Several years earlier, when Reynolds was contemplating giving up on what he deemed was an unsuccessful acting career, Jocko had given him encouragement to hang in there. A few years after that, Reynolds landed the *Deliverance* (1972) role that would catapult him into leading man stardom on the big screen.

During Jocko's time in a wheelchair following his stroke he had learned to take a stunt fall from it. Reynolds knew of Jocko's skill and devised a nifty cameo for him. Jocko played a man in a wheelchair who encounters Reynolds on a bridge. The scene culminates with Jocko taking a 12-foot stunt fall off the bridge while remaining in a seated position. He landed on his back in four feet of water, nailing the stunt in one take. Reynolds and the crew gave him a standing ovation. Jocko was especially grateful to Reynolds for putting him back in a mainstream movie. Unfortunately additional scenes with Jocko ended up on the cutting room floor as did veteran actor Sam Jaffe's entire part. Before they parted ways, Reynolds signed a photo of the two of them together and wrote to Jocko, "You're only the best."

Burt Reynolds had high praise for Jocko. He shared his thoughts in a letter, commenting: "Jocko, without a doubt, was the best stuntman who ever lived. He could do it all: High falls, horse falls, any fight ever put on film. No stunt was too tough for him. When other people said no, he said 'you got it.' There will never be another like him."[10]

Performing a stunt again after his stroke was a triumphant moment for Jocko. He told the *Santa Ana Register*, "It was a ball." Despite the brevity of his acting part, the role in *The End* gave Jocko some much-needed publicity. He spoke at length to reporter Nancy Anderson in a 1977 nationally syndicated newspaper article about his stroke and his return to acting, saying: "I'm still in the process of recovery. If you've ever had Novocaine, you know how your mouth feels as the anesthetic begins to wear off, as though it were being pricked by 1000 needles. Well, that's how I feel all over now. And as a result I tire easily. But I'm coming along. I know I'm going to recover completely."

Hooper (1978) was a tribute to the motion picture stuntman and highly autobiographical on the part of both Hal Needham and Burt Reynolds. The plot involved an up-and-coming stunt tyro (played by Jan-Michael Vincent) who is seeking to dethrone Reynolds' Sonny Hooper as the greatest stuntman alive. Reynolds' character had done much the same thing to his own mentor, the father of his love interest Sally Field. The part of Field's father Jocko Doyle was based on Jock Mahoney himself. The character even wears a *Range Rider*–inspired buckskin fringe jacket. Both Reynolds and stuntman-turned-director Needham were Jocko fans, but the studio didn't want Jocko in the part. Jocko Doyle was played by the rugged actor Brian Keith, a former U.S. Marine whom Jock Mahoney conceded to *Filmfax* magazine has "a much bigger name than I have."

There is some misconception that Jocko was still periodically wheelchair-bound at this point in time and was unable to take on the strenuous role, in part due to his cameo in *The End*. The truth is that Jocko was not offered the part of Jocko Doyle. Jocko was involved in the making of the film in an advisory capacity, and Needham and Reynolds sought out many "Mahoneyisms" from both Sally Field and Princess O'Mahoney to incorporate into the picture. Keith, a Jocko crony from way back, had many of his own Jocko stories to bring to the role. Keith says Jocko's personal mantra "Your body is a temple" as a line in the film and felt honored to be playing his friend. The colorful Keith had many of the film's best moments as the bourbon-toting Jocko Doyle, including a vulnerable scene with Field and Reynolds where he lies in a hospital bed following a stroke.

Jocko and Sally might have had their differences over the years, but their mutual involvement in the film is a testament to the admiration they held for one another. Sally's quotes over the years regarding Jocko tend to run hot and cold. In a 1995 *TV Guide* interview she said of Jocko, "I thank him every day, because he taught me to be a fighter." In 2000 she told *The Toledo Blade*: "I had a stepfather who, bless his heart, was terribly colorful and larger than life, and I either adored him or despised him. There was no middle ground." In 2008 she told the *Academy of Achievement* website, "He was probably one of the finest stuntman that ever lived, athletically gifted beyond belief, and a gorgeous male."

Jocko was tremendously proud of the strides that Sally had made in her acting career. He told *Favorite Westerns*, "I raised Sally from the time she was five years old, until she left home at 18. She's paid her dues and deserves all of the awards and attention she's now getting." Even though Jocko did not appear on screen, *Hooper* was still a positive experience for him. He told the *Santa Ana Register* he was "flattered" at being fictionalized and honored in the movie.

Hooper sparked a tremendous public interest in the life of stuntmen and prompted many a hopeful young man and woman to journey to Hollywood to become a stunt professional. The overall effect unfortunately was a watering-down of the industry with unqualified people passing themselves off as professional stunt performers. Still, the film brought public awareness and much recognition to the profession. No longer did stunt performers go without being listed in the closing credits. The popularity of *Hooper* set the television networks into motion to develop a series about a professional stuntman. This evolved into the 1981 Lee Majors series *The Fall Guy*, which Jocko also played an important role in.

Another byproduct of the popularity was a flurry of television specials highlighting the work of stunt performers. Some of these shows contained stunt competitions where the top stuntmen tried to one-up each other. *Super Stunt Two* aired in the spring of 1979 and featured extraordinary high falls, car chases, and car rolls. The show was hosted by Rock Hudson and directed by stuntman Max Kleven. It also had a special salute to the career of the legendary Jock Mahoney, hosted by Burt Reynolds and Sally Field.

Jocko gradually began to become more active but was always mindful of never going at 100 percent. One of his favorite activities was attending horse shows with lifelong friend Don Burt. He helped groom the horses and lent a hand any way he saw fit. Jocko loved being around animals again. When Burt opened the L.A. Equestrian Center, Jocko became a familiar presence with the horse crowd. Ever the practical joker, he sometimes got a personal chuckle by hiding Burt's tiny wife Ardys with his large frame. Burt would be searching for his wife among the crowd as Jocko casually leaned against a fence surveying the horses. When Burt had finally reached his wit's end, Jocko would step aside with a long-suppressed laugh to reveal Ardys. Wearing an ever-present cowboy hat, Jocko always cut an amusing figure with any arrival as he stretched his big body out of the tiny German-made Opel he drove around.

Burt was instrumental in getting Jocko back up on a horse on a regular basis. Jocko often rode with Burt around Griffith Park and Forest Lawn Cemetery. The area used to be the Hudkins' Ranch, site of many a filmed western. They would ride over the swinging suspension bridge that connected Burbank with the park. Jocko often stopped to reminisce with Burt and point out areas where he had once performed Durango Kid stunts. Jocko couldn't risk riding full-out any more, but it was good for him to be back in the saddle. "He had to be careful with what he did," Burt said.[11]

On occasion Burt got together with the legendary trio of Jocko, Yakima Canutt, and Ben Johnson to ride and reminisce about the good old days. When dining at a restaurant they would lay a shock on the waitress by ordering "one of everything." Jocko and Autumn spent much of their free time with the Burts. If Don was out of town, Jocko called or stopped by every day to make sure Ardys was doing okay. In his book *Horses and Other Heroes,* Don said of Jocko, "His burly individuality was only a front for the many kindnesses he bestowed upon my wife and me."

Jocko continued to make personal appearances wherever and whenever he was asked. In the late 1970s he attended two National slingshot tournaments in Toulon, Illinois. He was a big hit with the audiences and even competed in the show. In California he appeared with Roy Rogers, Rex Allen, and Ben Johnson at the KLAC Days Party at the Montie Montana Ranch. Playing up his association with Tarzan, Jocko rode an elephant down Hollywood Boulevard for the 1978 Santa Claus Lane Parade. Nineteen seventy-nine saw Jocko serve as the grand marshal for a parade celebrating the grand opening of the Sam's Town Casino in Las Vegas. He called his old friend John Hagner to bring some stuntmen along and stage fight scenes for the crowds. Hagner and his crew fought on a flatbed float while Jocko rode a horse ahead of them.[12] Hagner wrote that Jocko was "one of the most outstanding stuntmen ever."

Jocko found another favored activity in hot-air ballooning and flew with the Blue Angels after serving as the master of ceremonies for a number of their dinners. Jocko was allowed to take the controls of a Cougar jet, initiate a roll, and land the aircraft after he flew over the ocean. Around this time Jocko became involved as the president of Pacific Air Transport International, a paper company that never actually made it into the air freight business despite good intentions. The company's business address could be traced to Lido Peninsula in Newport Beach where a 136-foot motor yacht named the *Nisco 1* was moored. The former minesweeper was in the slip next to John Wayne's yacht *The Wild Goose.* The venture was indicative of Jocko's far-ranging interests. He was not a man prone to sitting on his hands.

Jocko and Autumn planned a mammoth cross-country horseback trip that would start at the Canadian border, come down through Washington to California, then cut across Nevada all the way to Miami and up the East Coast. It would be the longest horseback ride in history, but never came to be largely due to funding. Another ambitious Jocko project that didn't make it to completion was a film series to be called *The Magic World of Horses* that would trace the history of 96 different horse breeds beginning with a 90-minute segment on the Arabian. These projects absorbed a lot of Jocko's time, energy, and finances at the close of the decade. In 1979 he was hired to host a TV special entitled *University of the Third Age* for the San Diego station KCST-TV. The documentary looked at an experiment combining young college students with elderly ones returning to academia. The experiment was a success and became a worldwide organization.

At the invitation of writer David Rothel, Jocko journeyed to Florida in 1979 to serve as a guest artist for the Sarasota Visual and Performing Arts Center. Jocko spent one week of daily classes interacting with the students and their teachers, discussing the business of being an actor and stuntman. By the end of the week he brought out mats and showed the students how to stage a fight scene for the cameras. The following year Jocko returned to visit Rothel as the guest of honor at the Orlando Comic Con. Rothel remembered Jocko in his book *Opened Time Capsules,* stating: "Jock Mahoney had impressed me with his outgoing, likable personality, his sense of humor, and his intellect. This big bear of a man was just fun to be around."

Jocko appeared at the 1979 National Film Society Awards and presented his fantastic stuntman counterpart Dave Sharpe with a Yakima Canutt Award. He recited a list of Sharpe's many athletic skills and accomplishments in the stunt field to the appreciative audience. Unfortunately, Sharpe had been diagnosed with Amyotrophic Lateral Sclerosis (aka Lou Gehrig's Disease) and was in ill health. Jocko and John Hagner visited him often in the Motion Picture Home. Johnny Weissmuller, who had suffered a series of strokes, was in the room next to him. Sharpe passed away in 1980, a shame considering his robust lifestyle and the physical skills he was capable of. Sharpe was still able to do handstands and back-flips into his sixties; then all of a sudden his body betrayed him. This was a scenario Jocko himself knew all too well.

Jocko still helped aspiring stunt performers at every opportunity. Ray Lopeman was a rodeo cowboy and former U.S. Marine who came to the fringes of the film industry rather late, after he was one of the finalists for a Marlboro Man print ad campaign. Jocko befriended Lopeman and gave him pointers in regard to stunt work and the film industry in general. Lopeman wrote: "I will never forget the first time I met him [in the late 1970s]. It was some kind of gathering in L.A. First thing I said to him, 'You sure have gained some weight.' He replied, 'You ain't no slim boy yourself.' We both laughed and felt comfortable the rest of the evening. I met him later at a frontier movie town somewhere in L.A. and several times he taught me some basics in stunt fighting and falling. It got me a few gags. Later he was a judge for the National Association of Old West Gunfighters in Calico, I believe. I won that one. I always enjoyed Jocko, though I did not spend lots of time with him. He always said it like it was. Could be tough, but a heart of gold."[13]

Another interesting character with ties to Jocko was stuntman Lenny Dee from Florence, Arizona. A minor stuntman in John Wayne films, Dee fronted a touring Wild West Show during the late 1970s and early 1980s. Dee told the *Casa Grande Dispatch* he was a member of the Marine Corps Hall of Fame, a Hells Angel, and the first stuntman to be honored with an Academy Award. That sole distinction actually belongs to the legendary Yakima Canutt, who was honored for his lifetime of achievement in 1966. There is no mention of Dee in any Academy history (or even the Internet Movie Database for that matter). Dee also claimed that he was one of the only stuntmen to successfully duplicate Yakima Canutt's famous stunt from *Stagecoach* (1939) where Canutt fell between the running six-up horse team and is dragged beneath the stage. Dee boasted the only other man to have done that stunt was none other than Jock Mahoney. Actually, Dean Smith did it for the *Stagecoach* remake in 1966 and Terry Leonard performed it for *The Legend of the Lone Ranger* in 1981, but was injured in doing so. Dee claimed he trained with Jocko when he entered the industry, saying Jocko was "the greatest, the master of them all." In reality, Dee hardly made a dent in the stunt industry and should be considered more of a local character. He no doubt had ties to Jocko's stunt school, as did a number of working stuntmen and women from this period.

Jocko judged a stuntman competition in Salt Lake City and attended rodeo events and stunt competitions in Phoenix for stuntman Ron Nix. When asked about Jocko during a Q & A session at the annual Apacheland Days event, Nix shared a few brief memories. Nix had originally met the cowboy star at the age of ten when Jocko and Dick Jones came to Phoenix for one of their rodeo appearances. By the mid 1960s Nix had entered the profession as a resident stuntman for TV's *Death Valley Days* on episodes that filmed at the Arizona movie location. When Jocko made his 1967 appearance at Apacheland, Nix revealed his intention to someday build his own western town where he would put on stunt shows and lure film productions. He asked Jocko if he would consider being a judge for his competitions. Jocko put an arm around Nix's shoulder and said, "Son, if you build it, I'll be there."[14]

Ten years later, Nix made his dream a reality with the opening of A Day in the West Movie Ranch near Lake Pleasant, Arizona. Jocko held true to his word and served as Nix's Stuntmen's Rodeo judge for a number of years. Nix's A Day in the West eventually became known as Cowtown. Jocko met many aspiring stuntmen at these events and shared his knowledge and expertise on fights and falls, continually impressing the notion that if a stunt didn't feel right, one should abandon it. The events allowed Jocko an appropriate forum to preach stunt safety to the next generation.

Like Nix, Rodd Wolff initially met Jocko in the 1950s when he was only a small boy. Jocko and Dick Jones were making an appearance at a Phoenix rodeo and their hotel room air conditioning had gone out. Wolff's dad was called to the room to fix it and was surprised to find the Range Rider opening the door. Knowing his boy was a big fan of the duo, he asked if he could bring his son back. Jocko and Dick readily agreed. Young Rodney got to meet his heroes but forgot to bring a camera along. Jocko told them that he and Dick would be in a parade the next day and to get their attention then for the photo. During the parade, Rodney waved his arms to get the men's attention. Jocko and Dick saw the boy in the crowd and stopped the parade to get off their horses. Dick was behind the camera for the photo of Jocko and Rodney. Then Jocko took the camera and snapped a shot of Dick with the boy. Then Jocko and Dick got back on their horses and the parade resumed.

That experience would seem to be enough for any youngster, but Jocko also wrote down an address where Rodney could write him. Jocko always answered Rodney's letters and was especially impressed by the technical questions about stunt work. Even when Jocko changed addresses, he always made sure to send Rodney an update. Their letters continued back and forth for the better part of a decade until Rodd Wolff was ready to become a stunt professional. Wolff's stunt career followed a similar path to Ron Nix's on mostly Arizona-filmed productions dating back to late 1960s episodes of *Death Valley Days* and *The High Chaparral.*

In the early 1970s Wolff tried his luck in Hollywood, where he met and trained with Jocko. Wolff had become an expert horseman and struck up a strong friendship with Jocko, whom he considered his mentor. Jocko took Wolff around and introduced him to a number of people for prospective jobs. Knowing Wolff was a western buff, Jocko arranged a meeting at the home of the very private and reclusive Randolph Scott. He also took Wolff up to Big Bear to meet Woody Strode. Unfortunately westerns were on the way out in Hollywood. Wolff eventually returned to Arizona. Despite being out of the motion picture mainstream he was able to land work on a number of films, including *Rambo III* (1988), *Universal Soldier* (1992), and *The Getaway* (1994).[15]

For the *Screen Actors Guild Newsletter* Wolff wrote, "I've had some of the best people in the business impart their safety knowledge to me. One name stands tall above the rest, 6'4" tall, to be exact. He is Jacques O'Mahoney. Jock stands plenty tall as a stuntman and to those who know him personally, even taller as a valued friend and human being."

At the close of the decade, Jocko and Autumn moved out of their Carlsbad condominium and leased a five-acre ranch outside of San Marcos, California. Their hope was to eventually find the perfect horse ranch. In the meantime they looked for houses to purchase, refurbish, and resell. Their leased San Marcos property contained pheasants, peacocks, ducks, chickens, and geese. "We get a ton of eggs daily," Jocko told Frank Rhodes for his column in the *San Diego Union*. Through this time Jocko dabbled once again at writing an autobiography. He got about a quarter of the way through his life before he decided to land an agent and get back into acting. There were still far too many chapters to live before he could stop to write about them.

13

The Return of Jocko

In 1979 Jocko was instrumental in helping put together an ABC television special that reunited several of the old western stars. *When the West Was Fun: A Western Reunion* was set in a saloon and around a campfire with Glenn Ford hosting. The show was a folksy hour of long-time friends getting together to hash out the good old days. The former TV stars on display were staggering, and the majority of them all came courtesy of Jocko who made the necessary calls and coerced the men into working for peanuts for the sake of the good times. Jocko even receives a credit at the end of the show for casting. He was assisted in the endeavor by Gene Ryals. No one had a problem with Jocko's recruitment, even though the day of the filming Jocko expected to be put on the spot for more money by at least someone. He was not. All the assembled cowboy stars worked for scale, the lowest wage possible.

Appearing with Jocko on the show were Dick Jones, Clayton Moore, James Drury, Lee Van Cleef, Chuck Connors, John Russell, Guy Madison, Doug McClure, Will Hutchins, Slim Pickens, Denver Pyle, Dan Haggerty, Ty Hardin, Neville Brand, John Ireland, Rod Cameron, George Montgomery, Alan Hale, Jr., Jack Kelly, Barry Sullivan, Michael Ansara, Pat Buttram, Rex Allen, X Brands, Iron Eyes Cody, Ken Curtis, Milburn Stone, Larry Storch, Keenan Wynn, John Bromfield, Harry Lauter, Tony Young, Terry Wilson, Bill Williams, Joe Bowman, and even Roy Rogers and Dale Evans who sang "Happy Trails" at the end with everyone around a campfire. Jocko invited John Wayne, Gene Autry, Charles Starrett, Joel McCrea, and Richard Boone, but they were unable to attend. The entire cast agreed to dedicate the show to John Wayne, who was in failing health at the time.

Clips of the stars in their heyday were shown with new footage of them all together. Jocko is curiously introduced as Yancy Derringer, even though he is far more identified as Range Rider, and is clad in buckskin for the show. The highlight is a big saloon brawl which the cowboy actors obviously delighted in staging. During the brawl, Jocko let Glenn Ford smash him over the back with a breakaway chair. On camera Ford called Jocko "the best stuntman in Hollywood." The show was a nice trip down Memory Lane for both audiences and the performers. A clean-shaven Jocko appears healthy and robust.

Overall the show was great fun for Jocko, although he was a bit disappointed in the low budget and the insertion of a couple of musical segments with can-can dancers. The two long days allotted to filming proved tough on the performers. James Drury recalled the director Walter C. Miller desired to get as many stars as possible in each shot, and by the end they were all trying to get out of being seen on camera.[1] Filming went until 4:30 in the morning on the final day. Dick Jones found the premise interesting but thought the show itself was a bust because everyone sat around so long doing nothing but watching the director focus on the dancing girls.[2]

Jocko wanted to film another reunion special with the same group of stars in which the can-can girls were eliminated and all the performers were paid top-dollar and given a higher quality of production and less demanding shooting schedule. Even though the 1979 reunion was ABC's top-rated special for the season, Jocko tried for several years to get his follow-up show centering on a Roy Rogers barbecue off the ground to no avail. Despite its budgetary constraints, *When the West Was Fun* remains a popular collector's item for cowboy buffs.

Jocko appeared in a little-seen Bruce Richardson short film for the American Film Institute, *A.W.O.L.* (1980). There's not a lot of information on the production in which Jocko plays a character known as "the Cowboy." In the spring of 1980 he formed Big Sky Productions with J. David Siddon and Jim Lawrence. Jocko and Autumn relocated to Lolo Hot Springs, Montana, for the summer of 1980 to film *Reve Blue* (aka *Blue Dream*). In addition to producing chores, Jocko starred in the western as a mountain man. In real life Jocko was a mountain man buff and a black powder muzzle-loading enthusiast. Unfortunately, the low-budget independent film was never completed or released. This was another hit to Jocko's financial standing. Jocko and Autumn moved back to the San Diego area, settling in Solana Beach.

Jocko's next assignment was far more high-profile. One of the biggest stars of 1980 was a young actress named Bo Derek who had bared it all in the hit comedy *10* (1979). She was the current wife of veteran actor and filmmaker John Derek, former husband of Ursula Andress and director of *Once Before I Die* (1965), in which Jocko had done a cameo in the Philippines. The movie world was set abuzz when the Dereks announced that their next project would be tackling an updated version of *Tarzan, the Ape Man* (1981) that would focus more on Jane than Tarzan. They even offered the tentative title *Me, Jane*.

When it came time to cast the new Tarzan, John Derek approached Jocko to join in the auditioning process as a consultant. Jocko interviewed 125 men for the part and screen-tested a dozen of them. Some he filmed swinging through the trees at Hollywood Park while distracted local golfers looked on. He then narrowed it down to two and set about training them for the role at Bob Yerkes' backyard full of stunt and circus equipment. The man who won the job in Derek's eyes was Lee Canalito, a massive 6'4", 250-pound former heavyweight boxer who had earlier appeared opposite Sylvester Stallone in *Paradise Alley* (1978).

Derek planned to make the movie in the exotic location of Sri Lanka and the Seychelles Islands, but the movie became embroiled in all kinds of controversy. Much of the problem reportedly stemmed from the ego of Mr. Derek and his on-set paranoia. Derek was a complex, temperamental man who had burned through many professional and personal relationships since his leading man days in the early 1950s. Many crew members on the Tarzan film were fired or quit, including the star Canalito. When Derek sought Jocko's advice for a quick replacement, Jocko recommended a 6'3", 200-pound former Mississippi State football player turned male model named Miles O'Keeffe, who had impressed him greatly with his athleticism and sleekly muscled physique during the auditions. MGM had kept O'Keeffe on retainer. Jocko told the *Iowa City Press-Citizen*, "He was my concept of Tarzan. He was a beautiful, well-coordinated young man. Tarzan has to be visually appealing."

O'Keeffe was soon headed to Sri Lanka, and Jocko was enticed by John Derek to take over as the film's stunt coordinator. It seems the previous coordinator was fired after butting heads with Derek over the staging of a sequence the stuntman deemed too dangerous. The director wanted locals to make an ascent up a sheer cliff face but when Jocko arrived and surveyed the situation he came to the same conclusion. What Derek wanted was far too dangerous. Jocko offered alternative solutions and other bits of action. However, Derek didn't use any of Jocko's suggestions. He seemed more intent on photographing his wife's naked body than presenting Edgar Rice Burroughs' creation effectively on the screen. Derek subsequently relieved Jocko of his stunt coordinator duties by leaving a note on his pillow saying his services were no longer needed.[3] Considering their friendship went back three decades, Jocko was tremendously disappointed with Derek and his callous handling of the situation.

Legend has it that a departing Jocko met an arriving O'Keeffe at the Sri Lanka airport. O'Keeffe took that as a bad omen but tried to make the best of a bad situation in his first film. For O'Keeffe's first scene, John Derek wanted him to perform a stunt swinging from a vine and dropping into a lake next to Bo. There was no stuntman or coordinator at all at this point. O'Keeffe remembered his training with Jocko and was able to get the shot in two takes. When it came to action, John Derek filmed a few other bits in ineffective slow-motion. He definitely could have used Jocko's presence and vast experience on the set. O'Keeffe discussed his training for the *Memphis Commercial-Appeal*, saying of Jocko, "He was a big guy, but he moved like a cat. He taught me how to throw a tomahawk. He was amazing."

Jocko was reportedly unpaid for his location work as the production descended further into chaos. O'Keeffe was forced to sign an order of silence, which meant he was unable to speak about the film until months after its release. The public and press assumed he was all muscle and no brain. The Burroughs estate sued the filmmakers and MGM, demanding cuts be made to the film. Derek's *Tarzan*, which Jocko was initially enthusiastic about, became a subject Jocko preferred not to discuss. When finally released, the film did indeed focus on Bo Derek's character and remained heavy on nude shots of the actress. *Tarzan, the Ape Man* was a moneymaker but was widely ridiculed for its accent on naked nonsense.

Jocko had initially hoped the movie might lead to more stunt coordinating gigs and second unit directing work in the same manner that Yakima Canutt had distinguished himself after a stellar stunt career. However, stunt coordination jobs for the big studios did not materialize. No doubt the shift in Hollywood over the previous decade away from westerns and into urban action fare hurt Jocko's chances. It's perplexing that a man known for taking such safety precautions was not hired to front stunt crews and design stunts. The most plausible explanation is that Jocko wasn't actively out there selling himself and that his long sabbatical from motion pictures left him an unknown quantity with the new producers and directors within the industry.

There were more than likely a couple of other factors at play. Jocko's macho posturing and propensity for salty language may have unintentionally offended some power brokers in a changing Hollywood. One other scenario is that Jocko's reputation for safety might have had those in power afraid to have him on the typical 1980s set. Jocko was extremely vocal and justifiably angry when actor Vic Morrow and two Vietnamese children were killed by a crashing helicopter during the making of *Twilight Zone: The Movie* (1983).[4] At this point in time the film industry had become permeated with cocaine, and Jocko was a known safety hawk who would not tolerate such activity, especially when it came to stunt work. It's likely many a crew member didn't want to have Jocko looking over their shoulder ready to blow the whistle. Jocko had a favorite saying that went, "Never take the call, if you can't take the fall"[5] and it was a creed he lived by. "He did everything the way you should do it," veteran stuntman Loren Janes said. "I don't think he ever got hurt doing a stunt."[6]

One benefit of the Derek film was that Jocko met MGM production assistant Esther Beardsley while working on the project. The two became fast friends, with Jocko reminding Esther of her father. Jocko was quick to lend his help when Esther hosted a dinner for a group of foreign USC students in her home. When she became engaged to location manager Larry Luttrell, it was Jocko who gave away the bride during the wedding ceremony. Jocko and Autumn became so friendly with the Luttrells that holidays were often spent with one another. One year Jocko wrote a special Christmas story and shared his creation with his friends while reading from an armchair.[7] Esther eventually made a name for herself as a writer and mentions Jocko in her book *Murder in the Movies*, calling him "one of the most respected professionals in the business."

Jocko began acting again in several episodic TV shows, among them *BJ and the Bear*, *The Fall Guy*, *Simon and Simon*, and *The Master* with his good friend Lee Van Cleef. The 1982 *Simon and Simon* episode was no more than an extended special appearance during a barroom brawl scene, but it was great to see Jocko throwing punches again. Veteran TV cowboy John Russell and stuntman Hal Needham also appeared, as do Broderick Crawford, Alan Hale, and Pat Buttram in a Burt Kennedy–directed episode in which Stuart Whitman plays a former TV cowboy named Buck Yancey. A 1983 episode of *The A-Team* focused on *Range Rider* and used old clips of Jocko in action. Rather surprisingly, Jocko was not asked to appear in the episode, despite the fact that star George Peppard was a good friend.

On the truck driver show *BJ and the Bear* a bearded Jocko first appeared in the 1979 episode "Fly a Wild Horse," playing a crooked rancher endangering a herd of wild horses. Jocko underplays menacingly throughout until the final chase scene, when he lets out an odd maniacal laugh that fits in with a silly show where the lead's sidekick is a chimpanzee. Jocko got a kick out of his character becoming crazed. Jocko later had a running role on the series as heavy Jason T. Willard, the head of Trans-Cal Trucking. He appeared in a pair of two-part episodes in 1981.

Jocko acted with premier tough guy villain William Smith in the continuing *BJ and the Bear* episode "The Fast and the Furious." Smith claimed Jocko was his "mentor" dating back to 1940s Burbank when a young Smith cleaned the horse manure out of Jocko's stalls at Riverside Stables and exercised his five horses. They met up years later after Smith had served in the Air Force, and Jocko couldn't believe Smith was the same skinny kid who once worked for him. Jocko taught the muscular and athletic Smith the tools of the stunt trade. All the fancy mounts and vaults Smith made onto his horse Buttermilk on the popular western *Laredo* (1965–1967) were taught to him by Jocko. On the second season of that show Smith wore a Range Rider buckskin outfit. From the 1970s on, Smith sported the special ring on the pinky finger of his left hand that was given to him by Jocko.[8] Smith told *Filmfax* that Jocko was "a great guy and a good friend."

The 6'2" Smith had slim hips and long legs that didn't respond to weight training the way his upper body did. He caught good-natured flack from some of his buddies over his lack of leg development to the point that he twice turned down the role of Tarzan because he was embarrassed to be running around in a breach cloth with his skinny calves. Denny Miller and Ron Ely took those Tarzan parts. Smith was very proud, however, of the great spring in his legs that aided him in his many athletic feats. Smith could get seven feet into the air with his flying karate kick and was able to stand flat-footed next to a five-foot stepladder and jump over it. Smith recalled that no one else in Hollywood could do that except Jock Mahoney.[9]

The television series *The Fall Guy*, starring macho Lee Majors as bounty hunter–stuntman Colt Seavers, was a product of the cinematic success of *Hooper*. It premiered in the fall of 1981 to great popularity despite silly storylines. Episodes featured outstanding stunt work from the best in the business, and it was only natural that Jocko found a role both on screen and off. He appeared in the first season episode "Charlie" as veteran stuntman Gus Flint, who serves as emcee to a stunt convention. He played a similar role as the special guest star in a two-part episode during the second season, "Colt's Outlaws" and "Colt Breaks Out." Jocko's character Wild Dan Wilde, the stuntman mentor of Majors, was unabashedly autobiographical and great fun for Jocko.

Jocko got along well with Majors and was surrounded by a crew of stuntmen who respected him and his life's work. Despite being in his early sixties, Jocko was still game for doing as much of his own stunt work as possible when it came to fights and falls for the show. He also returned to working behind the scenes as a stunt performer. There were no fantastic leaps and bounds, but these small stunt gags still required a professional. Veteran stuntman Gene LeBell worked regularly on *The Fall Guy* and recalled, "He was a great guy. I worked with him many times. Fantastic athlete and did most of his own stunts. He was the real deal."[10]

Under stunt coordinators Bill Catching and Mickey Gilbert, Jocko helped work out many stunts for the show and performed as much as he could, mostly automobile and horse work. An astute viewer will notice that Jocko appears to be the horseback double for Pat Buttram in the 1983 Roy Rogers episode "Happy Trails." Stuntman Robert Potter recalled having worked with Jocko 15 to 20 times on the show. On one episode Jocko was behind the wheel of a semi truck that Potter laid a motorcycle underneath. On an episode filmed in Big Bear, Jocko and Potter drove snowmobiles into a mini-avalanche and nonchalantly strolled out of the snow banks. "Everybody thought we were two of the most lunatic characters," Potter said laughing. "He was very admired by Lee Majors. I remember Jock and I used to walk beside Lee Majors on the set to keep the women from throwing themselves at him."[11]

The stunt process was always memorable because Jocko kept the mood so light beforehand as they hashed out and analyzed the action. Whenever laughter was heard on *The Fall Guy* set amongst cast and crew, Jocko was usually at the center of it. Potter recalled, "Over the years we used to get together and joke around. Jock was one of the funniest guys you ever met. He knew how to make people laugh. Whenever he walked on a set it would end up being a pretty silly situation. Jock would have the whole cast and crew cracking up during rehearsals. He was down to earth and had a great sense of humor. Yet he wasn't afraid to pray before a big stunt. He was a humble screwball."

Neil Summers, another stuntman who worked regularly on *The Fall Guy*, was a historian for his profession and the western genre. Summers admired Jocko and they became close friends. In the early 1980s Summers served behind the scenes on a short-lived magazine entitled *Blazing West* for which Jocko contributed a guest column. Jocko also wrote the introduction to Summers' *The Official TV Western Book Vol. 2*. Summers wrote of Jocko within that book's pages: "Jock is one of this writer's idols, and I am proud to call him my friend. He is a most gracious man to his fans and as such, he is much loved and respected."

Jocko revealed his own appreciation for cowboy heroes in the Summers book, writing:

> One thing that hasn't changed is my deep abiding love and respect for my friends, the gentlemen in the white hats. I heartily recommend them for succeeding generations to emulate, and I heartily recommend the book of Neil's. What fun it is to go through the photos and once again see so many of my saddle pals smiling back at me. I am proud to have been a part of the history of television and a cowboy to boot. If I entertained one of your readers even a little bit, then it was worth it.

Summers wrote further on Jocko in *Western Clippings*:

> Jock and I once lived in the same complex in Sherman Oaks, California. He would often call me to come visit him or walk around the block with him after his stroke. To be in his presence and to be his friend was my honor. He was one of a kind. A superb athlete and a consummate stuntman that made every actor he doubled look better. He made everything he did look so easy and effortless, when indeed these stunts are not. He often joked, "I was born a cat." Jock's passing December 14, 1989, left a giant void in my life. I still think of him often.

A heavyweight Jocko returned on screen for one final episode during the 1983–84 season of *The Fall Guy*. In "King of the Cowboys" he played himself in an episode that starred Roy Rogers. Former cowboy stars John Russell and Peter Breck also play themselves from the series *Lawman* and *The Big Valley*. In the climax Jocko got to involve himself in the action, galloping on his horse and engaging in a fistfight although he looked to be carrying at least 250 pounds across his gigantic frame. He also got to flirt in a good-natured way with pretty blonde Heather Thomas, resulting in the big guy getting flipped onto his back.

Jocko and Roy Rogers had been friends since meeting at horse trainer Glen Randall's stables in the early 1940s. Outside of *When the West Was Fun*, the only other time they had worked with one another was in November of 1981 when Jocko guest starred on the variety show *The Nashville Palace*, hosted by Roy and Dale Evans. That episode was in celebration of Roy's fiftieth year in the entertainment business. Other guests included Lash LaRue, George Montgomery, Iron Eyes Cody, Sunset Carson, Montie Montana, Pat Buttram, Monte Hale, Eddie Dean, and Rex Allen. In all Jocko played three different characters in four episodes over the course of three seasons of *The Fall Guy*. They were all essentially Jocko cast as himself, a living legend stuntman.

Jocko guest starred on *The Master* in 1984. The show was short-lived largely due to the ridiculous premise of having an aged Lee Van Cleef doing ninja moves courtesy of his stunt doubles. Nevertheless, it was a guilty pleasure for many viewers. Jocko played the main heavy; a greedy land developer who will resort to murder. At the climax he engaged in a short fight scene with Van Cleef, but unfortunately both men were doubled. The current filmmakers were not aware of the significance of Van Cleef and Jocko continuing a 30-year on-screen war that had begun in the days of *The Range Rider*. Nevertheless, the show was great fun for Jocko, and he was quite pleased to be on screen with his old pal.

Esther Luttrell was working on the series and actually had a part in getting him cast, although it was Van Cleef who personally called and asked Jocko to appear as the top guest. "Lee was glad to make it happen," Luttrell said.[12]

Jocko tried to get several other movie projects off the ground with no success. He developed a script with X Brands titled *Shining Through* and tried to get a Louis L'Amour-style western made. He was also attached as stunt coordinator for a picture on the life of his early cowboy hero Tom Mix that was being put together by Jocko's stuntman friend Rex Rossi. The movie eventually fell through in development as so many prospective films do when it comes to financing. Jocko did do a 1983 radio show revival of the old *Tom Mix* show that was sponsored by Ralston Purina. Jocko played the part of a troubled rancher. The show was heard on radio stations around the country.

Jocko hoped to land a steady job on a TV series, preferably a western, but nothing materialized for him. Jocko's agent Steve Stevens handled Chuck Connors' career during this period, as well as Jack Palance, Leo Gordon, Slim Pickens, Forrest Tucker, Rod Cameron, Alan Hale, and Claude Akins. Unfortunately, having so many similar types beneath one banner meant that many of Stevens' clients were competing amongst themselves for the same roles. Stevens recalled:

> Besides being one of the greatest stuntmen in the business, he was a pretty good actor. There was a likability about him. Good-looking, and a man's man. He was not easy to represent because he couldn't stand or want to put up with the young people who ran the business who had never been on a hot dusty location. Like so many of his peers, he was living in the past and could not understand why I wanted him to get me several recent photos. Don't get me wrong. I really liked Jocko and continued to do the best I could for him as his agent.
>
> One of my favorite Jocko stories was when I got him a meeting with the producers of the TV series *Fame*. They were looking for a former cowboy movie or TV star for a special episode. He had to audition, and I got him the script a week ahead of time so he could work on the two scenes they wanted him to read for the producers and director. One of the producers had written this episode and was excited to meet Jocko and have him audition. I was told by the casting director that Jocko showed up on time, entered the meeting, and promptly asked, "Who wrote this crap?" Well, that was the end of that. He was one of a kind.[13]

Jocko, Chuck Connors, and Leo Gordon all appear in the 1985 low-budget western *The All-American Cowboy*. Gordon even had a hand in writing the project. The sepia-tinted docudrama stars James Drury and features Ben Johnson, Clint Walker, Johnny Crawford, Iron Eyes Cody, Gene Autry, and *Gunsmoke* alumni Ken Curtis and Buck Taylor. The movie was made on location outside Fort Worth, Texas, at the western town Storybook Ranch. Jocko plays a bartender who throws Drury a rifle for the final shootout. "He did it perfectly," Drury recalled.[14]

Reflecting the times, *All-American Cowboy* from the independent production company Studio of Illumination failed to find distribution or even a network to air it. Twenty years later it briefly found an outlet as a mail-order DVD. It just as quickly disappeared and became an expensive collector's item due to the many classic western stars involved. Short clips from the film have found their way onto the Internet.

The film's stunt coordinator, a young local named Grady Bishop, saw Jocko on the set and nearly turned down the job in deference to the veteran. Bishop was ready to work on the film for free simply to learn from a stunt master with Jocko's credentials. Jocko took Bishop on a short walk and talked him into staying on at full pay to coordinate the climactic gunfight and saddle falls, offering to help Bishop only if he needed it. Jocko ultimately helped Bishop and the director Howell Upchurch in placing the camera for the action scenes. "I followed him around like a puppy dog on that set," Bishop said. "I wanted to be a sponge and soak up anything that leaked out. Jocko helped me out a ton, but he pulled my chain a lot."[15]

As can be expected, there were plenty of practical jokes being played amongst the cast of old-timers. Jocko was front and center in many of the gags. When Drury was being interviewed on camera by *Entertainment Tonight*, Jocko came up behind him with what Bishop remembers was "a grin like a Cheshire cat." Everyone on the set knew Jocko was up to something. Jocko tipped up Drury's hat as he put his arm around him, telling the camera that their next film together was going to be *Fairies on the Prairie*. Drury, with his forehead exposed and the interview ruined, gave Jocko a good-natured elbow to the gut.

Bishop was the victim of one practical joke. Chuck Connors was having his makeup done in the western town's barbershop when the assistant director called for Connors to come to the set. An angry Connors came to the barbershop door and yelled that he was still in makeup. Bishop was standing in the street with a rifle in hand, while Jocko was across the street. Jocko called out, "Connors, you big faggot, get yourself on the set!" Connors went ballistic and stormed toward Jocko, who paced forward with fists clenched to meet the 6'6" storm head on. Caught in the middle was Grady Bishop. He dropped his rifle in a panic as Connors and Jocko collided in front of him. Suddenly the veteran actors were arm and arm and skipping off to the set together all smiles.

Bishop became a friend and another in a long line of stuntmen who considered Jocko his father figure and mentor. Jocko imparted his wisdom to Bishop in many ways, stressing how important it was to always stand up for the little guy and treat others the way you wanted to be treated yourself. It was important to share the craft and make time for others. Bishop spent one memorable evening having dinner with Jocko and Iron Eyes Cody where they traced Bishop's entire Cherokee ancestry. Shortly after making *All-American Cowboy*, Bishop lost his mother, and Jocko was there to help him through a difficult time.

"I owe everything to that man," Bishop said. "I wouldn't be where I am today if it wasn't for Jocko Mahoney. He was a great man, greater than a lot of people realize. Everything he did touched your heart. He watched over me, and I think he still does today. Every day I'm on the set I whisper to myself and say out loud, 'Thanks, Uncle Jocko.'"

Bishop's résumé notes Jocko gave him training in screen fights and fire gags. Jocko also filmed a video dedication for Bishop that the stuntman used on his demo reel. After *All American Cowboy* Jocko began serving on the advisory board for the Texas-based Third Coast Stuntman's Association, an organization fronted by Bishop and Ray Barrow. Whenever Bishop had a problem or a question on any film he was coordinating, Jocko was only a phone call away. Jocko's vast experience and connections solved many a professional difficulty for Bishop. The Third Coast organization awarded Jocko a plaque of appreciation and thanks for his advisory role.

Jocko and fellow stuntman Dean Smith helped Bishop in training falling horses for a medieval film called *The Radicals* (1988) made in Germany, Switzerland, and France. Bishop spent two days with Jocko and Smith in Los Angeles learning to fall the horses. Once in Europe, Bishop encountered problems with the lack of western saddles available for the warmblood horses they used. Bishop talked back and forth with Jocko and Smith on the phone during this period to solve the difficulties and save their shooting schedule. "I could call him any time I had a problem and it got fixed," Bishop said. "He taught me a lot. He was big into safety. He taught me how to shoot around stuff if you can't get the stunt; how to deal with the D.P. and still make the shot look good."

Jocko saw Bishop whenever he made personal appearances in Texas at Ben Johnson's charity rodeos and helped with Bishop's live Wild West shows at the Fort Worth Stockyards during such events as the Pioneer Days and the Chisholm Trail Days. At one of Yakima Canutt's last appearances for Ben Johnson in Fort Worth, Bishop was determined to duplicate Canutt's famous *Stagecoach* stunt for the arena crowd. Jocko and Johnson gave him some pointers. Bishop successfully completed the fall and drag between the horses but was unable to pull himself back up onto the coach as his ribs had been stepped on. Jocko took the microphone and explained to the appreciative audience the difficulty of what they just witnessed. The arena crowd gave Bishop a standing ovation as he walked off.

At one Fort Worth show Jocko led John Wayne's horse Dollor around the arena with an empty saddle to the delight of the fans. Jocko also judged a gunfight competition involving Bishop and Barrow's stunt crew and served in the same capacity for the Texas Motion Picture Stuntman's Competition Bishop put on in the late 1980s. During one lean period Bishop was working at the Alamo Village in Brackettville and unsure if he could make a decent living doing stunt work in Texas. "Stick with it, Boo Boo," Jocko lectured. "It will pay off."

Bishop stuck with it and eventually became a well-respected stunt coordinator not only in Texas, but also in Florida and Los Angeles. He later created a tribute to Jocko called *The Friends of Jock O'Mahoney* on his Facebook website. Bishop shared many of Jocko's teachings and mantras and provided space for Jocko's friends to honor the stunt legend's memory with photos and recollections. In 2012 Bishop formed Jocko Productions in hopes of one day filming a remake of *Slim Carter*. "Anything for Jocko," Bishop said. "I wouldn't be in this business if not for him."

Ray Barrow was another Third Coast stuntman who worked on *All-American Cowboy* and *The Radicals* and recalled his life and professional lessons from Jocko with fondness[16]:

> What I got from Jocko, I've kept with me my whole life. Good, bad, or indifferent. Don't tell the director what you're going to do. Let him tell you what he wants you to do. Always pay attention to what's going on. Don't get hurt. Never do any more than you have to. I wish I'd been around him a little sooner. He was a pretty awesome guy to be around, and it felt like he was about eight feet tall.
>
> He was very interesting and kind of a dad figure. I did a high fall tribute to Dar Robinson and Jocko spoke to the audience and said, "That's my kid down there." It was more of a cool thing he was talking to them about me than the stunt itself. I used his name quite a bit when I went to Los Angeles, and I talked to him a couple times out there. He was always real honest and a big mentor. He wasn't real involved in the business much any more, but he'd say, "I'll do what I can for you." I still carry a lot of him with me.

It's a little surprising that Jocko didn't make more TV and film appearances during this period. With his full beard, he'd have seemed a natural to play a character part as a Confederate or Union officer in one of the epic Civil War mini-series such as *The Blue and the Gray* (1982) or *North and South* (1985). Country singer Kenny Rogers made a series of TV movie westerns that employed many older cowboy players. Given his status as a former TV western star, Jocko might have found a role here. It also seems a TV movie about the life of Errol Flynn titled *My Wicked Wicked Ways* (1985) could have found employment for Jocko as actor or stunt coordinator. These opportunities, however, would have amounted to little more than bit parts.

Jocko would have loved to have sunk his teeth into a meaty character role, something such as his former stuntman friend Richard Farnsworth landed with *The Grey Fox* (1983). Unfortunately, nothing materialized for Jocko. Word in the industry was that he was having trouble remembering his lines because of the stroke, and that became the kiss of death to his acting career. Producers are reluctant to hire actors who will cost them production time. It's to Jocko's credit that he resisted accepting roles in horror or cheap exploitation films that could have top-lined his name but gone against his values. Low-budget director Fred Olen Ray wanted to employ Jocko in one of his first crudely made films in the early eighties, but Jocko turned the part down on principle. He really wanted to make things he could be proud of.

One show Jocko enjoyed in the early 1980s was the syndicated TV series *Fishing Fever* with host Robert Fuller. Jocko spent ten days in the Bahamas scuba diving and deep sea fishing off a 53-foot yacht with his pal for the cameras. The show tied in an interview on the transom of the boat with Jocko as he and Fuller fished for marlin, tarpon, shark, or whatever game fish came their way. Fuller spent a year hosting the pleasantly diverting show and inviting pals Doug McClure, Ron Ely, Richard Jaeckel, Patrick Wayne, Dan Haggerty, Slim Pickens *et al.* to angle with him. "We had a wonderful time," Fuller said of the days he spent on the show with Jocko.[17]

Upon turning 65, Jocko began to settle into his retirement from acting and spent most of his off-hours taking care of his new horse named Lady. He had not owned a horse in many years and considered her his prized possession. Jocko and Autumn especially enjoyed taking leisurely rides with one another. Ever the enterprising businessman, Jocko became a partner in an effort to build equestrian centers in California, New Mexico, and Missouri. He returned to the land of horse breeding as he served as a spokesperson for a breed called a National Show Registry, a combination of Arabian and American saddle-bred horses. In connection with this position, Jocko still tried to get his film series *The Magic World of Horses* off the ground.

Jocko had many irons in the fire. He discussed producing arena shows at the ranch of veteran trick rider Montie Montana and made plans with his close friend Jack Iversen to build a film studio to be named Viking Studios, in the Simi Valley. The intention was to return old-fashioned adventure to the movies with Jocko acting, producing, and directing. His friend Gene Ryals would have been head of security for the studio. Often times Jocko's endeavors had no positive impact on his own wallet. He was ever ready to lend his name to a cause he strongly believed in and felt that simply mingling with others was beneficial to his own well-being. Ryals claimed, "He would give you the shirt off his back if you asked for it."[18]

Jack Iversen, a former U.S. Marine and noted animator for both Walt Disney and Warner Bros. cartoons, wrote of his friendship with Jocko in the pages of *The Burroughs Bulletin*:

> In all my years in Hollywood, I have never met anyone quite like Jock Mahoney. He was unique in many ways because of his multi-talents, and due to his awesome agility, sincerity, abject pro-fessionalism, sense of humor and humility, he stood out from the rest of the western stars in a

very refreshing way. Strangely enough Jocko had basically the same sense of humor as I have which made our friendship a very fun thing to say the least, since we sparked each other's wit, which was sometimes devastating…. We were together constantly, and I really got to know the complexity of the man from every angle.

Due to a sporadic income, Jocko and Autumn moved around often. For a time they lived in a house in Van Nuys owned by Sally Field's ex-husband Steve Craig, who remained friendly with his children's grandfather. At one point Jocko lived on Huston Street in Sherman Oaks next to Gene Autry's old comedian sidekick Pat Buttram, who became yet another of Jocko's very good friends. Buttram kept Jocko laughing with his good humor. Although Jocko was often silent about events of his past, in the here and now he was an extroverted riot and made no attempt to shy away from the public. Jocko and Autumn could often be found eating alongside their friend Esther Luttrell at the popular Jerry's Deli in Studio City.

On occasion Jocko still managed to get his name in the paper. Along with Gordon Scott and Denny Miller, Jocko jokingly formed the Past Tarzan's Association and attended the Christopher Lambert Tarzan film *Greystoke: The Legend of Tarzan, Lord of the Apes* (1984) with the two. The classy production from English director Hugh Hudson was the most serious Tarzan film ever presented on screen. Jocko told the *Los Angeles Times*, "I think Burroughs would have been happier with this movie than any of them. Tarzan was an animal. Lambert played him beautifully."

More honors came Jocko's way. In 1981 the National Film Heritage Society gave him the Yakima Canutt Award for stunt excellence. In October of 1984 he was awarded a Hollywood Stuntmen's Life Achievement Award at the Century Plaza Hotel. He also received an award from the Hollywood Appreciation Society. The life achievement award was in connection with the Hollywood Stuntmen's Lupus Foundation, an organization for which Jocko did a lot of charity work. The Jocko event was hosted by Ron Ely and chaired by Gene Autry. It featured the participation of Robert Fuller, Sally Field, Princess O'Mahoney, Burt Reynolds, Charles Bronson, Ben Johnson, Lee Van Cleef, Peter Breck, George Montgomery, Sammy Davis, Jr., Gene Kelly, Frances Bergen, Beverly Garland, Barbara Stanwyck, Loretta Young, Ruta Lee, Denver Pyle, Pat Buttram and Alan Hale, and stuntmen Fred Krone, Boyd "Red" Morgan, Chuck Courtney, Richard Farnsworth *et al.* California Governor George Deukmejian sent Jocko a letter of congratulations.

By 1982 Jocko was serving on the Board of Directors for the Hollywood Appreciation Society and was instrumental in getting his old serial director Spencer Gordon Bennet inducted. Denver Pyle and Iron Eyes Cody served alongside chairman Jocko, helping to induct otherwise overlooked talents such as rodeo cowboy Montie Montana and B-western star Sunset Carson. Jocko told the *Los Angeles Times*, "Basically, the whole idea is to get together and have fun. We primarily honor little legends. A lot of these people have never been honored in any way, shape, or form."

Jocko's former co-star Terry Frost regularly attended the Hollywood Appreciation Club with his wife and invited his writer friends Tom and Jim Goldrup to attend the award functions. Tom met Jocko there. They shook hands and Tom told Jocko he watched him on *The Range Rider* when he was a kid. Jocko eyed the premature graying in Tom's hair and beard and with a gleam in his eye said, "Don't give me any of that 'when you were a kid' shit." Tom recalled Jocko as "a nice man with a sense of humor."[19]

Movie critic Leonard Maltin interviewed Jocko about his remarkable stunt career for

Entertainment Tonight, coming away with the impression that Jocko might have been a little full of himself but rightfully so. In his book *Leonard Maltin's Movie Encyclopedia* he called Jocko "one of the greatest stuntmen who ever lived." Jocko was also interviewed for the documentary *Stooge Snapshots* (1984) and the baby boomer nostalgia shows *Our Time* (1985) and *Our World* (1986), and appeared on *The Sally Jesse Raphael Show* with Pierce Lyden for a segment about films of the 1940s.

In February 1985 he was honored at his alma mater in Iowa City for a Jock Mahoney–Hawkeye Fantasy Film Festival where *Tarzan Goes to India, The Land Unknown,* and one of his Three Stooges shorts were shown. In connection with the festival, Jocko served as the honorary coach for both a swim meet and a wrestling match between Iowa and Iowa State at the Carver-Hawkeye Arena. These were important sporting events, and the University of Iowa athletes received an extra boost of adrenaline from having Tarzan speak words of encouragement. Jocko had long followed Iowa Hawkeye athletics and had the pleasure to meet swimming coach Glen Patton, legendary wrestling coach Dan Gable, and athletic director Bump Elliott. "Once a Hawkeye, always a Hawkeye," Jocko told the *Iowa City Press-Citizen.*

When announced to the crowd of over 12,000, he walked onto the gym floor to a standing ovation. Photos from the event show a clean-shaven and slimmed-down Jocko looking the best he had in years. He had lost 20 pounds especially for the event. During his visit, Jocko met Edgar Rice Burroughs scholar Erling Holtsmark, who while critical of the Tarzan films as a whole told the *Press-Citizen* he found Jocko to be "a nice guy, outgoing, a salt of the earth type, very unpretentious." Holtsmark gave Jocko a copy of his latest book on Burroughs' life. Jocko also had the opportunity to reminisce with Jim Zabel about their days at Davenport High.

As was Jocko's custom, he stayed in touch with Mike Chapman, a local Iowa writer and wrestling historian who was instrumental in arranging Jocko's invitation and appearance for the event. Chapman and his family spent nearly two and a half days with Jocko and Autumn, forming a lasting bond of friendship in the process. Chapman had a strong knowledge of the Tarzan films and Jocko's overall importance to that franchise, liking the way he portrayed the character as faithful to Burroughs. Chapman later authored a well-received biography of Herman Brix entitled *Please Don't Call Me Tarzan,* which explored Brix's life-long battle with distancing himself from the character.

After his return to California, Jocko sent Chapman a seven-page handwritten letter in which he outlined his philosophy on life and the importance of always coming up with tests and new challenges. Jocko did not believe in luck affecting one's fortunes but felt that a person must prepare themselves physically and psychologically for any endeavor. A person had a lot to learn from failure. To Jocko, defeat was only a step up the ladder of success. Chapman had met celebrities as famous and diverse as Ronald Reagan and Muhammad Ali, yet he considered his weekend with Jocko to be one of his most memorable encounters. They continued to correspond by phone and mail.[20] Chapman wrote of his weekend with Jocko in the *Iowa History Journal:* "His optimism about life in general and his sense of adventure left an impact on me. I am proud that I was able to spend time with this intriguing Iowan from out of the past."

Jocko began to pile up so many personal appearances, one would need a scorecard to keep track of them. In 1983 he judged the Poway County Fair's gunfighter competition in

San Diego and rode in the East Los Angeles Parade. In 1984 he appeared with Ben Johnson and John Russell at the Western Chuck Wagon Bar-BQ and Wild West Show in connection with the 1984 Olympic Games in Los Angeles. That same year he rode in the St. Patrick's Day Parade with Rory Calhoun and Dan Haggerty. In 1985 he appeared in Orlando, Florida, for the Deborah Heart and Lung Center, a fundraiser for a New Jersey clinic offering medical aid for the financially needy. In Tombstone, Arizona he was sworn in as an honorary deputy marshal at the historic home of the famous O.K. Corral. He was guest speaker at LOSCON-12, a science fiction and fantasy convention staged at the Pasadena Hilton in late 1985. A photo of a buckskin-fringe Jocko and Iron Eyes Cody mugging for the camera at the Annual Directors Guild of America Dinner held at the Beverly Hills Hilton made it into the pages of *Life* magazine in 1985.

Jocko, Woody Strode, John Agar, and Harry Carey, Jr., were among those lobbying to get a star on the Hollywood Walk of Fame for veteran character actor Hank Worden. Despite a fundraiser called "The Hoedown for Hank," the Worden plaque was never approved because he was deemed not important enough by Hollywood. Jocko, Iron Eyes Cody, and Pat Buttram showed up for the ceremony when their late friend Smiley Burnette received a star in May of 1986. Jocko, Gene Autry, Denver Pyle, and Iron Eyes were there for Buttram's star in August of 1988. Pyle and Iron Eyes would both land stars on the sidewalk. Ironically, Jocko was never nominated for a star on the Hollywood Walk of Fame, despite the fact he was a film and television headliner. Fellow Tarzans Johnny Weissmuller and Buster Crabbe both have stars. Dick Jones received a star in 1960. Gene Autry has no less than five stars on the Walk of Fame.

In August of 1986 Jocko was honored with the coveted Golden Boot Award, the mark of a performer who had contributed greatly to the western genre. The award was sponsored by the Motion Picture and Television Fund and was conceived by Pat Buttram in 1983. Other cowboy stars receiving the honor at the Fourth Annual Award show held at the Warner Center Marriott in Woodland Hills included George Montgomery, Guy Madison, Fess Parker, James Arness, and Jocko's favorite western writer Louis L'Amour. Jocko became a mainstay at that yearly award and enjoyed mingling and honoring those actors and fellow stuntmen he had worked with throughout his career. He often attended the shows and the Pre-Boot party at the Sportsmen's Lodge on Ventura Boulevard with pals like Robert Fuller.

Few of those who entered motion pictures with Jocko remained active in the business, although Jocko's friend Ronald Reagan had ascended to the presidency of the United States in 1980. One publicity junket took Jocko, James Drury, and Doug McClure to the White House. Drury recalled they were in the catacombs of the building preparing to take press photos when Jocko stepped out of the reception line and grabbed the president of the United States by the lapels. Jocko "button-holed" President Reagan to the shock of all those present as McClure grinned and Drury rolled his eyes at Jocko's chutzpah. "I was horrified," Drury said, laughing at the memory. "Of course they were old friends. Jocko was crazy, but in a good sort of way."[21]

Many of Jocko's personal appearances took him to the state of Texas. In 1984 he was in Dallas for the Cattle Baron's Ball for cancer research. From that year on, he made a number of personal appearances alongside former stuntman pals Ben Johnson and Richard Farnsworth for the Y.O. Ranch near Kerrville, Texas. The ranch had the world's largest collection of roaming exotic animals and was noted for its huge parties. Jocko was a yearly regular at the Ben Johnson Celebrity Cutting and Roping events for abused children in Fort Worth and attended former Dallas Cowboy football player Walt Garrison's Rodeo for Multiple Sclerosis. In 1986 Jocko rode in the Gonzales, Texas, parade celebrating the state's war for independence. During this period, Jocko traveled to Houston to survey sites for the Great West Hero Museum, a project that never came to pass.

Dallas-based Marty Rendleman met Jocko at the Ben Johnson Celebrity Cutting and Roping event. At the time the music manager had started a side business called Celebrity Prints, Inc. She and her business partner set about getting hand and foot prints of as many of the celebrities as possible. Jocko became fast friends with the Texas lady. Whenever she came to Los Angeles he helped her as much as possible, literally coming to her hotel room with his phone book in hand. Every friend he called was soon at Rendleman's doorstep ready to contribute their prints.[22]

On one morning a rambunctious Jocko surprised Rendleman through her open window, giving out a loud Tarzan yell that could have woke the dead. Jocko roared with laughter as the entire hotel stirred awake. Grady Bishop also remembered that Jocko "would do that Tarzan yell in a hurry,"[23] recalling one late night ape call in a hotel lobby that drew a standing ovation from everyone present. Marty Rendleman recalled, "He had a smile that lit up the room, and a laugh that could be heard across the street."[24]

Whenever she was in Los Angeles, Jocko made time to invite Rendleman and her friends to breakfast or dinner with himself and Autumn. Rendleman called Jocko "quite a character and always entertaining." She remembered one dinner when he outlined his philosophy about finding something to like about every person you meet. "Even if it's only their socks," he laughed. In Rendleman's words, Jocko was "one of the most gregarious, wonderful men I've ever met. We enjoyed every minute with him."

In 1986 Jocko appeared at the V.P.R.A. grand opening of a video production company in Southern California. It was there that a young stuntman named Eric Dyck encountered Jocko in a filmed training session. Dyck was still in his teens but was fortunate to have already been taken under the wing of veteran stunter Boyd "Red" Morgan and the legendary Yakima Canutt. Through these men he had heard plenty of tales about Jocko and how he would chew out someone practicing unsafe stunt techniques. Dyck recalled, "He wasn't the big bad mean guy they made him out to be, but was very open when it came to your performance. I expected him to be 15 foot tall with fangs down to his chest. Imagine an 18-year-old meeting one of the big names with one set of impressions, and finding out he was one of the greatest people and down to earth one could meet."[25]

There were plenty more events for Jocko to occupy his time and energies. During the 1980s Jocko and Autumn became quite close with *Sugarfoot* TV star Will Hutchins and his wife Barbara Torres, a former student in Jocko's stunt classes at CBS-TV (she likened Jocko to Santa Claus). They often traveled together to the assorted film festivals, with Jocko teasingly calling Hutchins Sweet Toes. Hutchins had turned his back on his acting career but gave credit to Jocko for getting him back into circulation with the fans. Jocko had first contacted Hutchins for a cowboy photo shoot in the late 1970s. That photo shoot and the TV special *When the West Was Fun* were experiences Hutchins enjoyed, and it jump-started a second phase of his career. Hutchins said, "When I got hitched to Babs, Jocko, Autumn, and we shared many a joyous adventure at western film festivals and the like. I am not unaware that Jocko was an angel in my life."[26]

In May of 1986 Jocko and Hutchins traveled to Portsmouth, Ohio, for the Roy Rogers Wild West Days. Jocko put his hand and feet imprints in concrete for the Rogers festival. The event was filmed by the Nashville Network and aired as a segment of their *Country Notes* program. While being interviewed, Jocko recalled that one of his favorite stunts was the front flip he performed with guitar in hand for the Three Stooges in *Punchy Cowpunchers*. The next morning Hutchins woke up, turned on the TV, and was stunned to see that exact Stooges short being shown. The odds of such happenstance seemed unreal. "It could happen only with Jocko," Hutchins said. "Jocko was of another plateau of consciousness."

In addition to film festivals, Jocko and Hutchins served together as celebrity judges for gunfighter competitions everywhere from Bandera, Texas, to San Diego, California. Hutchins wrote:

> Going to gunfight contests with Jocko was always a treat. Once in Bandera, Texas, we visited the local saloon. Jocko said, "That isn't sawdust on the floor. It's last night's furniture." These gunfight contests were little playlets in which duded-up contestants would shoot it out, but not before setting it up in dramatic fashion. The costumes and acting played a big part in the scoring, as well as the gunmanship. Jocko was a stickler on gun safety. He kept a sharp eye out for any transgressors. He was a mighty strong supporter and worker for gun safety, stuntman safety, and animal safety.

"We had good fun in San Diego," Hutchins said of another gunfight event in which veteran character actor Keenan Wynn judged alongside them. The trip back involved an enjoyable diversion to see Jocko's director friend Budd Boetticher and his wife at their ranch. Hutchins continued: "It was late when we started our drive back to L.A. along dark, winding mountain roads. Jocko hadn't completely recovered from the after-effects of his stroke. Let me tell ya, there were no atheists in his car. He made our ride one hairy, scary stunt. God bless him."

At the 1987 Memphis Film Festival, Jocko was reunited publicly with Dick Jones to the delight of all involved. It was the only film festival appearance that Jocko and Jones made with one another. At this show Jocko was swamped by the fans and their requests for autographs. Jones knew that Jocko could be finicky at times about what he signed. Jocko preferred photos or programs to blank pieces of paper. Dick got in line and when it came his turn he shoved a crumpled gum wrapper onto the table and demanded, "Sign this." Jocko did a slow burn until he looked up and realized it was his old saddle partner. "Jocko jumped up on top of the table and we went at it for the fans," Jones recalled.[27]

Jocko continued to make the rounds of the western film festival circuit, attending events in Memphis; Williamsburg, Virginia; Ashland, Charlotte, and Raleigh, North Carolina; St. Louis; Orlando; Atlanta; and Ogden, Utah. He was always one of the most accessible stars at these conventions and loved the fans. Many of them he remembered by name during repeat visits. Jocko was especially good with kids, although when they weren't around Jocko could and did swear like a sailor. Writer David Rothel had an opportunity to catch up with Jocko at film festivals in Memphis and Charlotte and noted in his book *Opened Time Capsules* that Jocko "was still the devil-may-care joker and raconteur, always a funny story to tell or film anecdote to recall for those who clustered around him."

Bill Sasser was in charge of the Williamsburg Film Festival. He commented: "I met Jock twice at film festivals. He was a gentleman and was very nice to his fans. He was down to earth and did not appear to have an ego. Dick Jones loved him and swears that they did all their own stunts in *Range Rider*. At Charlotte he met a friend of mine who mentioned Tarzan to him. In the course of the conversation, my friend mentioned that he did not know how to swim. For the next four days, Jocko met him at the hotel swimming pool at 7 A.M. and taught him how to swim."[28]

Bobby Copeland, another film festival regular, encountered Jocko on a handful of occasions and came away with pleasant memories. He found it interesting that there was such a disparity between the real Jocko and his screen image: Copeland noted that on screen he found Jocko to be rather stiff and wooden. In person though, Jocko was energetic and a terrific guest. Jocko inevitably become "the King of the Panel" whenever questions were fielded from the audience. Copeland described Jocko as a "good-natured clown" who loved to pull practical jokes. For example, Jocko and Pierce Lyden were on a motel elevator full of people traveling to their respective floors. When Jocko got off at his floor he held the door open and turned to Lyden, saying loudly that if Lyden didn't shave his legs he wasn't sharing Jocko's bed that night. The door closed on a shocked and embarrassed Lyden as Jocko let out his booming laugh from the hallway.[29]

Gun, knife, and bullwhip stunt artist Gordie Peer had known Jocko since the 1950s, when he was making personal appearances on the rodeo circuit with their mutual friends Clayton Moore, Jay Silverheels, and Lash LaRue. The personal appearances were so lucrative that Peer gave up work as a film stuntman to concentrate on the live shows. Jocko found it ironic that Peer was making more money on the weekends than Jocko was earning during the week starring as the Range Rider. The two were occasionally in competition with one another for the live shows but had a healthy friendship.

"Jocko liked to call me a little pipsqueak," the 5'8", 156-pound Peer laughed. "He could jump from the ground to the saddle without using his hands. I could do that too. 'Don't you ever do that when I'm around,' he used to joke. 'That's supposed to be my thing.' He was one heck of a guy, not like some of them out there. I enjoyed the times I spent with him. He was a real enjoyable and down-to-earth person. Jocko was a practical joker. Several times he pulled practical jokes on me, though I got him back one time."

Jocko and Peer were doing publicity for an appearance at the Great Western Heroes film festival in Orlando, Florida. A TV interview was done in the Cheyenne Saloon, a western nightclub at the Church Street Station. Jocko and Peer were standing against the long bar for the interview. As Peer was interviewed, a wily Jocko draped his arm across the bar and reached down to surreptitiously rub Peer's backside. A visibly uncomfortable Peer began to fidget so much on camera that the interviewer asked if there was a problem. "Yes," Peer blurted out. "Jocko is playing with my butt!" Jocko was surprised by Peer's revelatory exclamation and his humorously shocked expression aired on the TV ads for the show.[30]

Atlanta-based character actor Don Young met Jocko at the Memphis Film Festival in the late 1970s and they hit it off right away. Horse lover Young was also a good friend of Ben Johnson, and he would see both Ben and Jocko whenever he was in California. When Jocko would travel to Memphis, Young would pick him up at the airport. At this point Young had never acted before, but he became interested in the business. Young never asked for it, but Ben and Jocko helped steer him on his way to a professional acting career that is still going strong in films like *Trouble with the Curve* (2012). He said of his friends,

They were some characters. Jock was awful nice and never met a stranger. He was easy to get to know. Jock was a big cut-up. I don't think Jock was ever serious. He played practical jokes all the time and was never serious for a minute. After I met him I couldn't enjoy his movies any more because I was always waiting for him to start cutting up. He always cut-up with kids. He liked to call them brats, but the next minute he'd be hugging them; then he'd turn around and cuss. He was great. He met my daughter and I told her beforehand, "Be prepared for anything." I think he loved kids more than anybody I've ever known.

Jock was a big ol' robust rascal. He wouldn't even drink cocoa. He'd say, "No, I can't put that in me." He was always eating fruit and health foods. That's why it was so surprising when he died. I thought he was the picture of health. I had a friend who was a policeman who told me this story. A man was hurt in an accident and Jock was there. Jock knelt down and was talking to the man. The man was hurt bad and didn't end up making it. Jock told him it was going to be all right. "Death is not to be feared," Jock said. "I've been there before." Jock said he had died and come back. I don't know the veracity of that story since it is second-hand. Jock never mentioned it to me, but I always found it interesting that Jock had said he had died and come back. I know he was interested in that kind of thing.[31]

Unfortunately, some of Jocko's colleagues and co-workers began to pass away with alarming frequency. In years past he'd lose the occasional pal: Errol Flynn in the late 1950s, Bill Elliott and Smiley Burnette in the late 1960s, and Rodd Redwing, Lane Bradford, Kelly Thordsen, and Charles Horvath in the 1970s, but at this point Jocko's friends began to fall too fast and too often. Stunt legends Dave Sharpe and Richard Talmadge both passed, and Jocko lost an especially good friend in singing cowboy star Jimmy Wakely in 1982. In a letter to Robert Callaghan, Wakely's son Johnny remembered Jocko's dedication and his countless visits to the hospital: "Jock Mahoney, what a great guy. He was a true man's man as they say and yet he was the sweetest, kindest man you can imagine."

Cancer finally took John Wayne in 1979 after a 15-year battle. Jay Silverheels died of a stroke in 1980. Marshall Reed and Slim Pickens died of brain tumor complications in the early 1980s. Richard Boone succumbed to throat cancer in 1981 at the age of 63. Buster Crabbe died of a heart attack in 1983 and Johnny Weissmuller of pulmonary edema in 1984. Rod Cameron died in 1983 and Ted Mapes in 1984. Charles Starrett and Yakima Canutt passed on in 1986 and Randolph Scott followed the next year. "Red" Morgan, Chuck Roberson, and Louis L'Amour died in 1988.

Although some of Jocko's contemporaries were reaching the end of the trail he continued to make new friends and acquaintances at a rapid pace. Many were just ordinary people from all walks of life. Jocko often initiated conversations with complete strangers as he was out and about. Gene Ryals recalled once being at the grocery store with Jocko, who became intrigued by a female shopper who was staring longingly at a canned good product on the shelf. Jocko approached the woman and told her the price of the item was going up the longer she looked at it. "She just stared at him like he was nuts," Ryals said. "It was very funny."[32]

One of Jocko's very good friends was Judy Pastorius, whom he had known since she was a young girl back in the 1950s. At the age of 14 she became intrigued with Jocko's handsome smile on the television set and joined a *Range Rider* fan club. Due to her location she was eventually asked to be their western representative. Through the fan club she met Jocko and began interviewing him regularly for the publication. A few years later Jocko invited her high school class onto the set of *Yancy Derringer* to see how a production was filmed. "He met us there and very graciously showed us all around," Pastorius recalled. "What a day.... Over the years our friendship grew and until the day of his passing I regarded him as one of my dearest friends."

Jocko and Pastorius made it a point to celebrate one another's birthdays through the years, even if it involved Jocko traveling to her home in Las Vegas for nothing more than cake and a short visit. On one occasion Jocko made his way through a downpour to see Judy and her husband off at the Los Angeles airport as they prepared to fly to Hawaii. "I met so many wonderful people through him that I'll always be grateful for," Pastorius said. "Even today I am still meeting people who knew him and they tell me of their experiences. He was never boring to be around; swimming parties, dinners or anything we did was such a memorable lifetime for me. I can't imagine my life without Jocko in it. There are just so many wonderful times, I couldn't mention them all."[33]

Much of Jocko's free time was spent reminiscing over breakfast about the good old days with former co-workers and contemporaries Pat Buttram, Denver Pyle, Dana Andrews, John Russell, Don Durant, Richard Webb, R.G. Armstrong, Terry Frost, Gregg Barton, Monte Hale, Peggy Stewart, Pierce Lyden, William Campbell, Gregg Palmer, Rand Brooks, and John Agar, to name but a few. They were often accompanied by Jocko's daughter Princess and veteran stuntmen such as Al Wyatt, John "Bear" Hudkins, Rodd Wolff, and Neil Summers. Sometimes they were even joined by Gene Autry. Jocko's friends Jack Iversen, Steve Kiefer, Herb Harris, John Church, and Jan Alan Henderson were regularly included as Jocko sipped coffee and held court at the head of the table. Photographer Steve Kiefer drove all the way from Palm Springs to have breakfast with Jocko and had special T-shirts made up for the group. "He was an extrovert's extrovert," Will Hutchins said of Jocko. "Boy, did he have a slew of pals."[34]

The group of Saturday morning regulars became known unofficially as Jocko Mahoney's Breakfast Club, an updated version of the B.S. and Grub Club that Jocko had formed in the early 1970s. They initially met at a Bob's Big Boy and later Charlie's Restaurant in Studio City. The Breakfast Club found a lasting home at the Sportsmen's Lodge, a popular spot with the older Hollywood crowd that was noted for its peaceful gardens and trout fishing pond on the grounds. Much of the group's talk inevitably centered on Jocko's legendary exploits. Veteran character actor Richard Webb of TV's *Captain Midnight* told the *Los Angeles Daily News* in 1986: "Jocko used to go out on the ground floor balcony of the house and dive from the balcony into the pool! Talk about macho! Anything he did was macho. The way he moved — it was just like water flowing to watch him."

The biggest rumbling in Jocko's retirement was stepdaughter Sally's revelations of 1960s domestic discord to *Playboy* in 1986, mentioning how tough Jocko was as a parent. Jocko chose not to defend against or counter Sally's interview. He no doubt had regrets about the way his marriage to Sally's mother turned out, but he kept them to himself. He still loved them as family. When asked about his stepdaughter at film festivals, he continued to speak of her with fondness and pride in her many accomplishments. He told the *St. Louis Dispatch*, "Sally is a fine girl, a genuinely nice person. We're still close."

The image of Jocko as a demanding authoritarian was in strong contrast to the fun-loving man that many of his friends had known both publicly and privately. "Everybody knew Jocko," Jim Martin said. "I never heard anyone say a bad thing about him except Sally Field. He was always a gentleman around me and would have done anything to be polite around women."[35] Longtime friend Judy Pastorius said, "I knew him from 1956 until his death in 1989 and never saw a negative side to him as some have reported."[36] Gene Ryals added, "I never heard Jocko say a bad word about Sally Field. Whenever he talked about her it was always like a proud Dad."[37] Esther Luttrell backed this up: "By the time I met him he was so very proud of her, but frankly, a little intimidated by her at the same time. Guilt probably had a lot to do with it. He really, really cared about her."[38] Grady Bishop said, "All I heard was praise for her. I saw it in person, the admiration he had for her when she was doing one of her hardest roles in *Punchline*."[39]

Jocko continued to seek out the slightly strange and extraordinary in hopes of bettering himself as a person. Will Hutchins recalled that Jocko was a very spiritual person with a keen interest in legitimate psychic phenomenon. Hutchins shared the following story: "One time, he, Autumn, Babs, and I went to some sort of psychic institute up by our apartment house in Los Feliz. We sat there for a spell, soaking in all the aura. Then, we were informed that the guru-swami-whatchamacallit was about to appear, robed, before our very eyes. We were asked each to make a contribution of $60. Jocko skedaddled mighty fast, we three in his wake."[40]

In November of 1987 Jocko was featured in a BBC documentary entitled *Hot House People*. Presented by author Jane Walmsley, the show looked at the controversial technique of Hot Housing, a method of enhancing mental and physical faculties to increase intelligence and extend the lifespan. The practice was gaining popularity with children's parents and even older adults as they attempted to ward off the effects of aging. Jocko was a proponent. He was also fond of Arizona doctor Sam Meranto's visualization techniques to overcome stress, depression, addiction, weight gain, and illness through the powers of positive thinking. Whenever he was in Phoenix he paid a visit to Meranto's meditation clinic.

In the late 1980s Jocko's health problems began to flare up again. He was forced to cancel a repeat appearance at the Ohio Roy Rogers Wild West Days Festival in Portsmouth due to a sudden illness in 1987. There were reports that he was plagued by arthritis, certainly conceivable given the many years he beat his body up for the movies. Far more troubling was the onset of cardiac problems. In 1988 he was operated on for five and a half hours for an aneurysm. In early 1989 he had two more minor strokes. During one of his hospital stays, Sally visited and gave him a giant Teddy bear. Esther Luttrell recalled the stuffed animal proved to be especially dear to Jocko and was one of his prized possessions. Despite his health setbacks, Jocko maintained a youthful twinkle in his eye. Luttrell said Jocko was "a big bear of a man, handsome right up to the end."[41]

There were a few more public appearances to be made career-wise and further examples of the special relationship Jocko created with his fans. In October of 1988 Jocko had his hand-and boot-prints immortalized for the Iverson Movie Location Ranch Walk of Fame near Chatsworth. Thirty other celluloid cowboys were there in what was billed as the largest celebrity printing in history. In regard to Iverson Ranch, Jocko told the *Los Angeles Times*, "I've dug up every foot of ground with my head."

Doug McAndrew, a Tarzan fan from England, was taking his daughter to Disneyland and cold-called Jocko. He found himself and his daughter Jocko's special guests that day at Iverson Ranch. For *The Fantastic Worlds of Edgar Rice Burroughs*, McAndrew wrote, "Considering that he was talking to a complete stranger, I have to say that his manner was most admirable. After introducing ourselves we were invited over for a chat. This was followed by some picture-taking. I think I can say quite confidently when I speak for my daughter that this day is one that neither she nor I will forget. I only wish now that I had the opportunity to know him better for he was one movie star for whom the word gentleman truly applied."

The producers of the CBS-TV movie *Tarzan in Manhattan* (1989) starring 6'3" Joe Lara as the ape man asked Phil Petras if he could bring any ex–Tarzans onto the Burbank set for publicity. Petras contacted Jocko and Denny Miller. Everyone was amazed when Jocko showed up with Gordon Scott in tow. Hardly anyone had seen or heard from the elusive Scott in the past 15 years. The three former Tarzans had fun beating their chests for the cameras and whooping up jungle calls. The dinner and conversation that followed were, in Petras' words, "a fan's dream."[42]

Despite the multitude of friends to talk to in Hollywood, Jocko began to grow restless again. The smog surrounding the city of Los Angeles and the San Fernando Valley bothered him and he wanted to breathe clean air again in light of his recent health maladies. Jocko and Autumn decided to move to the Puget Sound area in Poulsbo, Washington near Seattle, where she had children and grandchildren. The mountainous area was full of waterways offering plenty of opportunity for Jocko to indulge his love of sailing, although the frequent rain and damp surroundings no doubt bothered his old stunt injuries. Jocko's Breakfast Club had a huge send-off for the couple.

Realizing retirement in the Pacific Northwest could not have been easy for Jocko's psyche. He was accustomed to always pushing ahead with new plans and goals. Sitting on a rocker as a 70-year-old man listening to the rain pitter-patter on the roof would not have been his cup of tea. Living in Hollywood had kept the irons in the fire even though he had not had an acting role for several years. Interacting with those in the industry maintained the ideas dancing in Jocko's brain. In Washington he was out of the creative loop, left with only memories. During this period Jocko often called Rodd Wolff, Grady Bishop, and other friends to talk on the phone. Perhaps sensing he was now in the twilight of his life, he penned a poem entitled "Coming Home."

Jocko did new interviews for the movie magazines *Starlog* and *Filmfax* with his friend Jan Alan Henderson and invited writer Ronald Jackson to his home for dinner. Jocko presented the latter several photos from his private collection for a project on television westerns. Jocko was back around Hollywood for the 1989 Golden Boot Awards, where he presented his old sidekick Dick Jones with the award. Jones was given the opportunity to choose who presented and chose his old partner Jocko over Gene Autry or Roy Rogers. It was an especially gratifying moment for both Jocko and Dick. The Golden Boot Awards, the Reid Rondell Stunt Foundation Celebrity Race, the Texas Y.O. Ranch feast, and a Schuetzenfest single shot rifle shooting festival with John Russell in California would be the last of Jocko's public appearances.

On Tuesday, December 12, 1989, Jocko was driving his car east on Lincoln Road northeast of Poulsbo when he began to swerve and crashed into an embankment and drainage ditch near Stottlemeyer Road. "It busted him apart pretty bad," Dick Jones said.[43] Jocko was taken to Harrison Memorial Hospital in nearby Bremerton in serious condition but held on valiantly until his daughter Princess could make it up to Washington to talk with him. Jock Mahoney finally passed away two days later at 1 P.M. on December 14, 1989, with Autumn and his daughter Princess at his bedside. Jocko's good friend Robert Fuller spoke to Autumn, who said Jocko had opened his eyes to tell her he loved her and to please let him go. Then with a final goodbye wink, he left this world.[44]

The apparent cause of Jocko's car crash and death was another stroke. An autopsy was performed by Kitsap County's chief deputy coroner Jane Jermy, who came to the same conclusion. Jacques Joseph O'Mahoney was only 70 years old. Autumn wisely surmised that Jocko had lived about five normal lifetimes in those 70 years. Actor Lee Van Cleef, Jocko's good friend and fellow screen cowboy, learned of Jocko's passing on the evening of the 15th. Van Cleef had been battling throat cancer and took the news hard. He passed away from a heart attack shortly after midnight on December 16, 1989. The two movie tough guys died within hours of one another.

Jock O'Mahoney
1919 - 1989

The photograph distributed at Jocko's memorial (courtesy of Rodd Wolff).

The obituary syndicated around the nation's newspapers called Jocko "Hollywood's most famous stuntman turned actor." Writer Tim Ferrante had interviewed Jocko for *Starlog* magazine and penned a remembrance in that magazine's pages: "This *Starlog* contributor had the pleasure of joking, dining, and reminiscing with Mahoney in August 1987 at the Golden Boot Awards ceremony. The then 67-year-old legend, having already beaten one stroke, was as ruggedly handsome as ever. He spoke to one and all like old friends and one's immediate feeling was one of delight and awe. While Mahoney may have missed out on screen superstardom, he most assuredly was a star when dealing with fans."

Back in California, an Irish wake for Jocko was attended by hundreds at a chapel high in the Santa Monica hills. His ashes were ultimately scattered in the Pacific Ocean that he loved. As a final send-off, Autumn released a single balloon into the sky. Don Burt and his wife Ardys will never forget what happened next. The balloon hovered 50 feet over the crowd for several minutes, then rose to 100 feet and again stuck around as if it wasn't ready to leave. Finally, the balloon sped swiftly up into the sky, its tail seeming to wave goodbye to the friends and family beneath it. "It was uncanny the way that balloon circled," Burt said.[45]

On February 6, 1990, a memorial roast for Jocko was held at the Sportsmen's Lodge Regency Room in Studio City. More than 350 people attended to reminisce about their friend and raise a glass in his honor and memory. "He deserved it," Dick Jones said.[46] The four-hour event was sponsored by Jack Iversen and emceed by William Campbell. Among those attending were Jocko's extended family plus Jones, Robert Fuller, Woody Strode, John Russell, Will Hutchins, Peggy Stewart, X Brands, Iron Eyes Cody, Gene Ryals, Jack Lewis, Don Burt, John Agar, Gregg Palmer, Anthony Caruso, Wayde Preston, John Hart, Terry Frost, Gregg Barton, Pierce Lyden, Richard Webb, Don Durant, Hank Worden, Beverly Garland, and John Wayne's son Michael. Stuntmen such as Al Wyatt, Neil Summers, Hal Needham, Dean Smith, Chuck Courtney, and Rodd Wolff are but a small sampling of that profession's representation at the event. Gene Autry and members of Jocko's Breakfast Club turned out in force.

Attendees such as Dick Jones, X Brands, Woody Strode, John Russell, and Robert Fuller were asked to take the stage to share their favorite Jocko stories, guaranteeing the night would be full of laughter and tales of awe-inspiring feats. Gregg Palmer acted out a humorous skit involving John Wayne, Gary Cooper, Walter Brennan, and Gabby Hayes riding through Indian land to attend Jocko's memorial. Joe Bowman twirled his guns for the audience, saying of Jocko on his website: "He rode off into the sunset. And my life was made richer because he called me friend."

Jocko's sudden death was a great blow to his close friends. Over 20 years later his loss could still make a macho man grow misty-eyed thinking of his memory. James Drury said, "I miss him, and I think about him all the time."[47] Robert Fuller noted, "He left us too soon. He was not an old man by any means."[48] Rodd Wolff shared: "Jock was a wonderful guy. He was my mentor and friend."[49] Gene Ryals wrote, "We were good friends and I miss him greatly."[50] Don Burt called Jocko "as good a friend as I've ever had."[51] Neil Summers said, "I revere the memory of Jocko and the 20 years I was able to be his friend.... Long live Jocko's memory."[52] Grady Bishop revealed, "I cried for three days after Autumn told me we lost him. It left a big hole. Not a day goes by that I don't think about him. He was a great man."[53] Phil Petras remembered, "The last time I saw my friend was at a restaurant in the Los Angeles area, with a little get-together that was known as Jocko's Breakfast Club. Other oldtime celebrities were on hand, and a few lucky folks like me. Jocko sat at the head of the table, as it should have been."[54]

Will Hutchins wrote that the event was "one long love letter to Jocko on high. The tenderest moment at Jocko's roast at the Sportsmen's Lodge came at the end. Autumn Mahoney spoke. She said that when folks in awe asked Jocko how he did all those spine-tingling stunts, he said he just stepped out. Autumn looked upward—'Jocko just stepped out.' She kissed me goodbye. Jocko and Autumn will always be a part of us."[55] Autumn finished the evening by reading Jocko's self-penned poem "Coming Home." There wasn't a dry eye in the house.

Epilogue

Jock Mahoney's legacy is that of arguably the greatest action actor ever to have graced the screen. He was certainly one of the all-time top stuntmen despite the brief period in which he filled that role. He will best be known by audiences as the Range Rider, Yancy Derringer, and Tarzan, but there will also be those who remember him for his work with the Three Stooges or as the double for the Durango Kid or Errol Flynn. He may not have been a great actor, but he worked hard to make himself a competent and successful one. His films and TV appearances offer a little bit for everyone, as did the man himself. Jocko's countless personal appearances and the endless hours of availability made for his fans are a reflection of a dying breed of showman. Jocko had flaws as we all do. He also had perfections that the majority of us could only dream of. Jock Mahoney was one of a kind, and his legend lives on.

Appendix: Film and Television Credits

Film

Frontier Gun Law (1946) stunt double for Charles Starrett
Roaring Rangers (1946) stunt double for Charles Starrett
Throw a Saddle on a Star (1946) stunt double for Ken Curtis
Gunning for Vengeance (1946) stunt double for Charles Starrett
Galloping Thunder (1946) stunt double for Charles Starrett
Two Fisted Stranger (1946) stunt double for Charles Starrett
The Desert Horseman (1946) stunt double for Charles Starrett
Heading West (1946) stunt double for Charles Starrett
Son of the Guardsman (1946) (as Captain Kenley) serial stunts.
Landrush (1946) stunt double for Charles Starrett
Terror Trail (1946) stunt double for Charles Starrett
The Fighting Frontiersman (1946) (as henchman Waco) also stunt double for Charles Starrett
South of the Chisholm Trail (1947) (as henchman Thorpe) also stunt double for Charles Starrett
Over the Santa Fe Trail (1947) (as Deputy Sheriff)
The Lone Hand Texan (1947) stunt double for Charles Starrett
West of Dodge City (1947) stunt double for Charles Starrett
Out West (1947) (Three Stooges short) (as The Arizona Kid)
Law of the Canyon (1947) stunt double for Charles Starrett
Prairie Raiders (1947) stunt double for Charles Starrett
Swing the Western Way (1947) (as Chief Iron Stomach)
The Stranger from Ponca City (1947) (as henchman Tensleep) also stunt double for Charles Starrett
Slave Girl (1947) stunts
The Swordsman (1947) (as clansman) also stunts
Riders of the Lone Star (1947) stunt double for Charles Starrett
Buckaroo from Powder River (1947) stunt double for Charles Starrett
Last Days of Boot Hill (1947) stunt double for Charles Starrett
To the Ends of the Earth (1948) stunts
The Gallant Blade (1948) stunts (unconfirmed)
Tex Granger, Midnight Rider of the Plains (1948) serial stunts
The Prince of Thieves (1948) stunt double for Jon Hall
Six Gun Law (1948) stunt double for Charles Starrett
Phantom Valley (1948) stunt double for Charles Starrett
Squareheads of the Round Table (1948) (Three Stooges short) (as Cedric the Blacksmith)
The Black Arrow (1948) stunt double for George Macready

Adventures in Silverado (1948) stunt double for William Bishop & Forrest Tucker
West of Sonora (1948) stunt double for Charles Starrett
Whirlwind Raiders (1948) stunt double for Charles Starrett
Silver River (1948) stunt double for Errol Flynn
Coroner Creek (1948) stunt double for Randolph Scott, Forrest Tucker, and George Macready
Blazing Across the Pecos (1948) (as Bill Wheeler) also stunt double for Charles Starrett
Trail to Laredo (1948) stunt double for Charles Starrett
Triple Threat (1948) football player
El Dorado Pass (1948) stunt double for Charles Starrett
Return of the Bad Men (1948) stunt double for Randolph Scott
The Untamed Breed (1948) stunt double for Sonny Tufts
You Gotta Stay Happy (1948) stunt double for Willard Parker
Thunderhoof (1948) stunt double for William Bishop
The Plunderers (1948) stunt double for Rod Cameron
Adventures of Don Juan (1948) stunt double for Errol Flynn
Quick on the Trigger (1948) stunt double for Charles Starrett
Smoky Mountain Melody (1948) (as Buckeye)
Yellow Sky (1948) stunt double for Gregory Peck
Challenge of the Range (1949) stunt double for Charles Starrett
Desert Vigilante (1949) stunt double for Charles Starrett
Wake of the Red Witch (1949) stunt double for John Wayne
The Walking Hills (1949) stunt double for Randolph Scott
Riders of the Whistling Pines (1949) stunts
Home in San Antone (1949) stunts
Laramie (1949) stunt double for Charles Starrett
Canadian Pacific (1949) stunt double for Randolph Scott
Lust for Gold (1949) stunts
Colorado Territory (1949) stunt double for Joel McCrea (unconfirmed)
The Doolins of Oklahoma (1949) (as Tulsa Jack Blake) also stunt double for Randolph Scott
The Blazing Trail (1949) (as Full House Patterson) also stunt double for Charles Starrett
Rim of the Canyon (1949) (as Pete Reagan)
Fuelin' Around (1949) (Three Stooges short) (as Guard)
South of Death Valley (1949) stunt double for Charles Starrett
Jolson Sings Again (1949) (bit part)
The Fighting Kentuckian (1949) stunts
The Gal Who Took the West (1949) stunt double for Scott Brady
Riders in the Sky (1949) stunt double for Gene Autry
Barbary Pirate (1949) stunt double for Donald Woods
Bandits of El Dorado (1949) (as Texas Ranger Tim Starling) also stunt double for Charles Starrett
Horsemen of the Sierras (1949) stunt double for Charles Starrett
Renegades of the Sage (1949) (as Lt. Hunter) also stunt double for Charles Starrett
The Palomino (1950) stunt double for Jerome Courtland
Punchy Cowpunchers (1950) (Three Stooges short) (as Elmer)
The Nevadan (1950) (as Sandy) also stunt double for Randolph Scott
Montana (1950) stunt double for Errol Flynn
Dallas (1950) stunt double for Gary Cooper (unconfirmed)
Kim (1950) stunt double for Errol Flynn
The Rogues of Sherwood Forest (1950) stunts (unconfirmed)
Trail of the Rustlers (1950) stunt double for Charles Starrett
Cody of the Pony Express (1950) (as Lt. Jim Archer) starring role in Columbia serial
Outcasts of Black Mesa (1950) stunt double for Charles Starrett

Cow Town (1950) (as Tod Jeffreys) also stunt double for Steve Darrell

Hoedown (1950) (as Stoney Rhodes) starring role

Texas Dynamo (1950) (as Bill Beck) also stunt double for Charles Starrett

The Tougher They Come (1950) (as Jones) also stunt double for Wayne Morris and William Bishop

David Harding, Counterspy (1950) (as Brown)

Streets of Ghost Town (1950) stunt double for Charles Starrett

Across the Badlands (1950) stunt double for Charles Starrett

Raiders of Tomahawk Creek (1950) stunt double for Charles Starrett

The Kangaroo Kid (1950) (as Tex Kinnane) starring role

Frontier Outpost (1950) (as Lt. Peck) also stunt double for Charles Starrett

Lightning Guns (1950) (as Sheriff Ron Saunders) also stunt double for Charles Starrett

Short Grass (1950) stunt double for Rod Cameron

The Cariboo Trail (1950) stunt double for Randolph Scott

Al Jennings of Oklahoma (1951) stunts (unconfirmed)

Only the Valiant (1951) stunt double for Gregory Peck

Whirlwind (1951) stunt double for Harry Lauter and Gregg Barton

Ridin' the Outlaw Trail (1951) stunt double for Charles Starrett

Fort Savage Raiders (1951) stunt double for Charles Starrett

Roar of the Iron Horse, Rail Blazer of the Apache Trail (1951) (as Jim Grant) starring role

Santa Fe (1951) (as Crake) stunt double for Randolph Scott

Snake River Desperadoes (1951) stunt double for Charles Starrett

Bonanza Town (1951) stunt double for Charles Starrett

The Texas Rangers (1951) (as Duke Fisher) stunt double for George Montgomery

The Lady and the Bandit (1951) (as Tavern troublemaker) also stunt double for Louis Hayward

Cyclone Fury (1951) stunt double for Charles Starrett

The Kid from Amarillo (1951) stunt double for Charles Starrett

Pecos River (1951) (as Jack Mahoney) stunt double for Charles Starrett

The Barefoot Mailman (1951) stunt double for Jerome Courtland

High Noon (1952) stunt double for Gary Cooper (unconfirmed)

The World in His Arms (1952) stunt double for Gregory Peck

Against All Flags (1952) stunt double for Errol Flynn

The Prisoner of Zenda (1952) stunt double for Stewart Granger (unconfirmed)

Smoky Canyon (1952) (as Jack Mahoney) also stunt double for Charles Starrett

The Hawk of Wild River (1952) (as Jack Mahoney) also stunt double for Charles Starrett

Laramie Mountains (1952) (as Swift Eagle) also stunt double for Charles Starrett

The Rough Tough West (1952) (as Big Jack Mahoney) also stunt double for Charles Starrett

Junction City (1952) (as Jack Mahoney) also stunt double for Charles Starrett

The Kid from Broken Gun (1952) (as Jack Mahoney) also stunt double for Charles Starrett

The Old West (1952) stunts; fight scene from *Rim of the Canyon* lifted

Panhandle Territory (1953) star for Columbia Pictures in unreleased film

Gunfighters of the Northwest (1954) (as Sgt. Jim Ward) starring role

Overland Pacific (1954) (as Ross Granger) starring role

Knutzy Knights (1954) (Three Stooges short) (as Cedric the Blacksmith)

Hot Stuff (1956) (Three Stooges short) (as Guard)

Away All Boats (1956) (as Alvick)

A Day of Fury (1956) (as Marshal Allan Burnett) starring role

I've Lived Before (1956) (as John Bolan/Lt. Peter Stevens) starring role

Showdown at Abilene (1956) (as Jim Trask) starring role

Battle Hymn (1957) (as Major Moore)

The Land Unknown (1957) (as Commander Harold "Hal" Roberts) starring role

Joe Dakota (1957) (as Joe Dakota, the Stranger) starring role

Slim Carter (1957) (as Slim Carter, aka Hughie Mack) starring role
The Last of the Fast Guns (1958) (as Brad Ellison) starring role
A Time to Love and a Time to Die (1958) (Immerman)
Money, Women, and Guns (1958) (as Silver Ward Hogan) starring role
Tarzan the Magnificent (1960) (as Coy Banton)
Three Blondes in His Life (1961) (as Duke Wallace) starring role
Tarzan Goes to India (1962) (as Tarzan) starring role
California (1963) (as Don Michael O'Casey) starring role
Tarzan's Three Challenges (1963) (as Tarzan) starring role
Moro Witch Doctor (1964) (as Jefferson Stark) starring role
The Walls of Hell (1964) (as Lt. Sorenson) starring role
Once Before I Die (1965) (as the major) (cameo)
Marine Battleground (1965) (as Nick Rawlins) starring role
Runaway Girl (1965) (as Randy Marelli) starring role
Blood in the Sky (1965) director-writer-star
West of West (1965) director-writer-star
The Glory Stompers (1967) (as Smiley)
Bandolero! (1968) (as Stoner) (cameo)
The Love Bug (1968) (stunt driver)
Tarzan's Deadly Silence (1970) (as the colonel)
The Bad Bunch (1973) (aka *Tom*) (as Sgt. Berry)
Outlaw Legacy (1973) producer-co-star (unreleased)
Their Only Chance (1976) (aka *Spirits of the Wild*) (as Grizzly Bill/Marvin Latham)
The End (1978) (as old man)
A.W.O.L. (1980) (as the cowboy)
Reve Blue (1980) actor-producer (unreleased)
Tarzan, the Ape Man (1981) stunt coordinator
All-American Cowboy (1985) (as bartender)
The Radicals (1988) stunt advisor (uncredited)

Television

The Range Rider series star (as The Range Rider) 78 episodes (1951–1953)
The Adventures of Wild Bill Hickok (1951) stunt double for Guy Madison
Death Valley Days "Swamper Ike" (2/3/1953)
Death Valley Days "Husband Pro Tem" (3/27/1954)
The Loretta Young Show "The First Man to Ask Her" (4/4/1954)
The Loretta Young Show "No Help Wanted" (11/7/1954)
The Loretta Young Show "Decision" (1/16/1955)
The Loretta Young Show "Option on a Wife" (2/20/1955)
The Loretta Young Show "Tale of a Cayuse" (2/27/1955)
The Loretta Young Show "Mink Coat" (3/27/1955)
Private Secretary "The Boy Next Door" (6/26/1955)
Wagon Train "The Dan Hogan Story" (5/14/1958)
Yancy Derringer (as Yancy Derringer) 34 episodes (1958–1959)
The Christophers "Some Facts About Valley Forge" (Syndicated, 1959)
Rawhide "Incident of the Sharpshooter" (2/26/1960)
The Millionaire "Millionaire Vance Ludlow" (5/10/1960)
Simon Lash series star (as Simon Lash) pilot episode (1960)
77 Sunset Strip "The Laurel Canyon Caper" (10/28/1960)
Laramie "Man from Kansas" (1/10/1961)

Gunslinger "Rampage" (3/16/1961)
Rawhide "Incident of the Phantom Bugler" (4/14/1961)
Laramie "Ladies Day" (10/3/1961)
Charter Pilot pilot episode (1966)
Batman "The Purrfect Crime" (3/17/1966)
Batman "Better Luck Next Time" (3/18/1966)
Tarzan "The Ultimate Weapon" (9/16/1966)
Tarzan "The Deadly Silence" (10/28/1966, 11/4/1966)
Tarzan "Mask of Rona" (2/17/1967)
Daniel Boone "Secret Code" (12/14/1967)
Batman "I'll Be a Mummy's Uncle" (2/22/1968)
Hawaii Five-O "The Grandstand Play" (3/3/1971, 3/10/1971)
Emergency "The Mascot" (1/22/1972)
Banacek "Let's Hear It for a Living Legend" (9/13/1972)
Emergency "Boot" (3/3/1973)
Kung Fu "The Hoots" (12/13/1973)
The Streets of San Francisco "Blockade" (1/24/1974)
The Streets of San Francisco "One Last Shot" (9/12/1974)
When the West Was Fun ABC Special (7/6/1979)
BJ and the Bear "Fly a Wild Horse" (12/8/1979)
BJ and the Bear "B.J. and the Seven Lady Truckers" (1/13/1981)
BJ and the Bear "The Fast and the Furious" (1/20/1981, 1/27/1981)
The Fall Guy "Charlie" (4/7/1982)
The Fall Guy "Colt's Outlaws" (11/10/1982)
The Fall Guy "Colt Breaks Out" (11/10/1982)
Simon and Simon "Rough Rider Rides Again" (11/18/1982)
The Fall Guy "King of the Cowboys" (2/29/1984)
The Master "A Place to Call Home" (8/31/1984)

Jocko also made appearances on *At Home with the Harmon's*; *The Ed Sullivan Show*; *Time for Adventure*; *Tootsie Roll Hippodrome*; *Truth or Consequences*; *It Could Be You*; *About Faces*; *Dance Party*; *The Mike Douglas Show*; *The Merv Griffin Show*; *The Tonight Show*; *University of the Third Age*; *The Nashville Palace*; *Fishing Fever*; *Stooge Snapshots*; *Entertainment Tonight*; *The Sally Jesse Raphael Show*; *Our World*; *Our Time*; *Country Notes*; and *Hot House People*.

Chapter Notes

Chapter 1

1. Jim Zabel, phone conversation, January 2012.
2. Tom Warner, phone conversation, March 2012.

Chapter 3

1. Roydon Clark, phone conversation, May 2012.
2. Don Kay Reynolds, phone conversation, November 2012.
3. Grady Bishop, phone conversation, October 2012.
4. Jim O'Mahoney, e-mail correspondence, April 2012.
5. Lois-Laurel Hawes, e-mail correspondence, February 2012.

Chapter 4

1. Tom Warner, phone conversation, March 2012.

Chapter 5

1. Dick Jones, phone conversation, July 2012.
2. Dick Jones, phone conversation, July 2012.
3. Dick Jones, phone conversation, July 2012.
4. Ford, Peter phone conversation, March 2012.
5. Dick Jones, phone conversation, July 2012.
6. Stephen Burnette, phone conversation, January 2012.
7. Dick Jones, phone conversation, July 2012.
8. Dick Jones, phone conversation, July 2012.
9. Dick Jones, phone conversation, July 2012.
10. Dick Jones, phone conversation, July 2012.
11. Dick Jones, phone conversation, July 2012.

Chapter 6

1. Jack Young, e-mail correspondence, March 2012.
2. Robert Dix, e-mail correspondence, February 2012.
3. James Drury, phone conversation, May 2012.
4. Russell Johnson, written letter, October 2012.

Chapter 7

1. Rodd Wolff, personal meeting, Phoenix, Arizona February 2012.

2. Ruta Lee, e-mail correspondence, February 2013.
3. Loren Janes, phone conversation, June 2012.
4. Jim Martin, phone conversation, January 2012.
5. Jim Martin, phone conversation, January 2012.
6. Gene Ryals, e-mail correspondence, December 2012.
7. Gregory Walcott, written correspondence, February 2012.

Chapter 8

1. Rodd Wolff, personal meeting, Phoenix, Arizona February 2012.
2. Robert Fuller, phone conversation, July 2012.
3. Jim O'Mahoney, e-mail correspondence, April 2012.
4. John "Bud" Cardos, phone conversation, June 2012.
5. Jim Martin, phone conversation, January 2012.
6. Phil Petras, e-mail correspondence, January 2012.
7. James Drury, phone conversation, May 2012.
8. Phil Petras, e-mail correspondence, November 2011.
9. Camille "Caz" Cazedessus, e-mail correspondence, January 2012.
10. Phil Petras, e-mail correspondence, November 2011.

Chapter 9

1. Jim O'Mahoney, e-mail correspondence, April 2012.

Chapter 10

1. Robert Fuller, phone conversation, July 2012.
2. Robert Fuller, phone conversation, July 2012.
3. Kalai Strode, e-mail correspondence, October 2012.
4. Robert Potter, phone conversation, May 2012.

Chapter 11

1. Jim Martin, phone conversation, January 2012.
2. Al Fleming, e-mail correspondence, February 2012.

3. Robert Fuller, phone conversation, July 2012.
4. Clarke Lindsley, e-mail correspondence, March 2012.
5. Greydon Clark, e-mail correspondence, November 2011.
6. Rodd Wolff, personal meeting, Phoenix, Arizona February 2012.

Chapter 12

1. Stephen Burnette, phone conversation, January 2012.
2. Dick Jones, phone conversation, July 2012.
3. Donald Carl Eugster, phone conversation, October 2012.
4. Diane Miller, e-mail correspondence, February 2012.
5. Gene Ryals, e-mail correspondence, November 2012.
6. Patrick Culliton, e-mail correspondence, February 2012.
7. Denny Miller, written correspondence, March 2012.
8. D. Peter Ogden, e-mail correspondence, January 2012.
9. Phil Petras, e-mail correspondence, November 2012.
10. Burt Reynolds, written correspondence, June 2012.
11. Don Burt, phone conversation, January 2012.
12. John Hagner, e-mail correspondence, December 2011.
13. Ray Lopeman, written correspondence, January 2012.
14. Ron Nix, personal meeting, Apache Junction, Arizona January 2012.
15. Rodd Wolff, personal meeting, Phoenix, Arizona February 2012.

Chapter 13

1. James Drury, phone conversation, May 2012.
2. Dick Jones, phone conversation, July 2012.
3. Esther Luttrell, e-mail correspondence, October 2012.
4. Will Hutchins, written correspondence, October 2012.
5. Grady Bishop, phone conversation, October 2012.
6. Loren Janes, phone conversation, June 2012.
7. Esther Luttrell, e-mail correspondence, January 2012.
8. William Smith, personal meeting, Marina Del Rey, California July 1997.
9. William Smith, personal meeting, Marina Del Rey, California July 1997.
10. Gene LeBell, e-mail correspondence, April 2012.
11. Robert Potter, phone conversation, May 2012.
12. Esther Luttrell, e-mail correspondence, January 2012.
13. Steve Stevens, e-mail correspondence, October 2012.
14. James Drury, phone conversation, May 2012.
15. Grady Bishop, phone conversation, October 2012.
16. Ray Barrow, phone conversation, October 2012.

17. Robert Fuller, phone conversation, July 2012.
18. Gene Ryals, e-mail correspondence, November 2011.
19. Tom Goldrup, e-mail correspondence, April 2012.
20. Mike Chapman, phone conversation, January 2012.
21. James Drury, phone conversation, May 2012.
22. Marty Rendleman, phone conversation, January 2012.
23. Grady Bishop, phone conversation, October 2012.
24. Marty Rendleman, phone conversation, January 2012.
25. Eric Dyck, e-mail correspondence, January 2012.
26. Will Hutchins, written correspondence, October 2012.
27. Dick Jones, phone conversation, July 2012.
28. Bill Sasser, e-mail correspondence, January 2012.
29. Bobby Copeland, phone conversation, January 2012.
30. Gordie Peer, phone conversation, November 2012.
31. Don Young, phone conversation, October 2012.
32. Gene Ryals, e-mail correspondence, November 2011.
33. Judy Pastorius, e-mail correspondence, October 2012.
34. Will Hutchins, written correspondence, October 2012.
35. Jim Martin, phone conversation, January 2012.
36. Judy Pastorius, e-mail correspondence, January 2012.
37. Gene Ryals, e-mail correspondence, November 2011.
38. Esther Luttrell, e-mail correspondence, January 2012.
39. Grady Bishop, phone conversation, October 2012.
40. Will Hutchins, written correspondence, October 2012.
41. Esther Luttrell, e-mail correspondence, January 2012.
42. Phil Petras, e-mail correspondence, December 2012.
43. Dick Jones, phone conversation, July 2012.
44. Robert Fuller, phone conversation, July 2012.
45. Don Burt, phone conversation, January 2012.
46. Dick Jones, phone conversation, July 2012.
47. James Drury, phone conversation, May 2012.
48. Robert Fuller, phone conversation, July 2012.
49. Rodd Wolff, personal meeting, Phoenix, Arizona February 2012.
50. Gene Ryals, e-mail correspondence, November 2012.
51. Don Burt, phone conversation, January 2012.
52. Neil Summers, personal meeting, Glendale, Arizona October 2012.
53. Grady Bishop, phone conversation, October 2012.
54. Phil Petras, e-mail correspondence, December 2012.
55. Will Hutchins, written correspondence, October 2012.

Bibliography

Print

Aaker, Everett. *Television Western Players of the Fifties.* Jefferson, NC: McFarland, 1997.

"Actor Friends Take the Stump for Candidate Reagan." *Hayward Daily Review.* April 3, 1966.

Ames, Walter. "Mahoney Is Real Stunt Man." *Los Angeles Times.* November 8, 1951.

Anderson, Nancy. "Tarzan Jock Mahoney Back in Films." *Copley News Service.* October 23, 1977.

Archiblad, John J. "Snarling Villains and Stunt Men Re-Create Best of the Old West." *St. Louis Post-Dispatch.* June 27, 1985.

Barde, Steve. "Tarzan's Tips for Beginners." *Bow and Arrow.* December 1975.

Barnum, Michael. "William Reynolds: The Perfect Son." *Classic Images.* Retrieved from www.classicimages.com. July 2012.

Baxter, John. *Stunt: The Story of the Great Movie Stuntmen.* New York: Doubleday, 1974.

"Beat Up Stuntman Complains That Top Stars 'Get the Glory.'" *Independent Press Telegram.* April 8, 1952.

Beery, Susanne Melanie, Terri Craft, Craig Stecyk III, and Scott Starr. "James O'Mahoney." *Juice* #57, 2004.

Beifuss, John. "Action Actor O'Keeffe Does OK Without Critics' Esteem." *The Commercial Appeal.* February 12, 1999.

Biffle, Kent. "John Wayne Fans Show True Grit." *Dallas Morning News.* September 18, 1988.

Black, William. "William Black interviews Charles Starrett." *Paragon* #5, 1973.

Blackhawk Yearbook. Davenport High, 1936–1938.

Blottner, Gene. *Universal-International Westerns, 1947–1963: The Complete Filmography.* Jefferson, NC: McFarland, 2000.

Bonderof, Jason. *Sally Field: A Biography.* New York: St. Martin's, 1987.

Bruno, Joyce. "Saddle Partners." *Movie.* April 1953.

Burt, Don. *Horses & Other Heroes.* Guilford, CT: Lyons, 2002.

Carman, Bob, and Don Scapperotti. *The Adventures of the Durango Kid.* N.p.: R.C. Carman, 1983.

Carroll, Harrison. "Behind the Scenes." *Warsaw-Union Times.* June 5, 1956.

_____. "Husky Stuntman Is New Boy in Life of Yvonne." *The Dispatch.* March 22, 1949.

Cary, Kenwicke. "Around the Horn." *San Antonio Light.* July 23, 1962.

Cazedessus, Camille. "Jock 'Lord Greystoke' Mahoney." *Erb-dom* #8, December 1963.

Chapman, Mike. "King of the Jungle." *Iowa History Journal.* January/February 2010.

Cline, William C. *In the Nick of Time.* Jefferson, NC: McFarland, 1984.

Collura, Joe. "Jerome Courtland: The Boy Next Door." *Classic Images.* June 2012. Retrieved from www.classicimages.com. July 2012.

_____. "Jock Mahoney: Risking Life and Limb." *Favorite Westerns & Serials Plus.* #20, 1985.

Condon, George E. "Jacques O'Mahoney, Egg-headed Cowboy, Puts Press Agent in Shape for Head Shrinkers." *Plain-Dealer.* January 25, 1956.

_____. "Range Rider, Alias Jacques O'Mahoney Has Rib-Cracking Background as Stunt Man in Movies." *Plain-Dealer.* May 16, 1953.

Cook, Ben. "Film Star Says Adults Like Westerns, Too." *Kingsport News.* November 14, 1952.

Copeland, Bobby. *B-Western Boot Hill.* Madison, NC: Empire, 1999.

_____. "Dick Jones: From Child Star to Buffalo Bill, Jr." *Under Western Skies* #50, 1997.

_____. "Phyllis Coates: The Last Serial Queen." *Western Clippings.* March 1999.

Coriell, Vern. "Old Enemy Becomes Tarzan: Stuntman Jock Mahoney." *The Gridley Wave* #4, April 1962.

Coriell, Vern. *Jocko: Jungle Lord.* House of Greystoke, 1984.

Cotton, W.P. "Stunt Man: Jock O'Mahoney." *Movie Thrills.* July 1950.

"Cowboys Now Load Guns After Six Shots." *Independent Press Telegram.* December 5, 1957.

Cutts, Terry. *Armchair Cowboy.* Canterbury, England: Parkers Digital, 2012.

Danson, Tom E. "Former Swim Instructor Stars on 'Range Riders.'" *Long Beach Press Telegram.* August 10, 1951.

Danzig, Fred. "Man Gets Kicks from Belting Foes on TV Western." *Anderson Daily Bulletin*. February 11, 1959.

"Daring Derringer: He's His Own Stunt Man." *Milwaukee Journal*. December 6, 1958.

Davidson, Julie. "Hot House People." *Glasgow-Herald*. December 12, 1987.

Dawson, Angela. "Tarzans Swing by Burbank." *Los Angeles Daily News*. January 20, 1989.

Dean, Paul. "Telethon for Cerebral Palsy Sparks Factional Dissension." *Arizona Republic*. July 15, 1967.

Deaterla, Mike. "Jock Mahoney, Will Hutchins Recall Days as Film Cowboys." *Portsmouth Daily Times*. May 2, 1986.

De Carlo, Yvonne, and Doug Warren. *Yvonne: An Autobiography*. New York: St. Martin's, 1987.

DeMarco, Mario. *Charles Starrett: Gallant Defender, The Durango Kid*. Self-published, 1982.

_____. *Serial Aces of the Silver Screen*. Self-published, 1985.

De Roos, Robert. "Sally Field: Her Feet Are on the Ground." *TV Guide*. September 25, 1967.

"Derringer's Jock Mahoney." *TV Western Round-Up*. February 1959.

Dungan, Ron. "Lenny Dee: Stuntman Reflects on a Wild Career." *Casa Grande Dispatch*. December 10, 1983.

Elwood, Roger. "Hollywood's Newest Tarzan: Jock Mahoney." *Young Mr. America*. November, 1963.

Essoe, Gabe. *Book of Movie Lists*. Westport, CT: Arlington House, 1981.

_____. *Tarzan of the Movies*. New York: Citadel, 1968.

Fagen, Herb. *White Hats and Silver Spurs*. Jefferson, NC: McFarland, 1996.

Farkash, Mike. "Former Tarzan Still Swinging in Film World." *The Enterprise*. December 8, 1985.

Ferrante, Tim. "Jock Mahoney: Twice Upon a Tarzan." *Starlog*. November 1988.

Feuerstein, Rich. "Tarzan Goes to Solana Beach." *San Diego Union*. December 29, 1977.

Fidler, Jimmie. "Fidler in Hollywood." *Nevada State Journal*. September 17, 1955.

Finnigan, Joseph. "Sore Feet are Problem for Mahoney." *Advocate*. June 25, 1963.

Fisher, Scott M. *The Iron Men: The 1939 Hawkeyes*. Media, 1989.

Fitzgerald, Michael, and Boyd Magers. *Ladies of the Western*. Jefferson, NC: McFarland, 2010.

Fletcher, Dibi. "James O'Mahoney." *Juice* #62, 2007.

Flynn, Sean, and Jane Ardmore. "The Candid Confessions of Errol Flynn's Son." *Modern Screen*. September 1961.

Fogg, William. "William Smith: Always Ready for Action!" *Filmfax*. April/June 2008.

Freeman, Donald. "Johnny Weissmuller — The Tarzan's Tarzan: I Was No Hambone." *San Diego Union*. May 3, 1964.

Fury, David. *Kings of the Jungle*. Jefferson, NC: McFarland, 2001.

Goldrup, Jim, and Tom Goldrup. *Feature Players: The Stories Behind the Faces (Vol. 1–4)*. Self-published, 1986–2006.

Goodman, Martin. "The Mahoney Backyard." *TV People*. August 1956.

Graham, Sheilah. "Hedy Restricts Jock Mahoney from Film Set." *Deseret News*. May 22, 1957.

_____. "Yvonne's had 10 Ace Flames." *Pittsburgh Post Gazette*. September 11, 1949.

Grahame, Harry L. "Jock Mahoney to Advise Bo on Tarzan." *Santa Ana Register*. January 25, 1981.

Grobel, Laurence. "Sally Field: When Larry Met Sally." *Movieline*. July 1991.

Grossman, Gary H. *Saturday Morning TV*. New York: Dell, 1981.

Habblitz, Harry. "Jock Mahoney: In Memorium." *Erbania* #61, 1990.

Hagner, John. *Falling for Stars*. Self-published, 1964.

_____. *Kangaroo Legs: Jocko Mahoney*. Self-Published, 1994.

_____. "Saga of Jock Mahoney." *Falling for Stars Magazine*. July/August 1974.

Hahn, Robyn. "Jock Mahoney was a Hawkeye." *Iowa City Press-Citizen*. February 21, 1985.

Hail, Marshall. "New Tarzan Has Muscles, But He's a Cultured Fellow." *El Paso Herald Post*. July 15, 1963.

Hamm, Keith David. "Pipeline to the Glory Days of Surfing." *Los Angeles Times*. July 21, 2002.

Hartigan, Elizabeth. "Those Ol' Westerns Were Made for Saturdays." *Los Angeles Daily News*. September 6, 1986.

Henderson, Jan Alan, and Herb Harris. "Jocko Mahoney." *Filmfax*. May 1990.

Heyder, Harvey. *Ron Nix's Cowtown, AZ*. Phoenix: PBS, 1987.

Hopper, Hedda. "Jock Beats Bushes for Tarzan Film." *Chicago Tribune*. September 24, 1962.

_____. "Jock Mahoney Meets the Elephants." *Chicago Sunday Tribune*. July 15, 1962.

_____. "Range Rider Gets a Lot of Television Offers." *Chicago Tribune*. January 28, 1958.

"How to Ride a Horse." *TV*. January 1955.

Hudson, Berkley. "Tinsel Town it isn't, But a Movie Is Being Made at Dutchman's Flat." *Bend Bulletin*. February 5, 1975.

Humphrey, Hal. "TV Fame Can Be Fast But Fortune Can Be Fickle." *Oakland Tribune*. September 14, 1954.

Hutchins, Will. "A Touch of Hutch." *Western Clippings* #48, July/August 2002.

Hyams, Joe. "McQueen of West Challenged." *Corpus Christi Caller Times*. March 1, 1959.

Iversen, Jack. "Jock Mahoney: A Personal Remembrance." *Burroughs Bulletin* #2, April 1990.

Jackson, Greg. "An Interview with Marshall Reed." *Serial World* #9, 1984.

Jackson, Ronald, and Doug Abbott. *50 Years of the Television Western.* Bloomington, IN: Author House, 2008.

Jacques, Steve. "Ron Ely: Tarzan Exchanges Loin Cloth for Karate Gi." *Fighting Stars.* February 1974.

"Jock Mahoney Begins Fourth Film Career." *Daytona Beach Morning Journal.* October 13, 1958.

"Jock Mahoney Is One of TV's Most Colorful Actors." *Modesto Bee.* November 30, 1958.

"Jock Mahoney Proves to be Real Film Star in *Showdown.*" *Rocky Mountain Evening Telegram.* December 23, 1956.

Kampion, Drew, and C.R. Stecyk. *Dora Lives: The Authorized Story of Miki Dora.* Santa Barbara, CA: T. Adler, 2005.

Kennedy, Dana. "Sticking to It, One Way or Another." *The New York Times.* September 24, 2000.

Kountze, Denman, Jr. "Newest Tarzan from Iowa Prefers Elephants to Nags." *Omaha World Herald.* June 11, 1962.

Kozub, Linda. "Old West Lives Again at Poway County Fair." *San Diego Union.* June 5, 1983.

Johnson, B. "Jocko the Gymnast." *TV Guide.* March 14, 1959.

Kleiner, Dick. "The Girl with Something Extra." *The Morning Record.* November 3, 1973.

Lauer-Williams, Kathy. "Collection Is One of Largest." *Morning Call.* May 28, 1998.

Lee, Luaine. "Field of Dreams." *The Toledo Blade.* September 26, 2000.

Leonard, Rod. "Movie, TV Star Jack Mahoney Does Own Oats Opera Stunts." *Waterloo Daily Courier.* June 27, 1954.

Lewis, C. Jack. "Colt, Mare's Leg, and Derringer" *Leatherneck.* July, 1960.

_____. "Ultimate Stuntman." *Guns of the Old West.* November, 2006.

_____. *White Horse, Black Hat.* Lanham, MD: Scarecrow, 2002.

Lewis, Jack. "SUI Man Has Performed Wondrous Feats in Movies." *Cedar Rapids Gazette.* August 6, 1950.

_____. "A Tear for Jack Mahoney, Who Is Too Important to do Movie Stunts." *Cedar Rapids Gazette.* July 22, 1951.

Lilley, Tim. *Campfire Embers.* Akron, OH: Big Trail, 1997.

Lousararian, Ed. "The Camera in the Corral: A Photographer's View of Western Heroes." *Wildest Westerns* #1, 1998.

Luttrell, Esther. *Murder in the Movies.* Superior, WI: Port Town, 2008.

Lyden, Pierce. *Those Saturday Serials.* Self-published, 1989.

Magers, Boyd, and Michael Fitzgerald. *Westerns Women: Interviews with 50 Leading Ladies of Television and Film.* Jefferson, NC: McFarland, 2004.

Mahoney, Jock. "The Great, Glorious Grand National Quail Hunt." *Gun World.* May 1968.

_____. "Rid'n the Range." *Blazing West.* Vol. 1, #1, 1984.

_____. "Shadow and Substance." *Modern Screen.* January 1955.

_____. "Tarzan and the Crooked Arrow." *Bow and Arrow.* October 1965.

_____. *Who's Who Among Western Stars.* 1953.

_____, and Jack Lewis. "Confessions of a Fall Guy." *TV & Movie Westerns.* December 1959.

Maltin, Leonard. *Leonard Maltin's Movie Encyclopedia.* New York: Dutton, 1994.

Manchell, Frank. *Every Step a Struggle: Interviews with Seven who Shape the African-American Image in Movies.* Washington, D.C.: New Academia, 2007.

Mason, Tork. "The House the Hawks Built: Field House's 100 Year History Dimming Soon." *Daily Iowan.* December 13, 2011.

McAndrew, Doug, and Frank Westwood. "Jock Mahoney: A Tribute." *The Fantastic Worlds of Edgar Rice Burroughs* #23, February/March 1990.

McCann, Tom. "Jock Mahoney: A Man of Many Parts." *Santa Ana Register.* July 30, 1978.

McLeod, Michael. "Rick Field." *Orlando Sentinel.* December 14, 1986.

Mellette, Billy. "Versatile Tarzan Star Pays Another Visit to Florence." *Florence Morning News.* August 4, 1963.

Miller, Leo O. *The Great Cowboy Stars of Movies and Television.* New Rochelle, NY: Arlington House, 1979.

Molter, Harry. "Range Rider Was All-Around Athlete in College Days." *Christian Science Monitor.* October 22, 1953.

Moraine, Jacob. "In Tribute to Jock Mahoney." *Burroughs Bulletin* #31, 1973.

Mosby, Aline. "Jack Mahoney, Onetime Star in Davenport High Sports, Now Is Newest Television Films Idol." *Davenport Morning Democrat.* October 25, 1951.

"Movie and TV Cowboy Comes to Cedar Rapids." *Cedar Rapids Gazette.* June 20, 1954.

Nevins, Francis M. "Tommy Carr: Men Who Called the Shots." *Western Clippings* #85, September/October 2008.

Newbold, Nancy. "The Man Behind the Derringer" *Ocala Star Banner.* August 22, 1965.

Nisbet, Fairfax. "Latest Tarzan Is Also Hardest Working Trooper." *Dallas Morning News.* July 20, 1963.

O'Mahoney, Jock. "Break Your Neck for a Thrill." *Man.* September 1950.

Orshefsky, Milton. "Tarzan in Thailand." *Life.* June 14, 1963.

Parla, Paul, and Charles P. Mitchell. "Autumn Russell: Heroine of Mora Tau." *Scary Monsters, Monster Memories* #8, 2000.

_____, and_____. *Screen Sirens Scream! Interviews with 20 Actresses from Science Fiction, Horror, Film Noir, & Mystery Movies, 1930s to 1960s.* Jefferson, NC: McFarland, 2000.

Pate, Michael. "Along the Big Trail." *Western Clippings* #56, November/December 2003.

Perrin, Marlene. "Classical Tarzan: Scholar Meets Actor." *Iowa City Press-Citizen.* February 27, 1985.

"Police Circus Stars Range Rider." *Pittsburgh Press.* July 30, 1952.

Price, Annie. "Tarzan Visiting in City, May Have Lengthy Reign as King of the Jungle." *Advocate.* July 27, 1962.

"*The Range Rider:* A Former Movie Stunt Man Is the New Cowboy Sensation." *TV Guide.* August 1, 1952.

"Range Rider and Pal Dick West Promise Lots of Action at Rodeo." *Oakland Star Tribune.* September 11, 1953.

Remenih, Anton. "Cowboy Stuntman Is TV Hero in Own Right." *Chicago Daily Tribune.* April 26, 1952.

Rendleman, Marty. *Singing Your Way to Stardom.* Mustang, OK: Tate, 2011.

Reynolds, Burt. *My Life.* New York: Hyperion, 1994.

Richard, Julie. "Past Tarzan Assn. Has Vine Time at *Greystoke.*" *Los Angeles Times.* April 28, 1984.

Roberson, Chuck. *The Fall Guy.* North Vancouver, Canada: Hancock, 1980.

Rothel, David. *Opened Time Capsules.* Albany, GA: Bear Manor, 2010.

"Ruidoso Downs Hosts Tarzan." *El Paso Herald Post.* May 10, 1969.

Schrader, Gus. "Ice Cream Scooper Makes Good." *Cedar Rapids Gazette.* June 20, 1954.

Scott, Vernon. "Best Scene in Movie Can't Be Shown." *Deseret News.* November 2, 1957.

_____. "Ex-Stuntman Star Goes Out to Save Stuntman." *San Mateo Times.* October 3, 1957.

_____. "Mahoney Risks His Neck in Every Film He Makes." *Panama City News.* March 29, 1957.

_____. "Newest Tarzan Deserts African Locale." *Wisconsin State Journal.* December 13, 1961.

Shapiro, Marc. "Steve James: Street Fighter." *Action Heroes.* #3, 1990.

Smith, Diane. "Studio Backlot Site of Benefit." *Independent Press-Telegram.* May 20, 1973.

Smith, Don. "Tarzan Comes to Salisbury." *Salisbury Post.* July 30, 1963.

Smith, Doug. *Davenport.* Charleston, SC: Arcadia, 2007.

_____. "Davenport Native Jock Mahoney Starred in Movies, Television." *Quad-City Times.* July 17, 2012.

Smith, Jack. "Tarzan, Gidget Both Gymnast's Relatives." *Hayward Daily Review.* February 20, 1966.

Stewart, Ethan. "Santa Barbara Museum." *Santa Barbara Independent.* December 9, 2010.

Strode, Woody, and Sam Young. *Goal Dust.* Lanham, MD: Madison, 1990.

Stuart, Mary. *Both of Me.* Garden City, NY: Doubleday, 1980.

"Stunt Work Leads to *Range Rider* Show." *Daily Inter Lake.* January 21, 1955.

Subotnick, Nadine. "The Old Range Rider Comes a Lopin' in to Have a Swim." *Cedar Rapids Gazette.* June 24, 1954.

Sullivan, Meg. "Cowboy Stars Return for Iverson Ranch Roundup" *Los Angeles Times.* October 10, 1988.

Summers, Neil. "Jock Mahoney Memorial Tribute." *The Westerner* #14, 1990.

_____. *The Official TV Western Round-Up Book Volume 2.* TV Westerns, 1989.

_____. "*The Range Rider* TV Series." *Blazing West.* Vol. 1, #1, 1984.

Szuch, John. "Lt. John Szuch Meets Tarzan." *The Gridley Wave* #13, January 1964.

"Tarzan Comes to India: MGM Unit at Bangalore." *Indian Express.* January 24, 1962.

"Tarzan Day Set at Aquatic Club Here Thursday." *State Times Advocate.* August 5, 1963.

Thomas, Bob. "Mahoney Is Hollywood's New Tarzan." *Cedar Rapids Gazette.* March 13, 1962.

_____. "Range Rider Is Still Collecting from Television." *The Newark Advocate.* June 21, 1955.

"TV Range Rider Stars in Rodeo at Ft. Madison." *Muscatine Journal and News Tribune.* August 28, 1954.

TV Western Round-Up. "A Rangy Rider." Vol. 1, #1; 1957.

Vincent, Mal. "Jock New Type Tarzan." *Burlington Daily Times.* July 30, 1963.

Walker, Dale. *Burroughs Bulletin.* "Tarzan in El Paso: A Pictorial Interview with Jock Mahoney." Vol. 1, #15, 1964.

Warren, Bill. *Starlog.* "Tarzan the Magnificent." February 1993.

Warren, James. *Screen Thrills Illustrated.* "Tarzan 1962." January 1963.

Waters, Tim. "Hollywood Remembers Little Legends." *Los Angeles Times.* June 11, 1982.

Weaver, Tom. *Double Feature Creature Attack.* Jefferson, NC: McFarland, 2003.

_____. *Earth vs. the Sci-Fi Filmmakers.* Jefferson, NC: McFarland, 2005.

_____. *I Talked with a Zombie: Interviews with 23 Veterans of Horror and Sci-Fi Films and Television.* Jefferson, NC: McFarland, 2009.

_____. *Return of the B-Science Fiction and Horror Heroes.* Jefferson, NC: McFarland, 2000.

_____. *Wild Wild Westerners.* Duncan, OK: Bear Manor, 2012.

Western, Johnny. "Filmland Horsemen: Jock Mahoney." *Western Horseman*. January, 1959.

Whitney, Dave. "Adventurous Jock Mahoney Here on Four Week Visit." *Ocala Star-Banner*. August 1, 1965.

_____. "Youth Camp on Edge of National Forest." *Ocala Star-Banner*. August 29, 1965.

Wiggins, Walt. "Let's Hunt Hawaii!" *Guns Magazine*. November 1959.

_____. "Tarzan's Pickup Camper." *Mobile Home Journal*. September 1963.

Wilson, David. *American Classic Screen*. "Kicking Away Gravity: The Saga of Four Great Hollywood Stuntmen." Vol. 5, #5, 1980.

Winfrey, Oprah. "Sally Field." *Oprah*. March, 2008.

Wise, James E., and Anne Collier Rehill. *Stars in the Corps*. Annapolis, MD: Naval Institute Press, 1999.

Witbeck, Charles. "When the West Was Fun." *The Miami News*. June 5, 1979.

Wolff, Rodd. "Stunt & Safety." *Screen Actors Guild Newsletter*. Summer 1986.

Wolters, Larry. "Jack Mahoney Will Head Cast of *Range Rider*." *Chicago Daily Tribune*. May 8, 1951.

_____. "The Mahoney Story: From Medicine to TV." *Chicago Daily Tribune*. November 30, 1958.

Word, Rob, and Bill Black. "From Stuntman to Star: *The Range Rider* Jock Mahoney." *TV Western*. #1, 2001.

Zabel, Jim, and Rich Wolfe. *65 Years of Fun and Games: I Love It! I Love It! I Love It!* Phoenix: Lone Wolfe, 2010.

Zolotow, Maurice. *Shooting Star: A Biography of John Wayne*. New York: Simon & Schuster, 1974.

Online

www.accomics.com (Bill Black's blogs about Jocko)

www.achievement.org (Sally Field interview)

www.ancestry.com (newspaper archive)

www.b-westerns.com (Chuck Anderson's Old Corral site)

www.erbzine.com (Edgar Rice Burroughs Tarzan site)

www.facebook.com (Friends of Jock O'Mahoney Fans Page by Grady Bishop)

www.filesofjerryblake.com (Jerry Blake's serial site)

www.genealogybank.com (newspaper archive)

www.googlenews.com (newspaper archive)

www.honolulusurfmuseum.com (Jim O'Mahoney site)

www.imdb.com (Internet Movie Database)

www.joebowman.com (Jocko tribute site)

http://members.shaw.ca/mahoney13/jm1.html (Bob Callaghan's Jock Mahoney tribute site)

www.newspaperarchive.com (newspaper archive)

www.riflemanconnors.com (Judy Pastorius memories)

www.sbsurfingmuseum.com (Jim O'Mahoney site)

www.tcm.com (Turner Classics Movie database)

www.terrororstralis.com (Irish McCalla site)

www.transformetrics.com (free-hand exercise site)

www.westernclippings.com (Boyd Magers site)

www.wikipedia.org

Index

Numbers in **bold italics** indicate pages with photographs.